RICHARD II

The RSC Shakespeare

Edited by Jonathan Bate and Eric Rasmussen

Chief Associate Editors: Héloïse Sénéchal and Jan Sewell

Associate Editors: Trey Jansen, Eleanor Lowe, Lucy Munro,
Dee Anna Phares

Richard the Second

Textual Editing: Eric Rasmussen

Introduction and Shakespeare's Career in the Theater: Jonathan Bate

Commentary: Ayako Kawanami and Héloïse Sénéchal

Scene-by-Scene Analysis: Esme Miskimmin

In Performance: Maria Jones (RSC stagings), Peter Kirwan (overview)

The Director's Cut (interviews by Jonathan Bate and Kevin Wright):
Claus Peymann and Michael Boyd

Playing Richard: Fiona Shaw

Editorial Advisory Board

The RSC Shakespeare

William Shakespeare

RICHARD II

Edited by Jonathan Bate and Eric Rasmussen

Introduction by Jonathan Bate

The Modern Library
New York

CONTENTS

INTRODUCTION

LYRIC TRAGEDY

In the second act of *The Life and Death of King Richard the Second*, the queen weeps after her husband departs to fight a war in Ireland. She is comforted by Bushy, one of the king's courtiers:

> Each substance of a grief hath twenty shadows,
> Which shows like grief itself, but is not so,
> For sorrow's eye, glazèd with blinding tears,
> Divides one thing entire to many objects,
> Like perspectives, which rightly gazed upon
> Show nothing but confusion: eyed awry
> Distinguish form. So your sweet majesty,
> Looking awry upon your lord's departure,
> Find shapes of grief, more than himself to wail,
> Which, looked on as it is, is naught but shadows
> Of what it is not. Then, thrice-gracious queen,
> More than your lord's departure weep not. More's not seen;
> Or if it be, 'tis with false sorrow's eye,
> Which for things true weeps things imaginary.

Tears glaze the eyes and distort our vision, fragmenting what we see. The emotions are at odds with the work of reasoning. The "substance" of the queen's grief—Richard himself—is away in Ireland. What she holds in her head is a "shadow," or rather many shadows, of him. When we are away from those we love, we fear that something bad may be happening to them. But the pictures of those bad things are not a reality: they are "things imaginary."

Strong emotions and imagined images are themselves the substance not only of grief and foreboding, but also of fiction and theater. The Richard and the queen whom we witness on stage, or conjure into our minds in the act of reading, are "shadows" rather than substances. They are brought into being by performance, by the impersonation of roles, by playacting. When we think more deeply about the roles of king and queen in historical reality, we might consider this question of "substance" and "shadow" further. Which is the substance and which the shadow? The office or the man? The king in his capacity as embodiment of the nation and God's representative upon earth assumes his role by means of costumes and props (robe, crown, scepter, orb, throne on which to sit) and of a highly theatrical ceremony (coronation, anointing, ritualized words, the blessing of the Church). Is there some sense in which that role is no more than a performance, in which a king is an actor-like "shadow," whereas the true "substance" is the flesh-and-blood body of the mortal individual whose name is Richard? Or is it the other way around: does Richard become a mere "shadow" of himself when he loses the name of king?

These are some of the questions with which the Shakespeare of *Richard II* was fascinated. The play is the most static and inward-looking of his histories, and perhaps for that reason it has always been one of the less frequently staged. Yet its visual images are striking: a shattered mirror, a king stripped of everything and mired in a dark prison cell. And its verbal music is of startling beauty. The exploration of shadows and substances, selves and roles, public and private, is conducted in intensely lyrical, formal language. Bushy's speech is typical. It proceeds in the form of a complex, balanced argument, rendered vivid by poetic imagery, such as the figure of the "perspective" glass, a kind of distorting mirror. And it is made memorable for both the actor learning the lines and the audience hearing the play by the resolution in rhyme at the close and by the beat of the iambic pentameter throughout. The pattern is of unstressed followed by stressed syllables five times over, with occasional reversals for variety and surprise. "Find shápes of gríef, móre than himsélf to wáil." The contrast between the "shapes of grief" and Richard "himself" is highlighted by the stress on "more," which breaks up the regular rhythm that would lead us to expect a stress on "than."

Richard II is the most poetic of Shakespeare's history plays. The extreme formality of its rhetoric and verse forms perhaps represents the high point, and the end point, of his early style. Hereafter, his forms will become more fluid, less formal, more conversational. He will use less rhyme. *Richard II* is indeed a very rare example of Shakespeare writing a play entirely in verse. In the history plays he had written before—the *Henry VI* sequence and *Richard III*—and those he would go on to write soon after—the two parts of *Henry IV* and *Henry V*—the march of verse-speaking kings and courtiers is peppered with interruptions from the prose voices of the commoners. But in this play even the gardeners speak in polished and elaborate verse as they make an allegorical comparison between the overgrown garden and the kingdom run to seed.

THE ESSEX CONNECTION

The 1580s was a decade of war in Flanders, where the English fought with the Dutchmen against the might of Catholic Spain. The 1590s was a decade of war in Ireland, where the Earl of Essex struggled in vain to quell the rebellion of the irrepressible Hugh O'Neill, Earl of Tyrone. For the first half of his career, all through the last years of old Queen Elizabeth's reign, Shakespeare was a war poet. He had an obsessive interest in military life. Richard III, Titus Andronicus and all his sons, Othello, Iago and Cassio, Macbeth and the other Thanes, Hamlet's armored father and young Fortinbras, King Lear, Julius Caesar, Brutus and Cassius, Mark Antony and Octavius Caesar, Coriolanus, Alcibiades, Henry IV and Sir John Falstaff, dozens of dukes, earls, and knights in the ranks of the history plays, Benedick and his colleagues in *Much Ado About Nothing*: all are soldiers, some by profession and others by force of circumstance. All are defined to a greater or lesser degree by the hunger to fill the vacuum left by battle and by war as the defining male action (which is not to say that Shakespeare failed to create a good line in female soldiers—Queen Margaret, Tamora Queen of Goths, Joan of Arc, Cleopatra, Cordelia and her sisters). But the most famous of all his soldiers would be King Henry V.

Having completed a sequence of four plays about the Wars of the Roses, then the rise and fall of Richard III, ending with the establishment of the Tudor dynasty following the battle of Bosworth Field, Shakespeare turned his mind to the preceding period of English history. In writing *Richard II*, which inexorably moves toward Henry

Bullingbrook's ascent of the throne as King Henry IV, Shakespeare was setting himself up for another cycle of plays that would inevitably climax in the short but triumphant reign of Bullingbrook's son, King Henry V, victor over the French.

At the beginning of the fifth act of King Harry's play, the Chorus describes his triumphal procession through the streets of London upon his return to England after his astonishing victory on the field of Agincourt. In the course of this speech, Shakespeare makes the most open and striking topical allusion anywhere in his works:

> . . . But now behold,
> In the quick forge and working-house of thought,
> How London doth pour out her citizens.
> The mayor and all his brethren in best sort,
> Like to the senators of th'antique Rome,
> With the plebeians swarming at their heels,
> Go forth and fetch their conqu'ring Caesar in:
> As by a lower but by loving likelihood,
> Were now the general of our gracious empress,
> As in good time he may, from Ireland coming,
> Bringing rebellion broachèd on his sword,
> How many would the peaceful city quit,
> To welcome him? Much more, and much more cause,
> Did they this Harry. . . .

When these lines were first spoken on the stage of the newly built Globe Theatre in the summer of 1599, few audience members could have had any doubt what the Chorus was talking about. The "gracious empress" is Queen Elizabeth and "the general" is the Earl of Essex—the queen's sometime favorite, embodiment of the martial code of chivalry and honor, leader of the war party in the long-standing debate at court over how to proceed in relation to Spain. At this moment he was leading his campaign against Tyrone in Ireland. The allusion is unmistakable.

Shakespeare does not let go of his habitual political caution. It is a "likelihood," not a certainty, that Essex will bring rebellion broached on his sword and it is an open question how many people will turn out to cheer him. But there is still a boldness in the comparison. When "conqu'ring Caesar" crossed the Rubicon and returned to Rome, there was talk of him seizing an imperial crown and Brutus and his friends had to take drastic action to save the republic. Conversely, there were moments in late Elizabethan court politics when exasperation with the old childless queen's refusal to name an heir led some to wonder whether there might not be a future for England in some form of Roman-style republican government, with the Privy Council serving as its Senate and a strong man such as Essex in the role of Consul. Shakespeare wrote *Julius Caesar* that same year of 1599.

But *Richard II*, written a few years before, is another powerful shadow behind the allusion to Essex and Tyrone. After all, that too is a play in which an Irish war is of pivotal importance in demonstrating an English monarch's failing grip on the handle of national power. Essex was often perceived as a Henry Bullingbrook figure, a no-nonsense military man greeted with acclaim whenever he rode through the streets of London, as he did before heading off on his French campaign in 1591. What is more, he claimed descent from Bullingbrook, which made some people worry that he had aspirations to the throne himself.

Shakespeare seems to have been aware of the Essex/Bullingbrook identification. At the climax of *Richard II*, he describes Bullingbrook in London, portraying him in a manner that draws on the public image of Essex:

> . . . the duke, great Bullingbrook,
> Mounted upon a hot and fiery steed
> Which his aspiring rider seemed to know,
> With slow but stately pace kept on his course.
> While all tongues cried 'God save thee, Bullingbrook!'
> You would have thought the very windows spake,
> So many greedy looks of young and old
> Through casements darted their desiring eyes
> Upon his visage, and that all the walls
> With painted imagery had said at once
> 'Jesu preserve thee! Welcome, Bullingbrook!'
> Whilst he, from one side to the other turning,

Bareheaded, lower than his proud steed's neck,
Bespake them thus: 'I thank you, countrymen',
And thus still doing, thus he passed along.

There is no precedent in Shakespeare's historical sources for this striking image of Bullingbrook's popularity. It has been invented in order to establish a contrast with the deposed Richard, who follows in after with no man crying, "God save him," and dust and rubbish being thrown out of the windows on his head. Shakespeare thus illustrates the process of the two cousins being like two buckets, one descending down a well as the other rises up. He also highlights the fickleness of the common people. At the same time, the close concentration on Bullingbrook's management of his proud horse makes a point about his strong statecraft: good horsemanship was a traditional image of effective government. This sequence in the play was explicitly quoted apropos of Essex in more than one political intervention of the period.

In the *Henry IV* plays, however, Shakespeare conspicuously dropped the image of Bullingbrook, now king, as a popular figure. Far from showing himself among his people and exemplifying strong government, Henry IV skulks in his palace as his kingdom disintegrates around him, the penalty for his usurpation of his throne. The horseman and populist is his son Hal, who goes on to become Henry V, leading his men to triumph in battle. The description of his return to London after the victory at Agincourt clearly echoes that of the speech about his father at the corresponding moment in *Richard II*. As so often in Shakespeare, the wheel of history comes full circle.

Regardless of Shakespeare's semiconcealed political intentions in making the allusion—one gets the sense that he is only somewhere a little over halfway to being an Essex man—it is easy to see how the two remarkably similar passages in *Richard II* and *Henry V* could have been perceived as pro-Essex. This perception drew him into exceptionally dangerous political territory. Things came to a head in 1601 and if they had gone just a little differently, his career—and indeed his life—would have come to an abrupt end. He could have found himself in the Tower of London or even in the hands of the public executioner.

How do we measure the worth of our rulers? By th claim to power or the quality of their actions at the helm. King Richard II has wasted public funds and is under the influen self-serving flatterers. He has arranged the murder of his uncle, Thomas of Woodstock. Yet he is the rightful king, anointed by God. Are his failures so great that it will be in the interest of the state to get rid of him? Or is the removal of a king from his throne a crime against God and the order of nature? In the central scene of Shakespeare's play, the king is forced to participate in a ceremony in which he formally removes himself from the throne. Deposition was a matter so sensitive that a large segment of this scene may have been censored out of the early printed editions of the play. And in the last years of Queen Elizabeth's reign, the contemporary resonances of the story of Richard II's deposition were so powerful that the followers of the Earl of Essex took a particularly close interest in Shakespeare's play.

The Essex faction, including the young Earl of Southampton to whom Shakespeare had dedicated his narrative poems *Venus and Adonis* and *The Rape of Lucrece*, considered the old queen to be as bad as Richard. Like him, they murmured, she was surrounded by flatterers, raising too many taxes, and conducting a disastrous Irish policy. Could she be ripe for Richard's bloody fate?

Early in February 1601, Sir Charles Percy, a descendant of the Percy family who had joined with Bullingbrook to overthrow King Richard, had a bright idea. Along with Southampton, he had joined the group of aristocratic malcontents who hung around Essex House and voiced their frustration at Elizabeth's policies and preferments. The Earl of Essex himself was plotting to march against the court and confront the queen with demands for change. Percy, together with Lord Mounteagle and one or two others, slipped over the river to the Globe. They asked the players to put on a special production of *Richard II*. Shakespeare's men were reluctant: the play was so old and had not been staged for so long that there would be little or no audience. Essex's gentlemen responded with an offer that the players couldn't refuse: an immediate down payment of forty shillings to supplement their takings. Lines were relearned overnight and the next afternoon, the show was staged, with a large number of Essex's followers prominent in the audience.

At supper after the show, rumors began to fly, and the next morning the Essex men armed themselves and headed for the palace, vainly hoping to gather popular support along the way. It didn't come. They were roundly defeated and the ringleaders tried for high treason. Augustine Phillips, the actor who served as business manager of Shakespeare's theater company, was immediately brought in for interrogation. His story about their reluctance to perform such an old play as *Richard II*, together with the fact that Essex himself was not present at the performance, provided an escape route. The tribunal was persuaded that they had only revived the show for the sake of the money.

To judge from the choices that Shakespeare made in dramatizing his historical source materials, he seems to have been more interested in the human story of Richard's fall than the politics of rebellion. It is likely that the Essex faction commissioned the special performance not so much for its actual content—we cannot be sure that the full deposition scene was actually staged at this time in the play's life—as for the broad association between the rise of Henry Bullingbrook and the career of the charismatic earl. Essex's men were probably remembering a book originally dedicated to their master, Sir John Hayward's *The First Part of the Life and Reign of King Henry IV*. Published in 1599, it had caused much controversy as a result of its detailed treatment of Richard's removal from the throne. It was almost certainly Hayward's book rather than Shakespeare's play that led Queen Elizabeth to say, some time later, "I am Richard the Second. Know ye not that?"

Following the rebellion of 1601, Essex was sentenced to be hanged, drawn and quartered. That meant having his privy members cut off and draped around his neck. His sangfroid did not desert him. On hearing his sentence, he joked that since he had served Her Majesty in the four corners of the world, it was fitting that his body should be cut in quarters and driven through the four corners of London. The Earl of Southampton, Shakespeare's sometime patron, was consigned to the Tower. Given their connections with him, it was a very close run thing for the players. Hayward the historian took the rap and Shakespeare was saved by the cool performance of his friend Phillips under interrogation.

THE KING'S TWO BODIES

Richard II was very attractive to Essex and his followers not only because it seemed to give good reasons for taking action against an ineffective, vacillating monarch, but also because it appeared to lament the decline of chivalric England. One of Essex's chief strategies during his rise to prominence at court in the 1590s was to portray himself as a hero from a nobler age that had gone. He invoked the code of "honour" and made himself synonymous with such displays as the Accession Day tilts, in which courtiers would joust like knights of old.

The beginning of the play, so redolent of medieval rites of knighthood, would have been very much to Essex's taste. Mowbray and Bullingbrook throw down their gages and prepare for single combat with sword and lance. They are concerned above all with "spotless reputation"; "Mine honour is my life; both grow in one," says Mowbray, "Take honour from me, and my life is done." Honor is seen as the hallmark of the "trueborn Englishman." The feuding dukes regard themselves as true patriots, appealing to "English earth" and lamenting that in exile they must forgo their "native English" language. Richard's native language, by contrast, was French (which was also the nationality of his wife) and his court is implicitly seen as a place of French affectation. One of the most cultured of English kings, Richard was a munificent patron of poetry and the arts; Shakespeare does not exploit this, but he may imply it through the way in which he gives such eloquent and rhetorically elaborate poetry to the king, whereas Bullingbrook speaks a blunter English idiom, albeit still in finely honed verse. Near the end of the play, when the Yorks kneel before the new King Henry and ask pardon for their son Aumerle, the duke suggests that he should take on the French manners associated with the court and say "*pardonnez-moi*," but the duchess, a better judge of character, is the one who wins the pardon because she knows that Bullingbrook will stick to English ("Speak 'pardon' as 'tis current in our land: / The chopping French we do not understand").

King Richard stands accused of wasting the patrimony of the English nation. He has been fleeced by his flatterers, and costly Irish wars have required him to "lease out" the land. Given that Queen Elizabeth's exchequer was also heavily overdrawn as a result of the Irish problem, Shakespeare was probably being diplomatic as well as practical in not attempting to stage Richard's military campaign in Ireland, which is described at great length in his source, Holinshed's *Chronicles*. The focus remains firmly on the English land, imagined metaphorically as a sea-walled garden "full of weeds, her fairest flowers choked up."

Within two years of the play appearing in print, John of Gaunt's "this sceptred isle" speech was ripped from its context and included in an anthology called *England's Parnassus* as an exemplar of patriotic writing. It appears there as an unfinished sentence, lacking the sting in the tail: "this England . . . Is now leased out . . . That England, that was wont to conquer others, / Hath made a shameful conquest of itself." True patriotism, the original context reveals, involves fierce criticism of bad government as well as rhetorical praise of the land.

But if the bad governor is sacredly endowed as God's anointed deputy on earth, then is it permissible to remove him, even in the name of England and "true chivalry"? If the king is synonymous with the law, then to turn the law against him may seem a contradiction in terms: "What subject can give sentence on his king?" The monarch was traditionally imagined to have two bodies: as body politic, the king was the incarnation of the nation; as body natural, he was a mortal like anyone else. This was what made possible the paradoxical words "The king is dead, long live the king." When Richard stages his own unthroning, he inverts the words of the coronation service, shatters a mirror and gives up one of his two bodies.

What is left for the private self when the public persona is stripped away? Without "honour," according to the contentious dukes, "Men are but gilded loam or painted clay." But what would a king be without his crown, without a name and a title? Once Richard has broken the mirror, he turns from his image to his inner self. Whereas monarchy depends on exterior show, inwardness is explored through the medium of words. Richard is by far the most inward-looking of Shakespeare's kings. By focusing on the individual consciousness, considering Richard's fate in psychological terms, Shakespeare neatly sidesteps the alarmingly destabilizing political consequences of the moment when a subject gives sentence on a king.

"I had forgot myself. Am I not king?" In the very act of asking this question, Richard reveals that the answer is "no": since a king has two bodies, he has the right to speak in the royal "we," but here Richard is no more than an "I." In speaking of himself he veers between "I," "we," and "he" ("What must the king do now? Must he submit?"). Inconsistent pronouns are the surest sign of the instability of his self.

Richard speaks between a quarter and a third of the text; he soliloquizes frequently and at length. One of the key respects in which he and Bullingbrook function as dramatic opposites is that Bullingbrook never reveals his motivation and feelings in soliloquy: he is symbolically the man of action, whereas Richard is the man of feeling. Bullingbrook is defined by what he does; Richard anticipates Hamlet in defining himself through his obsessive talking about, and to, himself. "The play throughout is a history of the human mind," observed Samuel Taylor Coleridge, a self-confessed Hamlet of real life. The American poet Robert Lowell developed the analogy between Coleridge and Richard II in a taut sonnet exploring "the constant overflow of imagination / proportioned to his dwindling will to act."

Soliloquy and rhetorical elaboration are forms of self-dramatization. Richard sustains himself through a bravura linguistic performance: "Let's talk of graves . . ." He makes himself the object of his subjective musings: ". . . Must he lose / The name of king?" He watches himself losing his grip on his role: "Ay, no; no, ay, for I must nothing be." And he becomes more and more aware that to be is also to act, that we are all role-players: "Thus play I in one prison many people, / And none contented" ("one prison" is the Folio text's interesting variant on the original Quarto's "one person"—"prison" nicely suggests both Richard's confined location and the traditional idea of the body as prison of the soul, which is then released to eternity in death). He leaves the stage in the manner of "a well-graced actor."

Though the Folio text is entitled *The Life and Death of King Richard the Second*, the earlier Quarto edition was called *The Tragedy of King Richard the Second*. The structure of the drama answers to a very traditional idea of tragedy as a story in which a powerful figure falls from earthly prosperity and in so doing rises to greatness of soul. Pity for Richard is the prevailing tragic emotion in the closing scenes. "It seems to be the design of the poet to raise Richard to esteem in his fall, and consequently to interest the reader in his favour," wrote Dr. Johnson. Note "the reader" there, not the *spectator*—this is a play that has been more admired on page than stage. Johnson continues: "He gives him only passive fortitude, the virtue of a confessor, rather than of a king. In his prosperity we saw him imperious and oppressive; but in his distress he is wise, patient, and pious."

By concentrating on the inner life of Richard, Shakespeare diminishes some of the major elements of the play that was his structural model, Christopher Marlowe's *Edward II*. The flatterers Bushy, Bagot, and Green are given very small roles and the exclusion of the queen from the king's affections is not fully developed. In Marlowe's dramatization of the fall of a weak king and the rise of his rival, the minions—first Gaveston and then Spencer—are central not only to the politics but also to the sexuality of the play. They are explicitly the king's lovers. The abused queen becomes a lead player in the rebellion against the king. Shakespeare's Richard by contrast seems too self-absorbed to be powerfully driven by sexual desire. Coleridge spoke intriguingly of the character's *feminine friendism*, but that is not quite a euphemism for homoerotic feeling.

As the man who rises when Richard falls, Bullingbrook's story remains unfinished. But Shakespeare anticipates the civil war that will wrack his reign. The role of Northumberland, who cooperates with Bullingbrook but will eventually turn against him, is greatly expanded from its seed in Holinshed's *Chronicles*. Richard delivers a prophecy that "The time shall not be many hours of age / More than it is ere foul sin, gathering head, / Shall break into corruption" and predicts rightly that Northumberland will seek to pluck King Henry IV from his usurped throne. As he wrote these words, Shakespeare must have been thinking of how he was going to continue the story in another play. He was getting ready for a sequel: *Henry IV Part I*.

ABOUT THE TEXT

Shakespeare endures through history. He illuminates later times as well as his own. He helps us to understand the human condition. But he cannot do this without a good text of the plays. Without editions there would be no Shakespeare. That is why every twenty years or so throughout the last three centuries there has been a major new edition of his complete works. One aspect of editing is the process of keeping the texts up to date—modernizing the spelling, punctuation, and typography (though not, of course, the actual words), providing explanatory notes in the light of changing educational practices (a generation ago, most of Shakespeare's classical and biblical allusions could be assumed to be generally understood, but now they can't).

But because Shakespeare did not personally oversee the publication of his plays, editors also have to make decisions about the relative authority of the early printed editions. Half of the sum of his plays only appeared posthumously, in the elaborately produced First Folio text of 1623, the original "Complete Works" prepared for the press by Shakespeare's fellow actors, the people who knew the plays better than anyone else. The other half had appeared in print in his lifetime, in the more compact and cheaper form of "Quarto" editions, some of which reproduced good quality texts, others of which were to a greater or lesser degree garbled and error-strewn. In the case of a few plays there are hundreds of differences between the Quarto and Folio editions, some of them far from trivial.

If you look at printers' handbooks from the age of Shakespeare, you quickly discover that one of the first rules was that, whenever possible, compositors were recommended to set their type from existing printed books rather than manuscripts. This was the age before mechanical typesetting, where each individual letter had to be picked out by hand from the compositor's case and placed on a stick (upside down and back to front) before being laid on the press. It was an age of murky rushlight and of manuscripts written in a secretary hand that had dozens of different, hard-to-decipher forms. Printers' lives were a lot easier when they were reprinting existing books rather than struggling with handwritten copy. Easily the quickest way to have created the First Folio would have been simply to reprint those eighteen plays that had already appeared in Quarto and only work from manuscript on the other eighteen.

But that is not what happened. Whenever Quartos were used, playhouse "promptbooks" were also consulted and stage directions copied in from them. And in the case of several major plays where a reasonably well-printed Quarto was available, the Folio printers were instructed to work from an alternative, playhouse-derived manuscript. This meant that the whole process of producing the first complete Shakespeare took months, even years, longer than it might have done. But for the men overseeing the project, John Hemings and Henry Condell, friends and fellow actors who had been remembered in Shakespeare's will, the additional labor and cost were worth the effort for the sake of producing an edition that was close to the practice of the theater. They wanted all the plays in print so that people could, as they wrote in their prefatory address to the reader, "read him and again and again," but they also wanted "the great variety of readers" to work from texts that were close to the theater life for which Shakespeare originally intended them. For this reason, the *RSC Shakespeare*, in both *Complete Works* and individual volumes, uses the Folio as base text wherever possible. Significant Quarto variants are, however, noted in the Textual Notes.

Written and first performed in 1595 or 1596, *Richard II* was published in Quarto format in 1597 and reprinted twice in 1598. The printed text excluded a sequence of about 160 lines in which King Richard formally hands over his throne, inverting the sacred language of the coronation ceremony and smashing a mirror. Scholars usually assume that this omission was because the scene was too politically sensitive for print, but there is no evidence of active censorship. The idea that it must have been censored is an enduring misapprehension even among some distinguished Shakespeareans. The scene appeared as a "new addition" in the 1608 reprinting of the quarto and again, in a better quality text, deriving from the theater promptbook, in the 1623 Folio version of the play. Arguably, the sequence in which King Richard says, "With mine own tears I wash away my balm, / With mine own hands I give away my crown . . ." makes the play *less* subversive, turning a deposition into an abdication.

This raises the possibility, generally neglected by scholars, that Shakespeare may have written it as an addition after the real-life drama of February 1601, in order to give the impression of a formal, stately handing over of power, as opposed to the presumption and hugger-mugger of the original version that was now tarred by association with the trial of Essex and his accomplices. Nor can we wholly rule out the possibility that, to freshen up the play and as a little treat for Sir Charles Percy and his friends in return for their forty shillings above the ordinary, Shakespeare dashed off the addition on the Friday and gave it to his actors to learn overnight, allowing them to rehearse it in the morning run-through before including it in the afternoon performance.

Richard II, then, is a play that nearly all modern editors print in a hybrid text that never appeared in print in Shakespeare's lifetime. They base the text on the First Quarto of 1597, but insert into it the deposition (or abdication) scene that first appeared in print many years later. The Folio-based policy of the RSC edition means that we do not have to conflate different source texts in this way. The price for this choice is that our text prints the Folio's watered-down oaths (typically "Heaven" instead of "God") that were the result of a parliamentary act passed in 1606, whereby players were fined for blaspheming (i.e. mentioning the name of God) on stage. Modern producers wishing to restore the more robust oaths of the Quarto may reinsert them by consulting the list of variants that we include after the textual notes that follow the text.

The following observations highlight various aspects of the editorial process and indicate conventions used in the text of this edition:

Lists of Parts are supplied in the First Folio for only six plays, not including *Richard II*, so the list here is editorially supplied. Capitals indicate that part of the name which is used for speech headings in the script (thus "John of GAUNT, Duke of Lancaster, Richard's uncle").

Locations are provided by the Folio for only two plays, not including *Richard II*. Eighteenth-century editors, working in an age of elaborately realistic stage sets, were the first to provide detailed locations. Given that Shakespeare wrote for a bare stage and often an imprecise sense of place, we have relegated locations to the explanatory notes at the foot of the page, where they are given at the beginning of each scene where the imaginary location is different from the one before.

Act and Scene Divisions were provided in the Folio in a much more thoroughgoing way than in the Quartos. Sometimes, however, they were erroneous or omitted; corrections and additions supplied by editorial tradition are indicated by square brackets. Five-act division is based on a classical model, and act breaks provided the opportunity to replace the candles in the indoor Blackfriars playhouse that the King's Men used after 1608, but Shakespeare did not necessarily think in terms of a five-part structure of dramatic composition. The Folio convention is that a scene ends when the stage is empty. Nowadays, partly under the influence of film, we tend to consider a scene to be a dramatic unit that ends with either a change of imaginary location or a significant passage of time within the narrative. Shakespeare's fluidity of composition accords well with this convention, so in addition to act and scene numbers we provide a *running scene* count in the right margin at the beginning of each new scene, in the typeface used for editorial directions. Where there is a scene break caused by a momentary bare stage, but the location does not change and extra time does not pass, we use the convention *running scene continues.* There is inevitably a degree of editorial judgment in making such calls, but the system is very valuable in suggesting the pace of the plays.

Speakers' Names are often inconsistent in Folio. We have regularized speech headings, but retained an element of deliberate inconsistency in entry directions, in order to give the flavor of Folio. Thus BULLINGBROOK is always so-called in speech headings but "the Duke of Hereford" on occasion in entry directions.

Verse is indicated by lines that do not run to the right margin and by capitalization of each line. The Folio printers sometimes set verse as prose, and vice versa (either out of misunderstanding or for reasons of space). We have silently corrected in such cases, although in some instances there is ambiguity, in which case we have leaned toward the preservation of Folio layout. Folio sometimes uses contraction ("turnd" rather than "turned") to indicate whether or not the final "-ed" of a past participle is sounded, an area where there is variation for the sake of the five-beat iambic pentameter rhythm. We use the convention of a grave accent to indicate sounding (thus "turnèd" would be two syllables), but would urge actors not to overstress. In cases where one speaker ends with a verse half line and the next begins with the other half of the pentameter, editors since the late eighteenth century have indented the second line. We have abandoned this convention, since the Folio does not use it, nor did actors' cues in the Shakespearean theater. An exception is made when the second speaker actively interrupts or completes the first speaker's sentence.

Spelling is modernized, but older forms are occasionally maintained where necessary for rhythm or aural effect.

Punctuation in Shakespeare's time was as much rhetorical as grammatical. "Colon" was originally a term for a unit of thought in an argument. The semicolon was a new unit of punctuation (some of the Quartos lack them altogether). We have modernized punctuation throughout, but have given more weight to Folio punctuation than many editors, since, though not Shakespearean, it reflects the usage of his period. In particular, we have used the colon far more than many editors: it is exceptionally useful as a way of indicating how many Shakespearean speeches unfold clause by clause in a developing argument that gives the illusion of enacting the process of thinking in the moment. We have also kept in mind the origin of punctuation in classical times as a way of assisting the actor and orator: the comma suggests the briefest of pauses for breath, the colon a middling one, and a full stop or period a longer pause. Semicolons, by contrast, belong to an era of punctuation that was only just coming in during Shakespeare's time and that is coming to an end now: we have accordingly only used them where they occur in our copy texts (and not always then). Dashes are sometimes used for parenthetical interjections where the Folio has brackets. They are also used for interruptions and changes in train of thought. Where a change of addressee occurs within a speech, we have used a dash preceded by a period (or occasionally another form of punctuation). Often the identity of the respective addressees is obvious from the context. When it is not, this has been indicated in a marginal stage direction.

Entrances and Exits are fairly thorough in Folio, which has accordingly been followed as faithfully as possible. Where characters are omitted or corrections are necessary, this is indicated by square brackets (e.g. "[*and Attendants*]"). *Exit* is sometimes silently normalized to *Exeunt* and *Manet* anglicized to "remains." We trust Folio positioning of entrances and exits to a greater degree than most editors.

Editorial Stage Directions such as stage business, asides, indications of addressee and of characters' position on the gallery stage are only used sparingly in Folio. Other editions mingle directions of this kind with original Folio and Quarto directions, sometimes marking them by means of square brackets. We have sought to distinguish what could be described as *directorial* interventions of this kind from Folio-style directions (either original or supplied) by placing them in the right margin in a different typeface. There is a degree of subjectivity about which directions are of which kind, but the procedure is intended as a reminder to the reader and the actor that Shakespearean stage directions are often dependent upon editorial inference alone and are not set in stone. We also depart from editorial tradition in sometimes admitting uncertainty and thus printing permissive stage directions, such as an **Aside?** (often a line may be equally effective as an aside or as a direct address—it is for each production or reading to make its own decision) or a **may exit** or a piece of business placed between arrows to indicate that it may occur at various different moments within a scene.

Line Numbers in the left margin are editorial, for reference and to key the explanatory and textual notes.

Explanatory Notes at the foot of each page explain allusions and gloss obsolete and difficult words, confusing phraseology, occasional major textual cruces, and so on. Particular attention is given to non-standard usage, bawdy innuendo, and technical terms (e.g. legal and military language). Where more than one sense is given, commas indicate shades of related meaning, slashes alternative or double meanings.

Textual Notes at the end of the play indicate major departures from the Folio. They take the following form: the reading of our text is given in bold and its source given after an equals sign, with "Q" indicating that it derives from the First Quarto of 1597, "F" from the First Folio of 1623, "F2" a correction introduced in the Second Folio of 1632, and "Ed" from the subsequent editorial tradition. The rejected Folio ("F") reading is then given. We have also included noteworthy rejected readings, for example Act 5 Scene 5 line 31: "**5.5 31 prison** = F. Q = person." This indicates that we have preferred the Folio reading "prison" but noted the frequently adopted and interestingly different Quarto reading "person."

KEY FACTS

MAJOR PARTS (*with percentage of lines/number of speeches/scenes on stage*): King Richard II (27%/98/9), Henry Bullingbrook (15%/90/8), Duke of York (10%/54/8), John of Gaunt (7%/28/4), Northumberland (5%/38/6), Mowbray (5%/13/2), Queen (4%/25/4), Aumerle (3%/38/7), Duchess of York (3%/28/2), Bishop of Carlisle (2%/6/2), Duchess of Gloucester (2%/4/1), Gardener (2%/6/1).

LINGUISTIC MEDIUM: 100% verse, with high proportion of rhyme.

DATE: 1595–96. Registered for publication August 1597. Written after Samuel Daniel's *First Four Books of the Civil Wars* (registered October 1594, apparently published 1595); perhaps postdates renowned Accession Day tilts of November 1595. Described in February 1601 as "old and long out of use."

SOURCES: Primary source is the account of the last two years of Richard's reign in Raphael Holinshed's *Chronicles* (1587 edition), supplemented—especially for various details in the final act—by Samuel Daniel's *First Four Books of the Civil Wars Between the Two Houses of Lancaster and York* (1594–95). Christopher Marlowe's *Edward II* (1592?) was a major dramatic influence, both structurally (the fall of a weak king and the rise of his rival) and thematically (flatterers, Irish wars, a marginalized queen). Some scholars also detect the influence of the anonymous chronicle play of *Woodstock*: as well as verbal parallels, there are resemblances between Shakespeare's John of Gaunt and this play's Thomas of Woodstock, Duke of Gloucester, but recent scholarship suggests that Shakespeare's play precedes *Woodstock*, not vice versa. The garden scene is apparently without source, though the comparison between a disordered state and an overgrown garden was traditional.

TEXT: First printed in Quarto in 1597, with text deriving from Shakespeare's working manuscript or a transcription of it; the deposition scene was, however, omitted for reasons of censorship. The First Quarto was reprinted several times (Second and Third Quartos, 1598; Fourth Quarto, 1608; Fifth Quarto, 1615). These later Quartos correct a few obvious errors in the First Quarto, but introduce many misprints. The Second Quarto was one of the first printed play texts to include Shakespeare's name on the title page. The Fourth Quarto printed the deposition sequence for the first time, but in a defective text. The Folio text seems to have been printed from the Third Quarto (though a few editors argue that it was based on either the Fifth Quarto or a defective copy of the Third Quarto with the missing final leaves made up from the Fifth Quarto), but the Folio editor also consulted a manuscript closely related to theatrical production, perhaps the company "playbook." The Folio restored many First Quarto readings that had been corrupted in later Quartos, printed a good text of the deposition scene for the first time, added and systematized stage directions, made some alterations to staging for the sake of clarification, introduced act divisions, replaced "God" with "heaven" in accordance with the 1606 Act to Restrain Abuses, made a few verbal alterations, and omitted about fifty lines (these mostly seem to be deliberate theatrical cuts, though a clutch of individual lines might have been dropped inadvertently). Most modern editions are based on the First Quarto, with the deposition scene, stage directions, and many individual readings taken from the Folio. Our text resists this sort of conflation and is based on Folio, with the correction of manifest printers' errors. The Quarto-only passages are given at the end of the play.

GENEALOGY: See *William Shakespeare: Complete Works*, pp. 2476–7.

THE LIFE AND DEATH
OF KING RICHARD
THE SECOND

LIST OF PARTS

KING RICHARD II of England

QUEEN, Richard's wife

John of GAUNT, Duke of Lancaster, Richard's uncle

Henry BULLINGBROOK, Duke of Hereford, John of Gaunt's son, later King Henry IV

Duke of YORK, Edmund of Langley, Richard's uncle

DUCHESS OF YORK, his wife

Duke of AUMERLE, their son and Earl of Rutland

DUCHESS of Gloucester, widow of Thomas of Woodstock, Duke of Gloucester (Richard's uncle)

Thomas MOWBRAY, Duke of Norfolk

Earl of SALISBURY

Duke of SURREY

Lord BERKELEY

Bishop of CARLISLE

ABBOT of Westminster

Sir Stephen SCROOP

BUSHY

BAGOT

GREEN

Earl of NORTHUMBERLAND

Harry PERCY, Northumberland's son

Lord ROSS

Lord WILLOUGHBY

Lord FITZWATERS

Sir Piers of EXTON

LORD

LORD MARSHAL

TWO HERALDS

CAPTAIN of the Welsh army

TWO LADIES attending the Queen

GARDENER

SERVANT to the Gardener

SERVANT to York

KEEPER of the prison at Pomfret Castle

TWO SERVANTS to Exton

GROOM of Richard's stable

Various Soldiers, Attendants, Lords

QUEEN unnamed on stage; the historical Richard's wife at the end of his reign was Isabel of Valois, a child; in portraying an adult queen and a close marriage, the play seems to conflate Isabel with Richard's deceased first wife, Anne of Bohemia.

Act 1 Scene 1

Enter King Richard, John of Gaunt, with other Nobles and Attendants

KING RICHARD   Old John of Gaunt, time-honoured Lancaster,
 Hast thou according to thy oath and band
 Brought hither Henry Hereford thy bold son,
 Here to make good the boist'rous late appeal,
5 Which then our leisure would not let us hear,
 Against the Duke of Norfolk, Thomas Mowbray?
GAUNT I have, my liege.
KING RICHARD   Tell me, moreover, hast thou sounded him,
 If he appeal the duke on ancient malice,
10 Or worthily, as a good subject should,
 On some known ground of treachery in him?
GAUNT As near as I could sift him on that argument,
 On some apparent danger seen in him
 Aimed at your highness, no inveterate malice.
15 KING RICHARD   Then call them to our presence.   [*Exit an Attendant*]
               Face to face,
 And frowning brow to brow, ourselves will hear
 Th'accuser and the accusèd freely speak;
 High-stomached are they both, and full of ire,
 In rage deaf as the sea, hasty as fire.
Enter Bullingbrook and Mowbray
20 BULLINGBROOK   Many years of happy days befall
 My gracious sovereign, my most loving liege!
MOWBRAY Each day still better other's happiness
 Until the heavens, envying earth's good hap,
 Add an immortal title to your crown!

1.1 ***Location: the court of King Richard II***   *John of Gaunt* was named after his place of birth, Ghent   **2 Hast thou** have you—the familiar form used to intimates and inferiors   **band** bond   **3 Henry Hereford** i.e. Bullingbrook; he had been created Duke of Hereford (pronounced as two syllables) by Richard In 1397   **4 boist'rous** violent   **late** recent **appeal** binding accusation   **5 our** Richard uses the plural royal pronoun   **leisure** i.e. lack of leisure   **7 liege** lord, superior entitled to feudal allegiance and service   **8 sounded** inquired of   **9 on ancient** out of long-standing   **11 ground** motive, cause   **12 sift** find by questioning **argument** topic   **13 apparent** manifest, obvious   **14 inveterate** long-standing   **18 High-stomached** proud/high-spirited/courageous/angry   **ire** anger   **21 gracious** full of divine grace, holy/benevolent   **22 still** always   **23 hap** fortune   **24 immortal title** i.e. immortality (in heaven)

25 KING RICHARD   We thank you both. Yet one but flatters us,
         As well appeareth by the cause you come,
         Namely, to appeal each other of high treason.
         Cousin of Hereford, what dost thou object
         Against the Duke of Norfolk, Thomas Mowbray?

30 BULLINGBROOK   First, heaven be the record to my speech!
         In the devotion of a subject's love,
         Tend'ring the precious safety of my prince,
         And free from other misbegotten hate,
         Come I appellant to this princely presence.

35   Now, Thomas Mowbray, do I turn to thee,
         And mark my greeting well, for what I speak
         My body shall make good upon this earth,
         Or my divine soul answer it in heaven.
         Thou art a traitor and a miscreant;

40   Too good to be so and too bad to live,
         Since the more fair and crystal is the sky,
         The uglier seem the clouds that in it fly.
         Once more, the more to aggravate the note,
         With a foul traitor's name stuff I thy throat;

45   And wish — so please my sovereign — ere I move,
         What my tongue speaks my right drawn sword may prove.

     MOWBRAY   Let not my cold words here accuse my zeal:
         'Tis not the trial of a woman's war,
         The bitter clamour of two eager tongues,

50   Can arbitrate this cause betwixt us twain.
         The blood is hot that must be cooled for this.

---

25 but only   26 well appeareth is plainly apparent   you come i.e. about which you come
27 appeal accuse of a crime which the accuser undertakes to prove (especially of treason)
28 object charge   30 record witness   32 Tend'ring cherishing   33 misbegotten wrongfully
conceived   34 appellant (as an) accuser   36 mark note, pay attention to   38 answer
answer for   39 miscreant wretch, villain   40 good high-ranking   41 crystal clear, bright
(heavenly bodies were thought to be contained within rotating crystal spheres)   43 aggravate
emphasize, magnify   note reproach, mark of disgrace   45 ere before   46 right justly,
rightfully   47 cold deliberate, unimpassioned   accuse i.e. diminish, cast doubt on   zeal
powerful feelings/loyalty   48 trial judgment, test   49 eager sharp, biting   50 Can arbitrate
that can reach a judicial decision on   cause matter of dispute   betwixt between   twain two
51 blood anger, passion/bodily blood   cooled calmed/let flow (either through medical
bloodletting or in death)

Yet can I not of such tame patience boast
As to be hushed and nought at all to say.
First, the fair reverence of your highness curbs me
55   From giving reins and spurs to my free speech,
Which else would post until it had returned
These terms of treason doubly down his throat.
Setting aside his high blood's royalty,
And let him be no kinsman to my liege,
60   I do defy him, and I spit at him,
Call him a slanderous coward and a villain,
Which to maintain I would allow him odds,
And meet him, were I tied to run afoot
Even to the frozen ridges of the Alps,
65   Or any other ground inhabitable
Wherever Englishman durst set his foot.
Meantime, let this defend my loyalty:
By all my hopes most falsely doth he lie.

BULLINGBROOK   Pale trembling coward, there I   *Throws down his gage*
throw my gage,
70   Disclaiming here the kindred of a king,
And lay aside my high blood's royalty,
Which fear, not reverence, makes thee to except.
If guilty dread hath left thee so much strength
As to take up mine honour's pawn, then stoop.
75   By that and all the rites of knighthood else,
Will I make good against thee, arm to arm,
What I have spoken, or thou canst devise.

MOWBRAY   I take it up, and by that sword I swear   *Takes up gage*
Which gently laid my knighthood on my shoulder,

---

54 fair reverence of proper respect for   **56 else** otherwise   **post** hasten   **58 Setting . . .
royalty** regardless of his royal blood (Bullingbrook is Richard's cousin, and grandson to Edward
III; **high blood** plays on the sense of "extreme anger")   **59 let** supposing   **60 defy** challenge
to combat   **62 odds** the advantage   **63 meet** encounter in combat   **tied** obliged
65 inhabitable not habitable   **66 durst** dares to   **67 this** i.e. the following accusation, or
possibly Mowbray indicates his sword   **69 gage** pledge signifying a commitment to combat
(usually a glove or gauntlet, thrown down to challenge the opponent)   **72 except** set aside
74 pawn gage   **76 make good** prove   **77 thou canst devise** you can invent   **79 gently**
nobly/kindly/softly

80   I'll answer thee in any fair degree,
       Or chivalrous design of knightly trial:
       And when I mount, alive may I not light,
       If I be traitor or unjustly fight!

    KING RICHARD   What doth our cousin lay to Mowbray's charge?
85   It must be great that can inherit us
       So much as of a thought of ill in him.

    BULLINGBROOK   Look what I said: my life shall prove it true,
       That Mowbray hath received eight thousand nobles
       In name of lendings for your highness' soldiers,
90   The which he hath detained for lewd employments,
       Like a false traitor and injurious villain.
       Besides I say, and will in battle prove,
       Or here or elsewhere to the furthest verge
       That ever was surveyed by English eye,
95   That all the treasons for these eighteen years
       Complotted and contrivèd in this land
       Fetched from false Mowbray their first head and spring.
       Further I say, and further will maintain
       Upon his bad life to make all this good,
100   That he did plot the Duke of Gloucester's death,
       Suggest his soon-believing adversaries,
       And consequently, like a traitor coward,
       Sluiced out his innocent soul through streams of blood:
       Which blood, like sacrificing Abel's, cries
105   Even from the tongueless caverns of the earth
       To me for justice and rough chastisement.
       And by the glorious worth of my descent,
       This arm shall do it, or this life be spent.

---

80 **in . . . degree** to any just, honorable extent   82 **light** alight, dismount (from my horse)
83 **unjustly** dishonorably/in an unjust cause   84 **lay . . . charge** accuse Mowbray of
85 **inherit us** put us in possession   87 **Look** attend to, note   88 **nobles** gold coins
89 **lendings** advances on payment   90 **lewd** improper/vile   91 **injurious** harmful   93 **Or**
either   96 **Complotted** plotted in conspiracy with others   97 **Fetched** drew/derived   **head**
source   100 **Duke of Gloucester** son of Edward III, hence Richard's uncle and John of
Gaunt's brother; he was murdered in 1397 at Calais, while in the custody of Mowbray and,
many believe, at Richard's prompting   101 **Suggest** tempt, incite   103 **Sluiced out** let flow,
flooded out   104 **sacrificing** sacrificial   **Abel** in the Bible, killed by his brother Cain, the
world's first murderer   106 **chastisement** correction, punishment

KING RICHARD   How high a pitch his resolution soars!
110   Thomas of Norfolk, what sayest thou to this?
MOWBRAY   O, let my sovereign turn away his face
            And bid his ears a little while be deaf,
            Till I have told this slander of his blood,
            How God and good men hate so foul a liar.
115   KING RICHARD   Mowbray, impartial are our eyes and ears.
            Were he my brother, nay, our kingdom's heir,
            As he is but my father's brother's son,
            Now, by my sceptre's awe, I make a vow,
            Such neighbour nearness to our sacred blood
120   Should nothing privilege him, nor partialize
            The unstooping firmness of my upright soul.
            He is our subject, Mowbray, so art thou.
            Free speech and fearless I to thee allow.
MOWBRAY   Then, Bullingbrook, as low as to thy heart,
125   Through the false passage of thy throat, thou liest.
            Three parts of that receipt I had for Calais
            Disbursed I duly to his highness' soldiers;
            The other part reserved I by consent,
            For that my sovereign liege was in my debt
130   Upon remainder of a dear account,
            Since last I went to France to fetch his queen.
            Now swallow down that lie. For Gloucester's death,
            I slew him not; but to mine own disgrace
            Neglected my sworn duty in that case.
135   For you, my noble lord of Lancaster,
            The honourable father to my foe,
            Once I did lay an ambush for your life —
            A trespass that doth vex my grievèd soul.
            But ere I last received the sacrament

---

109 **pitch** height (literally, the highest point in a falcon's flight)   113 **slander of** disgrace to
118 **my sceptre's awe** the reverence due to my scepter   119 **neighbour** neighboring, close
120 **partialize** make partial, bias   126 **receipt** amount received   130 **Upon . . . account** for
the balance of a large debt   131 **fetch** historically Mowbray was involved in marriage
negotiations on Richard's behalf, though Richard escorted the French princess Isabel to
England   135 **lord of Lancaster** i.e. John of Gaunt   138 **trespass** sin

140   I did confess it, and exactly begged
       Your grace's pardon, and I hope I had it.
       This is my fault. As for the rest appealed,
       It issues from the rancour of a villain,
       A recreant and most degenerate traitor
145   Which in myself I boldly will defend,
       And interchangeably hurl down my gage   *Throws down his gage*
       Upon this overweening traitor's foot,
       To prove myself a loyal gentleman
       Even in the best blood chambered in his bosom.
150   In haste whereof, most heartily I pray
       Your highness to assign our trial day.
    KING RICHARD   Wrath-kindled gentlemen, be ruled by me:
       Let's purge this choler without letting blood.
       This we prescribe, though no physician:
155   Deep malice makes too deep incision
       Forget, forgive, conclude and be agreed:
       Our doctors say this is no time to bleed.
       Good uncle, let this end where it begun:
       We'll calm the Duke of Norfolk, you your son.
160   GAUNT   To be a make-peace shall become my age:
       Throw down, my son, the Duke of Norfolk's gage.
    KING RICHARD   And, Norfolk, throw down his.
    GAUNT   When, Harry, when?
       Obedience bids I should not bid again.
    KING RICHARD   Norfolk, throw down, we bid; there is no boot.
165   MOWBRAY   Myself I throw, dread sovereign, at thy foot.   *Kneels*
       My life thou shalt command, but not my shame:
       The one my duty owes, but my fair name,

---

140 **exactly** in full detail/specifically   142 **appealed** with which I am charged   144 **recreant** cowardly (if an adjective)/coward (if a noun)   145 **Which** which accusation
146 **interchangeably** in exchange, reciprocally   147 **overweening** arrogant   149 **Even in** i.e. by shedding   **chambered** enclosed   150 **In haste whereof** to hasten which   153 **purge** cure medically (by bloodletting)   **choler** anger (literally yellow bile, the hot and dry "humor," one of four fluids in ancient and medieval physiology, believed to govern physical and mental qualities)   **letting** shedding; refers specifically to medical practice of phlebotomy (opening a vein so as to let blood flow)   156 **conclude** come to terms   157 **doctors** learned men, astrologers   160 **become** suit, befit   164 **boot** point, advantage (in refusing)
165 **dread** revered   167 **fair name** honorable reputation

Despite of death that lives upon my grave,
To dark dishonour's use thou shalt not have.
170   I am disgraced, impeached and baffled here,
Pierced to the soul with slander's venomed spear,
The which no balm can cure but his heart-blood
Which breathed this poison.

KING RICHARD   Rage must be withstood.
175   Give me his gage. Lions make leopards tame.

MOWBRAY   Yea, but not change his spots. Take but my shame,
And I resign my gage. My dear dear lord,
The purest treasure mortal times afford
Is spotless reputation: that away,
180   Men are but gilded loam or painted clay.
A jewel in a ten-times-barred-up chest
Is a bold spirit in a loyal breast.
Mine honour is my life; both grow in one:
Take honour from me, and my life is done.
185   Then, dear my liege, mine honour let me try.
In that I live and for that will I die.

KING RICHARD   Cousin, throw down your gage. Do you begin.

BULLINGBROOK   O, heaven defend my soul from such foul sin!
Shall I seem crest-fall'n in my father's sight?
190   Or with pale beggar-fear impeach my height
Before this out-dared dastard? Ere my tongue
Shall wound mine honour with such feeble wrong,
Or sound so base a parle, my teeth shall tear
The slavish motive of recanting fear,

---

170 impeached accused legally   baffled disgraced publicly   172 balm ointment
his . . . breathed the heart-blood of he who uttered   175 Lions make leopards the lion
symbolized the king and featured on the royal coat of arms; Mowbray's coat of arms bore a *lion
leopard*, i.e. walking and showing the full face   176 spots leopard spots/stains of dishonor
Take take responsibility for/take over   179 away gone   180 but gilded merely covered with
gold, superficially fair   loam earth, clay   181 ten-times-barred-up i.e. extremely secure
chest plays on the sense of "torso"   183 in one together, inseparably   185 try put to the test
189 crest-fall'n humbled/abashed   190 impeach my height discredit my high rank, stoop
191 out-dared cowed/terrified   dastard coward   193 parle truce (literally trumpet call
instigating negotiation)   194 motive instrument, i.e. tongue   recanting renouncing a
belief/making a public confession of error

195   And spit it bleeding in his high disgrace,
         Where shame doth harbour, even in Mowbray's face.

                                                                    Exit Gaunt

         KING RICHARD   We were not born to sue, but to command,
              Which since we cannot do to make you friends,
              Be ready, as your lives shall answer it,
200   At Coventry upon Saint Lambert's day:
              There shall your swords and lances arbitrate
              The swelling difference of your settled hate.
              Since we cannot atone you, we shall see
              Justice design the victor's chivalry.
205   Lord Marshal, command our officers at arms
              Be ready to direct these home alarms.   *Exeunt*

Act 1 Scene 2   *running scene 2*

         Enter Gaunt and Duchess of Gloucester

         GAUNT   Alas, the part I had in Gloucester's blood
              Doth more solicit me than your exclaims,
              To stir against the butchers of his life.
              But since correction lieth in those hands
5   Which made the fault that we cannot correct,
              Put we our quarrel to the will of heaven,
              Who, when they see the hours ripe on earth,
              Will rain hot vengeance on offenders' heads.
         DUCHESS   Finds brotherhood in thee no sharper spur?
10   Hath love in thy old blood no living fire?
              Edward's seven sons, whereof thyself art one,
              Were as seven vials of his sacred blood,

---

195 **his** its (the tongue's)   196 **harbour** dwell/shelter   197 **sue** beg   200 **Saint Lambert's day** September 17   202 **swelling** growing/inflated with pride   **settled** fixed, unchanging   203 **atone** set at one, reconcile   204 **design** designate, identify   **chivalry** valor or prowess in war   206 **home alarms** domestic calls to arms   **1.2** *Location: unspecified, probably assumed to be Ely House, London*   1 **part . . . blood** i.e. my kinship to Gloucester (who was John of Gaunt's brother)   2 **solicit** urge   **exclaims** outcries, exclamations   3 **stir** take action   4 **those hands** i.e. Richard's (whom Gaunt holds responsible for Gloucester's death)   11 **Edward** Edward III

Or seven fair branches springing from one root:
Some of those seven are dried by nature's course,
15   Some of those branches by the Destinies cut.
But Thomas, my dear lord, my life, my Gloucester,
One vial full of Edward's sacred blood,
One flourishing branch of his most royal root,
Is cracked, and all the precious liquor spilt,
20   Is hacked down, and his summer leaves all faded,
By envy's hand and murder's bloody axe.
Ah, Gaunt, his blood was thine! That bed, that womb,
That metal, that self-mould that fashioned thee
Made him a man. And though thou liv'st and breath'st,
25   Yet art thou slain in him. Thou dost consent
In some large measure to thy father's death,
In that thou see'st thy wretched brother die,
Who was the model of thy father's life.
Call it not patience, Gaunt, it is despair.
30   In suff'ring thus thy brother to be slaughtered,
Thou show'st the naked pathway to thy life,
Teaching stern murder how to butcher thee.
That which in mean men we entitle patience
Is pale cold cowardice in noble breasts.
35   What shall I say? To safeguard thine own life,
The best way is to venge my Gloucester's death.
GAUNT   Heaven's is the quarrel, for heaven's substitute,
His deputy anointed in his sight,
Hath caused his death, the which if wrongfully,
40   Let heaven revenge, for I may never lift
An angry arm against his minister.

15 **Destinies** the Fates in classical mythology who cut the thread of life with their shears
19 **liquor** liquid   20 **faded** faded, withered   21 **envy's** malice's   23 **metal** substance (puns
on "mettle," i.e. disposition)   **self-mould** selfsame mold/mold from which the self is made
25 **consent** assent, acquiesce   28 **model** copy, image   30 **suff'ring** allowing   31 **naked**
i.e. defenseless   33 **mean** lowly, humble   36 **venge** avenge   37 **Heaven's . . . deputy**
i.e. Richard who, as king, was held to be God's earthly representative   38 **anointed . . .**
sight i.e. marked with holy oil at Westminster Abbey, the part of the coronation ceremony that
signified the sacred nature of the king

DUCHESS Where then, alas, may I complaint myself?

GAUNT To heaven, the widow's champion to defence.

DUCHESS Why, then, I will. Farewell, old Gaunt.

45 Thou go'st to Coventry, there to behold
Our cousin Hereford and fell Mowbray fight.
O, sit my husband's wrongs on Hereford's spear,
That it may enter butcher Mowbray's breast!
Or if misfortune miss the first career,
50 Be Mowbray's sins so heavy in his bosom,
That they may break his foaming courser's back,
And throw the rider headlong in the lists,
A caitiff recreant to my cousin Hereford!
Farewell, old Gaunt: thy sometimes brother's wife
55 With her companion grief must end her life.

GAUNT Sister, farewell. I must to Coventry.
As much good stay with thee as go with me!

DUCHESS Yet one word more: grief boundeth where it falls,
Not with the empty hollowness, but weight.
60 I take my leave before I have begun,
For sorrow ends not when it seemeth done.
Commend me to my brother, Edmund York.
Lo, this is all. Nay, yet depart not so:
Though this be all, do not so quickly go.
65 I shall remember more. Bid him — O, what? —
With all good speed at Plashy visit me.
Alack, and what shall good old York there see
But empty lodgings and unfurnished walls,
Unpeopled offices, untrodden stones?
70 And what hear there for welcome but my groans?
Therefore commend me, let him not come there
To seek out sorrow that dwells everywhere.

---

42 **complaint myself** lodge a formal complaint   43 **champion** defender   46 **cousin** kinsman
fell cruel, fierce   49 **career** charge of the horse in combat   51 **courser** swift powerful horse
ridden in battle   52 **lists** area of combat (literally, the barriers enclosing it)   53 **caitiff**
cowardly, villainous   **recreant** faith-breaker   54 **thy sometimes** formerly your
58 **boundeth** rebounds   62 **brother** i.e. brother-in-law   63 **Lo** look   66 **Plashy** the Duke of
Gloucester's country estate in Essex   69 **offices** servants' quarters

Desolate, desolate, will I hence and die:

The last leave of thee takes my weeping eye.   *Exeunt*

Act 1 Scene 3   *running scene 3*

Enter [the Lord] Marshal and Aumerle

LORD MARSHAL   My Lord Aumerle, is Harry Hereford armed?

AUMERLE   Yea, at all points, and longs to enter in.

LORD MARSHAL   The Duke of Norfolk, sprightfully and bold,

Stays but the summons of the appellant's trumpet.

5   AUMERLE   Why, then, the champions are prepared, and stay

For nothing but his majesty's approach.

Flourish. Enter King, Gaunt, Bushy, Bagot, Green and others. [When

they are set,] then Mowbray in armour and [a] Herald

KING RICHARD   Marshal, demand of yonder champion

The cause of his arrival here in arms.

Ask him his name and orderly proceed

10   To swear him in the justice of his cause.

LORD MARSHAL   In God's name and the king's, say who thou art

And why thou com'st thus knightly clad in arms,

Against what man thou com'st, and what's thy quarrel.

Speak truly, on thy knighthood and thine oath,

15   As so defend thee heaven and thy valour!

MOWBRAY   My name is Thomas Mowbray, Duke of Norfolk,

Who hither comes engagèd by my oath —

Which heaven defend a knight should violate! —

Both to defend my loyalty and truth

20   To God, my king and his succeeding issue,

Against the Duke of Hereford that appeals me,

And, by the grace of God and this mine arm,

1.3   Location: the area of combat at Coventry   2 at all points completely, in every
respect   **3 sprightfully** full of high spirits   **4 Stays** awaits   **appellant** accuser, challenger
5 champions contenders   *Flourish* trumpet fanfare accompanying a person in authority
When . . . set a Quarto direction, omitted from Folio, indicating that the king, as umpire,
should be set upon a raised throne   **7 demand** ask   **9 orderly** duly, properly   **13 quarrel**
complaint   **18 defend** forbid   **20 succeeding** subsequent/who will inherit the throne
issue children

To prove him, in defending of myself,
A traitor to my God, my king, and me.
25   And as I truly fight, defend me heaven!
Tucket. Enter Hereford [Bullingbrook] and Herald
KING RICHARD   Marshal, ask yonder knight in arms,
    Both who he is and why he cometh hither
    Thus plated in habiliments of war,
    And formally, according to our law,
30   Depose him in the justice of his cause.
LORD MARSHAL   What is thy name? And wherefore
        com'st thou hither,   *To Bullingbrook*
    Before King Richard in his royal lists?
    Against whom com'st thou? And what's thy quarrel?
    Speak like a true knight, so defend thee heaven!
35   BULLINGBROOK   Harry of Hereford, Lancaster and Derby
    Am I, who ready here do stand in arms
    To prove, by heaven's grace and my body's valour,
    In lists, on Thomas Mowbray, Duke of Norfolk,
    That he's a traitor, foul and dangerous,
40   To God of heaven, King Richard and to me.
    And as I truly fight, defend me heaven!
LORD MARSHAL   On pain of death, no person be so bold
    Or daring-hardy as to touch the lists,
    Except the marshal and such officers
45   Appointed to direct these fair designs.
BULLINGBROOK   Lord Marshal, let me kiss my sovereign's hand,
    And bow my knee before his majesty.
    For Mowbray and myself are like two men
    That vow a long and weary pilgrimage,
50   Then let us take a ceremonious leave
    And loving farewell of our several friends.
LORD MARSHAL   The appellant in all duty greets your highness,
    And craves to kiss your hand and take his leave.

Tucket personal trumpet call   **28 plated** armored   **habiliments** clothing, attire
30 Depose him take his sworn deposition   **31 wherefore** why   **43 daring-hardy** recklessly
bold   **touch** i.e. interfere in   **45 fair** lawful, proper   **51 several** respective/various

KING RICHARD   We will descend and fold him in our arms.   *Comes*
55   Cousin of Hereford, as thy cause is just,   *down and embraces*
     So be thy fortune in this royal fight!   *Bullingbrook*
     Farewell, my blood, which if today thou shed,
     Lament we may, but not revenge thee dead.
BULLINGBROOK   O, let no noble eye profane a tear
60   For me, if I be gored with Mowbray's spear.
     As confident as is the falcon's flight
     Against a bird, do I with Mowbray fight.—
     My loving lord, I take my leave of you.—   *To Richard*
     Of you, my noble cousin, Lord Aumerle,
65   Not sick, although I have to do with death,
     But lusty, young, and cheerly drawing breath.
     Lo, as at English feasts, so I regreet
     The daintiest last, to make the end most sweet.—
     O thou, the earthy author of my blood,   *To Gaunt*
70   Whose youthful spirit, in me regenerate,
     Doth with a twofold rigour lift me up
     To reach at victory above my head,
     Add proof unto mine armour with thy prayers,
     And with thy blessings steel my lance's point,
75   That it may enter Mowbray's waxen coat,
     And furbish new the name of John a Gaunt,
     Even in the lusty 'haviour of his son.
GAUNT   Heaven in thy good cause make thee prosp'rous!
     Be swift like lightning in the execution,
80   And let thy blows, doubly redoublèd,
     Fall like amazing thunder on the casque
     Of thy amazed pernicious enemy,
     Rouse up thy youthful blood, be valiant and live.

---

55 as insofar as, to the extent to which   **56 royal fight** because held in the king's presence
57 my blood Richard's reference is ambiguous; Bullingbrook was his cousin but all subjects
were the king's and part of the body politic   **59 profane** wrongfully let fall   **66 lusty**
vigorous, robust   **cheerly** cheerfully   **67 regreet** salute, welcome   **68 daintiest** most
delicious   **70 regenerate** reborn, renewed   **71 twofold** i.e. father's and son's   **73 proof**
impenetrability   **75 waxen** i.e. soft, vulnerable   **76 furbish** polish   **77 'haviour** behavior,
actions   **81 amazing** stupefying/terrifying   **casque** helmet   **82 pernicious** ruinous

BULLINGBROOK   Mine innocence and Saint George to thrive!
85   MOWBRAY   However heaven or fortune cast my lot,
    There lives or dies, true to King Richard's throne,
    A loyal, just and upright gentleman.
    Never did captive with a freer heart
    Cast off his chains of bondage and embrace
90   His golden uncontrolled enfranchisement
    More than my dancing soul doth celebrate
    This feast of battle with mine adversary.
    Most mighty liege, and my companion peers,
    Take from my mouth the wish of happy years.
95   As gentle and as jocund as to jest
    Go I to fight. Truth hath a quiet breast.
KING RICHARD   Farewell, my lord. Securely I espy
    Virtue with valour couchèd in thine eye.
    Order the trial, marshal, and begin.
100   LORD MARSHAL   Harry of Hereford, Lancaster and Derby,
    Receive thy lance. And heaven defend thy right!   *Attendant gives*
BULLINGBROOK   Strong as a tower, in hope I cry 'Amen'.   *a lance to*
LORD MARSHAL   Go bear this lance to Thomas,   *Bullingbrook*
    Duke of Norfolk.   *Attendant gives a lance to*
FIRST HERALD   Harry of Hereford, Lancaster and Derby,   *Mowbray*
105   Stands here for God, his sovereign and himself,
    On pain to be found false and recreant,
    To prove the Duke of Norfolk, Thomas Mowbray,
    A traitor to his God, his king and him,
    And dares him to set forwards to the fight.
110   SECOND HERALD   Here standeth Thomas Mowbray, Duke of
    Norfolk,
    On pain to be found false and recreant,
    Both to defend himself and to approve
    Henry of Hereford, Lancaster and Derby,

---

84 **Saint George** patron saint of England   90 **enfranchisement** freedom   95 **gentle** pleasant, friendly, courteous   **jocund** joyful, cheerful   **jest** amuse oneself/act in a masque   97 **Securely** confidently   98 **couchèd** lodged/at rest   99 **Order** set in order/initiate   106 **recreant** cowardly/unfaithful to duty   108 **him** i.e. Bullingbrook   112 **approve** prove

To God, his sovereign and to him disloyal,
115   Courageously and with a free desire
Attending but the signal to begin.   *A charge sounded*
LORD MARSHAL   Sound trumpets, and set forward, combatants.
Stay, the king hath thrown his warder down.
KING RICHARD   Let them lay by their helmets and their spears,
120   And both return back to their chairs again.
Withdraw with us, and let the trumpets sound
While we return these dukes what we decree.   *A long flourish*
Draw near, and list what with our council we have done.
For that our kingdom's earth should not be soiled
125   With that dear blood which it hath fosterèd,
And for our eyes do hate the dire aspect
Of civil wounds ploughed up with neighbours' swords,
Which so roused up with boist'rous untuned drums,
With harsh resounding trumpets' dreadful bray,
130   And grating shock of wrathful iron arms,
Might from our quiet confines fright fair peace
And make us wade even in our kindred's blood:
Therefore, we banish you our territories.
You, cousin Hereford, upon pain of death,
135   Till twice five summers have enriched our fields
Shall not regreet our fair dominions,
But tread the stranger paths of banishment.
BULLINGBROOK   Your will be done. This must my comfort be:
That sun that warms you here shall shine on me,
140   And those his golden beams to you here lent
Shall point on me and gild my banishment.
KING RICHARD   Norfolk, for thee remains a heavier doom,
Which I with some unwillingness pronounce:
The sly slow hours shall not determinate

---

114 him i.e. Mowbray   116 Attending awaiting   *charge* trumpet call signaling the
beginning of combat   118 Stay halt, stop   warder staff or baton held by the king to
symbolize his authority over the combat   119 lay by put aside   122 return inform   123 list
listen to   124 For that because   125 dear beloved/costly   126 for because   aspect sight
128 boist'rous noisy, raucous/violent   130 shock clash in combat   136 regreet see again
137 stranger foreign   144 sly stealthy   determinate put to an end

145   The dateless limit of thy dear exile.
        The hopeless word of 'never to return'
        Breathe I against thee, upon pain of life.
        MOWBRAY   A heavy sentence, my most sovereign liege,
        And all unlooked for from your highness' mouth.
150   A dearer merit, not so deep a maim
        As to be cast forth in the common air,
        Have I deservèd at your highness' hands.
        The language I have learned these forty years,
        My native English, now I must forgo,
155   And now my tongue's use is to me no more
        Than an unstringèd viol or a harp,
        Or like a cunning instrument cased up,
        Or, being open, put into his hands
        That knows no touch to tune the harmony.
160   Within my mouth you have enjailed my tongue,
        Doubly portcullised with my teeth and lips,
        And dull unfeeling barren ignorance
        Is made my jailer to attend on me.
        I am too old to fawn upon a nurse,
165   Too far in years to be a pupil now.
        What is thy sentence then but speechless death,
        Which robs my tongue from breathing native breath?
        KING RICHARD   It boots thee not to be compassionate.
        After our sentence, plaining comes too late.
170   MOWBRAY   Then thus I turn me from my country's light
        To dwell in solemn shades of endless night.   *Starts to go*
        KING RICHARD   Return again, and take an oath with thee.
        Lay on our royal sword your banished hands;
        Swear by the duty that you owe to heaven —

---

145 **dateless limit** unlimited term   **dear** heartfelt/grievous   147 **life** i.e. loss of life
149 **unlooked for** unexpected   150 **merit** reward   **maim** wound   151 **common**
ordinary/open   157 **cunning** skillfully made/requiring skill to play   158 **open** not in its case
159 **touch** fingering/skill   161 **portcullised** shut in, as if with a portcullis (defensive iron
grille, usually of a castle)   168 **boots** profits   **compassionate** lamenting piteously
169 **plaining** complaining   171 **solemn** burdensome/dark/mournful

175 Our part therein we banish with yourselves —
To keep the oath that we administer:
You never shall, so help you truth and heaven,
Embrace each other's love in banishment,
Nor ever look upon each other's face,
180 Nor ever write, regreet, or reconcile
This louring tempest of your home-bred hate,
Nor ever by advisèd purpose meet
To plot, contrive, or complot any ill
Gainst us, our state, our subjects, or our land.

185 BULLINGBROOK I swear.

MOWBRAY   And I, to keep all this.

BULLINGBROOK Norfolk, so far as to mine enemy:
By this time, had the king permitted us,
One of our souls had wandered in the air,
190 Banished this frail sepulchre of our flesh,
As now our flesh is banished from this land.
Confess thy treasons ere thou fly this realm:
Since thou hast far to go, bear not along
The clogging burden of a guilty soul.

195 MOWBRAY   No, Bullingbrook. If ever I were traitor,
My name be blotted from the book of life,
And I from heaven banished as from hence!
But what thou art, heaven, thou, and I do know,
And all too soon, I fear, the king shall rue.
200 Farewell, my liege, now no way can I stray:
Save back to England, all the world's my way.   *Exit*

KING RICHARD Uncle, even in the glasses of thine eyes   *To Gaunt*
I see thy grievèd heart. Thy sad aspect
Hath from the number of his banished years
205 Plucked four away.— Six frozen winters spent,   *To Bullingbrook*
Return with welcome home from banishment.

175 Our part therein i.e. the duty you owe to me as king   180 regreet greet (one another) again   181 louring darkly threatening   182 advisèd considered, deliberate   183 complot conspire in   187 so far as let me say this much   190 sepulchre tomb   192 fly flee 194 clogging encumbering (like a clog, a block of wood attached to the neck or leg to prevent escape)   199 rue regret, lament   200 stray take the wrong road/go wrong   201 Save except   202 glasses windows   203 aspect look

BULLINGBROOK How long a time lies in one little word!
 Four lagging winters and four wanton springs
 End in a word: such is the breath of kings.
210 GAUNT I thank my liege, that in regard of me
 He shortens four years of my son's exile.
 But little vantage shall I reap thereby,
 For ere the six years that he hath to spend
 Can change their moons and bring their times about
215 My oil-dried lamp and time-bewasted light
 Shall be extinct with age and endless night.
 My inch of taper will be burnt and done,
 And blindfold death not let me see my son.
KING RICHARD Why uncle, thou hast many years to live.
220 GAUNT But not a minute, king, that thou canst give.
 Shorten my days thou canst with sudden sorrow,
 And pluck nights from me, but not lend a morrow.
 Thou canst help time to furrow me with age,
 But stop no wrinkle in his pilgrimage.
225 Thy word is current with him for my death,
 But dead, thy kingdom cannot buy my breath.
KING RICHARD Thy son is banished upon good advice,
 Whereto thy tongue a party-verdict gave.
 Why at our justice seem'st thou then to lour?
230 GAUNT Things sweet to taste prove in digestion sour.
 You urged me as a judge, but I had rather
 You would have bid me argue like a father.
 Alas, I looked when some of you should say
 I was too strict to make mine own away.
235 But you gave leave to my unwilling tongue,
 Against my will to do myself this wrong.

---

208 **wanton** abundant, flourishing   212 **vantage** advantage   214 **times** seasonal cycles
215 **oil-dried** empty of oil   **time-bewasted** used up by time   216 **extinct** extinguished
217 **taper** candle   218 **blindfold death** refers to the eyeless skull that symbolized death and/or
to the idea of death depriving Gaunt of the power to see   224 **pilgrimage** i.e. journey through
life   225 **current** valid, genuine (as a legitimate coin)   226 **dead** i.e. once I am dead
227 **advice** counsel, consideration, judgment   228 **party-verdict** share in the collective
decision (of the king's advisers)   229 **lour** frown, look gloomy   233 **looked when** expected
that, waited for   234 **make . . . away** banish my own child   235 **leave** permission

KING RICHARD   Cousin, farewell, and, uncle, bid him so.
  Six years we banish him, and he shall go.

                      Flourish.   *Exeunt [Richard and Attendants]*

AUMERLE   Cousin, farewell. What presence must not
  know,   *To Bullingbrook*
240   From where you do remain let paper show.

LORD MARSHAL   My lord, no leave take I, for I will ride   *To Bullingbrook*
  As far as land will let me, by your side.

GAUNT   O, to what purpose dost thou hoard thy
  words   *To Bullingbrook*
  That thou return'st no greeting to thy friends?

245 BULLINGBROOK   I have too few to take my leave of you,
  When the tongue's office should be prodigal
  To breathe th'abundant dolour of the heart.

GAUNT   Thy grief is but thy absence for a time.

BULLINGBROOK   Joy absent, grief is present for that time.

250 GAUNT   What is six winters? They are quickly gone.

BULLINGBROOK   To men in joy. But grief makes one hour ten.

GAUNT   Call it a travel that thou tak'st for pleasure.

BULLINGBROOK   My heart will sigh when I miscall it so,
  Which finds it an enforcèd pilgrimage.

255 GAUNT   The sullen passage of thy weary steps
  Esteem as foil wherein thou art to set
  The precious jewel of thy home return.

BULLINGBROOK   O, who can hold a fire in his hand
  By thinking on the frosty Caucasus?
260 Or cloy the hungry edge of appetite
  By bare imagination of a feast?
  Or wallow naked in December snow
  By thinking on fantastic summer's heat?

---

239 **presence . . . know** I cannot learn of you in person/what the royal court shall not know
240 **paper** i.e. letters   245 **few** i.e. few words   246 **office** function   **prodigal** extravagant
247 **breathe** utter   **dolour** sorrow   248 **grief** cause for grief (Bullingbrook shifts the sense to
"sorrow")   **time** short while   252 **travel** journey/labor   253 **miscall** wrongly call
255 **sullen** somber, melancholy   256 **Esteem as foil** regard as a setting for a jewel
259 **Caucasus** region bordering Asia Minor including the Caucasus Mountains, depicted by
Ovid as cold and stony   260 **cloy** satiate, gorge   263 **fantastic** imaginary

O, no, the apprehension of the good
265   Gives but the greater feeling to the worse.
Fell sorrow's tooth doth never rankle more
Than when it bites, but lanceth not the sore.

GAUNT   Come, come, my son, I'll bring thee on thy way.
Had I thy youth and cause, I would not stay.

270   BULLINGBROOK   Then England's ground, farewell. Sweet soil,
adieu.
My mother, and my nurse, which bears me yet!
Where'er I wander, boast of this I can,
Though banished, yet a trueborn Englishman.   [*Exeunt*]

Act 1 Scene 4   *running scene 4*

Enter King, Aumerle, Green and Bagot

KING RICHARD   We did observe.   Cousin Aumerle,
How far brought you high Hereford on his way?

AUMERLE   I brought high Hereford, if you call him so,
But to the next highway, and there I left him.

5   KING RICHARD   And say, what store of parting tears were shed?

AUMERLE   Faith, none for me, except the north-east wind,
Which then blew bitterly against our face,
Awaked the sleepy rheum, and so by chance
Did grace our hollow parting with a tear.

10   KING RICHARD   What said our cousin when you parted with him?

AUMERLE   'Farewell'. And, for my heart disdainèd that my
tongue
Should so profane the word, that taught me craft
To counterfeit oppression of such grief
That word seemed buried in my sorrow's grave.

15   Marry, would the word 'farewell' have lengthened hours

---

264 **apprehension** conception, awareness   266 **Fell** fierce, cruel   **rankle** cause festering
267 **lanceth** pierces (to relieve infection)   268 **bring** escort   270 **adieu** goodbye
1.4   *Location: the royal court*   1 We did observe Richard enters mid-conversation
2 **high** proud/of high rank   4 **next** nearest   5 **store** quantity, abundance   6 **for me** on my
part   8 **rheum** watery discharge, i.e. tears   9 **hollow** insincere   11 **for** because   12 **craft**
skill, cunning   13 **counterfeit** pretend, fake   15 **Marry** by the Virgin Mary

And added years to his short banishment,
He should have had a volume of farewells,
But since it would not, he had none of me.
KING RICHARD   He is our cousin, cousin, but 'tis doubt,
20   When time shall call him home from banishment,
Whether our kinsman come to see his friends.
Ourself and Bushy, Bagot here, and Green
Observed his courtship to the common people.
How he did seem to dive into their hearts
25   With humble and familiar courtesy,
What reverence he did throw away on slaves,
Wooing poor craftsmen with the craft of smiles
And patient underbearing of his fortune,
As 'twere to banish their affects with him.
30   Off goes his bonnet to an oyster-wench.
A brace of draymen bid God speed him well
And had the tribute of his supple knee,
With 'Thanks, my countrymen, my loving friends',
As were our England in reversion his,
35   And he our subjects' next degree in hope.
GREEN   Well, he is gone, and with him go these thoughts.
Now for the rebels which stand out in Ireland.
Expedient manage must be made, my liege,
Ere further leisure yield them further means
40   For their advantage and your highness' loss.
KING RICHARD   We will ourself in person to this war,
And, for our coffers with too great a court
And liberal largesse are grown somewhat light,
We are enforced to farm our royal realm,
45   The revenue whereof shall furnish us

---

19 **cousin** Aumerle's father is the Duke of York, Richard's uncle   **doubt** doubtful   **21 friends** relatives   **26 reverence** respect   **28 underbearing** endurance   **29 banish . . . him** take their affection into exile with him   **30 bonnet** soft brimless hat   **oyster-wench** girl who sells oysters   **31 brace of draymen** pair of cart drivers   **32 supple** easily bent   **34 in reversion** i.e. after my death (when leased land would revert to its true owner)   **35 our . . . hope** in terms of public expectation and favor, the nearest heir   **37 stand out** make a stand, hold out   **38 Expedient manage** swift management   **39 leisure** delay   **43 largesse** generosity   **44 farm** lease parts of the land to tenants who might then collect taxes on their own behalf

For our affairs in hand. If that come short,
Our substitutes at home shall have blank charters,
Whereto, when they shall know what men are rich,
They shall subscribe them for large sums of gold
50   And send them after to supply our wants,
For we will make for Ireland presently.

Enter Bushy

Bushy, what news?

BUSHY   Old John of Gaunt is very sick, my lord,
Suddenly taken, and hath sent post haste
55   To entreat your majesty to visit him.

KING RICHARD   Where lies he?

BUSHY   At Ely House.

KING RICHARD   Now put it, heaven, in his physician's mind
To help him to his grave immediately!
60   The lining of his coffers shall make coats
To deck our soldiers for these Irish wars.
Come, gentlemen, let's all go visit him.
Pray heaven we may make haste, and come too late!

[*Exeunt*]

Act 2 Scene 1   *running scene 5*

Enter Gaunt, sick, with York [and Attendants]

GAUNT   Will the king come, that I may breathe my last
In wholesome counsel to his unstaid youth?

YORK   Vex not yourself, nor strive not with your breath,
For all in vain comes counsel to his ear.

5   GAUNT   O, but they say the tongues of dying men
Enforce attention like deep harmony.
Where words are scarce, they are seldom spent in vain,

46 **come short** is insufficient   47 **substitutes** those appointed to govern during the king's absence   **blank charters** documents authorizing deputies to collect revenues, or forced loans; blank spaces were left for the names of those required to pay   49 **subscribe them** enter their names   50 **them** i.e. the sums collected   51 **presently** immediately   57 **Ely House** the Bishop of Ely's palace in Holborn, London   60 **lining** contents (puns on the sense of "lining of a coat")   **2.1   *Location: London, Ely House*   sick** Gaunt is probably carried on stage in a chair   2 **unstaid** uncontrolled

For they breathe truth that breathe their words in pain.
He that no more must say is listened more
10   Than they whom youth and ease have taught to gloze.
More are men's ends marked than their lives before.
The setting sun and music is the close,
As the last taste of sweets is sweetest last,
Writ in remembrance more than things long past.
15   Though Richard my life's counsel would not hear,
My death's sad tale may yet undeaf his ear.

YORK   No, it is stopped with other flatt'ring sounds,
As praises, of his state: then there are found
Lascivious metres, to whose venom sound
20   The open ear of youth doth always listen,
Report of fashions in proud Italy,
Whose manners still our tardy apish nation
Limps after in base imitation.
Where doth the world thrust forth a vanity —
25   So it be new, there's no respect how vile —
That is not quickly buzzed into his ears?
That all too late comes counsel to be heard,
Where will doth mutiny with wit's regard.
Direct not him whose way himself will choose.
30   'Tis breath thou lack'st, and that breath wilt thou lose.

GAUNT   Methinks I am a prophet new inspired
And thus expiring do foretell of him.
His rash fierce blaze of riot cannot last,
For violent fires soon burn out themselves.
35   Small showers last long, but sudden storms are short.
He tires betimes that spurs too fast betimes.
With eager feeding food doth choke the feeder.

9 listened listened to   10 gloze flatter, talk smoothly   11 marked paid attention to
12 close closing cadence of a piece of music   13 last at its end/for longest   16 sad serious,
solemn   18 state kingly splendor   19 metres verses   venom poisonous   21 proud
arrogant/showy/splendid   22 tardy apish belatedly imitating   24 vanity trifle   25 So
provided   there's no respect it does not matter   26 buzzed whispered busily   27 That so
that   28 will . . . regard desire rebels against reasoned consideration   31 new inspired newly
filled with divine influence (plays on the sense of "full of newly drawn breath")   32 expiring
dying/breathing out   33 riot wasteful, dissolute lifestyle   35 Small composed of fine drops
36 betimes early

Light vanity, insatiate cormorant,
Consuming means soon preys upon itself.
40 This royal throne of kings, this sceptred isle,
This earth of majesty, this seat of Mars,
This other Eden, demi-paradise,
This fortress built by nature for herself
Against infection and the hand of war,
45 This happy breed of men, this little world,
This precious stone set in the silver sea,
Which serves it in the office of a wall,
Or as a moat defensive to a house,
Against the envy of less happier lands,
50 This blessèd plot, this earth, this realm, this England,
This nurse, this teeming womb of royal kings,
Feared by their breed and famous for their birth,
Renownèd for their deeds as far from home,
For Christian service and true chivalry,
55 As is the sepulchre in stubborn Jewry
Of the world's ransom, blessèd Mary's son:
This land of such dear souls, this dear dear land,
Dear for her reputation through the world,
Is now leased out — I die pronouncing it —
60 Like to a tenement or pelting farm.
England, bound in with the triumphant sea,
Whose rocky shore beats back the envious siege
Of watery Neptune, is now bound in with shame,
With inky blots and rotten parchment bonds.
65 That England, that was wont to conquer others,
Hath made a shameful conquest of itself.

38 **Light vanity** frivolous foolishness   **cormorant** glutton (literally, greedy seabird)   39 **means** resources, means of sustenance   40 **sceptred** invested with regal authority   41 **earth of majesty** land fit for kings   **Mars** Roman god of war   45 **happy breed** fortunate race
47 **office** function   50 **plot** land for cultivation   51 **teeming** fertile   52 **by their breed** on account of their mighty ancestry   55 **sepulchre** cave outside Jerusalem in which Christ was buried   **stubborn Jewry** the residents of Jerusalem who resisted Christianity
56 **world's . . . son** i.e. Christ   60 **tenement** land or property held by a tenant   **pelting** paltry
61 **bound in** bordered, surrounded   62 **envious** malicious, hostile   63 **Neptune** Roman god of the sea   **bound** legally bound   64 **inky . . . bonds** i.e. the corrupt blank charters   65 **wont** accustomed

Ah, would the scandal vanish with my life,
How happy then were my ensuing death!

Enter King, Queen, Aumerle, Bushy, Green, Bagot, Ross and
Willoughby

YORK   The king is come. Deal mildly with his youth,
70   For young hot colts being raged do rage the more.

QUEEN   How fares our noble uncle Lancaster?

KING RICHARD   What comfort, man? How is't with agèd Gaunt?

GAUNT   O, how that name befits my composition!
Old Gaunt indeed, and gaunt in being old.
75   Within me grief hath kept a tedious fast,
And who abstains from meat that is not gaunt?
For sleeping England long time have I watched.
Watching breeds leanness, leanness is all gaunt.
The pleasure that some fathers feed upon,
80   Is my strict fast — I mean, my children's looks,
And therein fasting, hast thou made me gaunt.
Gaunt am I for the grave, gaunt as a grave,
Whose hollow womb inherits nought but bones.

KING RICHARD   Can sick men play so nicely with their names?
85   GAUNT   No, misery makes sport to mock itself.
Since thou dost seek to kill my name in me,
I mock my name, great king, to flatter thee.

KING RICHARD   Should dying men flatter those that live?

GAUNT   No, no, men living flatter those that die.
90   KING RICHARD   Thou, now a-dying, say'st thou flatter'st me.

GAUNT   O no, thou diest, though I the sicker be.

KING RICHARD   I am in health, I breathe, I see thee ill.

GAUNT   Now he that made me knows I see thee ill:
Ill in myself to see, and in thee seeing ill.
95   Thy death-bed is no lesser than the land
Wherein thou liest in reputation sick.

---

73 composition state of health   **76 meat** food   **77 watched** remained awake/kept guard
83 inherits receives   **84 nicely** ingeniously, precisely   **85 to mock** in mocking   **86 kill . . . me**
i.e. by banishing Gaunt's son and heir   **93 see thee ill** see you imperfectly (as my sight is
failing)/see the ill that is in you

And thou, too careless patient as thou art,
Commit'st thy anointed body to the cure
Of those physicians that first wounded thee.
100 A thousand flatterers sit within thy crown,
Whose compass is no bigger than thy head.
And yet, encagèd in so small a verge,
The waste is no whit lesser than thy land.
O, had thy grandsire with a prophet's eye
105 Seen how his son's son should destroy his sons,
From forth thy reach he would have laid thy shame,
Deposing thee before thou wert possessed,
Which art possessed now to depose thyself.
Why, cousin, were thou regent of the world,
110 It were a shame to let his land by lease.
But for thy world enjoying but this land,
Is it not more than shame to shame it so?
Landlord of England art thou and not king.
Thy state of law is bondslave to the law, and—
115 KING RICHARD   And thou, a lunatic lean-witted fool,
Presuming on an ague's privilege,
Dar'st with thy frozen admonition
Make pale our cheek, chasing the royal blood
With fury from his native residence?
120 Now, by my seat's right royal majesty,
Wert thou not brother to great Edward's son,
This tongue that runs so roundly in thy head
Should run thy head from thy unreverent shoulders.
GAUNT   O, spare me not, my brother's — Edward's — son,

---

101 compass circumference   102 verge limit, rim/the twelve-mile radius around the king's court/measure of land   103 waste wasteland/wastefulness/damage done to property by a tenant/waist   104 grandsire i.e. Edward III   105 his sons Edward's sons, Richard's uncles/Richard's own (as yet unborn) children   106 forth beyond   107 Deposing disinheriting, depriving   possessed in possession of the crown (sense then shifts to "inhabited by the devil")   109 cousin kinsman   regent ruler   111 for . . . land insofar as your world consists of this land   114 state . . . law absolute legal status (as king) is now subject to legal processes (as a result of leasing out land)   116 Presuming on taking advantage of   ague fever and shaking   117 frozen cold, hostile/chilled by illness   120 seat throne/status   122 roundly bluntly/fluently   123 unreverent disrespectful

125   For that I was his father Edward's son.
　　　That blood already, like the pelican,
　　　Thou hast tapped out and drunkenly caroused.
　　　My brother Gloucester, plain well-meaning soul —
　　　Whom fair befall in heaven 'mongst happy souls! —
130   May be a precedent and witness good
　　　That thou respect'st not spilling Edward's blood.
　　　Join with the present sickness that I have,
　　　And thy unkindness be like crookèd age,
　　　To crop at once a too long withered flower.
135   Live in thy shame, but die not shame with thee:
　　　These words hereafter thy tormentors be!
　　　Convey me to my bed, then to my grave:
　　　Love they to live that love and honour have.   *Carried off*

　　　　　　　　　　　　　　　　　　　　　　Exit   *by Attendants*

　　KING RICHARD　And let them die that age and sullens have,
140   For both hast thou, and both become the grave.
　　YORK　　　I do beseech your majesty, impute his words
　　　To wayward sickliness and age in him.
　　　He loves you, on my life, and holds you dear
　　　As Harry Duke of Hereford, were he here.
145   KING RICHARD　Right, you say true. As Hereford's love, so his;
　　　As theirs, so mine, and all be as it is.

Enter Northumberland

　　NORTHUMBERLAND　My liege, old Gaunt commends him to your
　　　majesty.
　　KING RICHARD　What says he?
　　NORTHUMBERLAND　Nay, nothing. All is said.
150   His tongue is now a stringless instrument.
　　　Words, life and all, old Lancaster hath spent.

---

125 **For that** because   126 **pelican** the bird's offspring were thought to feed on her
blood   127 **tapped out** drawn as from a barrel   **caroused** drunk heartily/drunk toasts
with   129 **fair** good, happiness   133 **unkindness** unnatural behavior   139 **sullens**
sulks, gloomy moods   140 **become** befit, suit   143 **dear As Harry** as dearly as Gaunt holds
Harry (but Richard interprets "as dearly as Harry holds Richard")   151 **spent** used up,
exhausted

YORK   Be York the next that must be bankrupt so!
            Though death be poor, it ends a mortal woe.
KING RICHARD   The ripest fruit first falls, and so doth he.
155   His time is spent, our pilgrimage must be.
            So much for that. Now for our Irish wars:
            We must supplant those rough rug-headed kerns,
            Which live like venom where no venom else
            But only they have privilege to live.
160   And for these great affairs do ask some charge,
            Towards our assistance we do seize to us
            The plate, coin, revenues and movables,
            Whereof our uncle Gaunt did stand possessed.
YORK   How long shall I be patient? O, how long
165   Shall tender duty make me suffer wrong?
            Not Gloucester's death, nor Hereford's banishment,
            Nor Gaunt's rebukes, nor England's private wrongs,
            Nor the prevention of poor Bullingbrook
            About his marriage, nor my own disgrace
170   Have ever made me sour my patient cheek,
            Or bend one wrinkle on my sovereign's face.
            I am the last of noble Edward's sons,
            Of whom thy father, Prince of Wales, was first.
            In war was never lion raged more fierce,
175   In peace was never gentle lamb more mild,
            Than was that young and princely gentleman.
            His face thou hast, for even so looked he,
            Accomplished with the number of thy hours.
            But when he frowned, it was against the French
180   And not against his friends. His noble hand
            Did win what he did spend and spent not that

---

155 pilgrimage i.e. journey through life   157 supplant get rid of   rug-headed shaggy-haired
kerns lightly armed foot soldiers   160 ask some charge require some expenditure
161 seize take possession (legal term)   162 plate gold or silver tableware   movables portable
property   167 Gaunt's rebukes the rebukes given by Richard to Gaunt   private wrongs
wrongs done to individuals   168 Bullingbrook . . . marriage Richard prevented the exiled
Bullingbrook from marrying a cousin of the French king   171 bend one wrinkle direct one
frown   178 Accomplished . . . hours i.e. when he was your age   Accomplished equipped

Which his triumphant father's hand had won.
His hands were guilty of no kindred's blood,
But bloody with the enemies of his kin.
185 O Richard, York is too far gone with grief,
Or else he never would compare between.

KING RICHARD   Why, uncle, what's the matter?

YORK   O my liege,
Pardon me, if you please; if not, I, pleased
190 Not to be pardoned, am content withal.
Seek you to seize and grip into your hands
The royalties and rights of banished Hereford?
Is not Gaunt dead? And doth not Hereford live?
Was not Gaunt just? And is not Harry true?
195 Did not the one deserve to have an heir?
Is not his heir a well-deserving son?
Take Hereford's rights away, and take from time
His charters and his customary rights:
Let not tomorrow then ensue today.
200 Be not thyself. For how art thou a king
But by fair sequence and succession?
Now, afore God — God forbid I say true! —
If you do wrongfully seize Hereford's right,
Call in his letters patents that he hath
205 By his attorneys-general to sue
His livery, and deny his offered homage,
You pluck a thousand dangers on your head,
You lose a thousand well-disposèd hearts
And prick my tender patience to those thoughts
210 Which honour and allegiance cannot think.

KING RICHARD   Think what you will, we seize into our hands

---

190 **withal** with that   191 **seize** take legal possession of   192 **royalties** rights granted by the king/rights due to one of royal blood   194 **true** loyal/legitimate (as heir)   198 **His** i.e. time's **customary rights** i.e. of inheritance and succession   199 **ensue** follow   204 **Call . . . patents** revoke the documents signed by the king granting land or titles   205 **By . . . livery** allowing him to sue, through his lawyers, for the right to his inheritance   206 **homage** avowal of allegiance, part of the formal process of receiving one's inheritance   207 **pluck** pull
209 **prick** spur

His plate, his goods, his money and his lands.

YORK   I'll not be by the while. My liege, farewell:

What will ensue hereof, there's none can tell.

215 But by bad courses may be understood

That their events can never fall out good.   *Exit*

KING RICHARD Go, Bushy, to the Earl of Wiltshire straight.

Bid him repair to us to Ely House

To see this business.— Tomorrow next

220 We will for Ireland, and 'tis time, I trow.

And we create, in absence of ourself,

Our uncle York Lord Governor of England,

For he is just and always loved us well.—

Come on, our queen. Tomorrow must we part.

225 Be merry, for our time of stay is short.

Flourish.   [Exeunt all] except Northumberland, Willoughby and Ross

NORTHUMBERLAND Well, lords, the Duke of Lancaster is dead.

ROSS   And living too, for now his son is duke.

WILLOUGHBY Barely in title, not in revenue.

NORTHUMBERLAND Richly in both, if justice had her right.

230 ROSS   My heart is great, but it must break with silence,

Ere't be disburdened with a liberal tongue.

NORTHUMBERLAND Nay, speak thy mind, and let him ne'er speak
     more

That speaks thy words again to do thee harm!

WILLOUGHBY Tends that thou wouldst speak to th'Duke of
     Hereford?

235 If it be so, out with it boldly, man.

Quick is mine ear to hear of good towards him.

ROSS   No good at all that I can do for him,

Unless you call it good to pity him,

Bereft and gelded of his patrimony.

---

213 **by** nearby, present   215 **courses** i.e. of action   216 **events** consequences   218 **repair**
come   219 **see** attend to   **Tomorrow next** tomorrow/tomorrow morning   220 **trow** believe
230 **great** swollen with emotion   **with silence** by keeping silent   231 **liberal** freely speaking
234 **Tends . . . to** does what you want to say relate to   239 **Bereft** forcibly deprived, robbed
gelded deprived of wealth/castrated

240 NORTHUMBERLAND Now, afore heaven, 'tis shame such wrongs
        are borne
      In him, a royal prince, and many more
      Of noble blood in this declining land.
      The king is not himself, but basely led
      By flatterers. And what they will inform,
245   Merely in hate, gainst any of us all,
      That will the king severely prosecute
      Gainst us, our lives, our children, and our heirs.
  ROSS   The commons hath he piled with grievous taxes,
      And quite lost their hearts. The nobles hath he fined
250   For ancient quarrels, and quite lost their hearts.
  WILLOUGHBY And daily new exactions are devised,
      As blanks, benevolences, and I wot not what.
      But what, o'God's name, doth become of this?
  NORTHUMBERLAND Wars hath not wasted it, for warred he hath
        not,
255   But basely yielded upon compromise
      That which his ancestors achieved with blows.
      More hath he spent in peace than they in wars.
  ROSS   The Earl of Wiltshire hath the realm in farm.
  WILLOUGHBY The king's grown bankrupt, like a broken man.
260 NORTHUMBERLAND Reproach and dissolution hangeth over him.
  ROSS   He hath not money for these Irish wars,
      His burdenous taxations notwithstanding,
      But by the robbing of the banished duke.
  NORTHUMBERLAND His noble kinsman. Most degenerate king!
265   But, lords, we hear this fearful tempest sing,
      Yet seek no shelter to avoid the storm.
      We see the wind sit sore upon our sails,
      And yet we strike not, but securely perish.

---

246 **prosecute** perform/pursue   248 **piled** most editors emend to "pilled" (stripped bare,
plunder ed)   250 **ancient** long-standing   251 **exactions** means of enforcing payment
252 **blanks** blank charters   **benevolences** forced loans   **wot** know   253 **this** i.e. all the
money that has been collected   255 **basely . . . compromise** made concessions in a cowardly
way   258 **in farm** for rent, on lease   259 **broken** financially ruined   267 **sore** sorely,
threateningly   268 **strike** draw in the sails/strike blows in opposition   **securely**
overconfidently, heedlessly

ROSS   We see the very wreck that we must suffer,
270   And unavoided is the danger now,
         For suffering so the causes of our wreck.
NORTHUMBERLAND   Not so: even through the hollow eyes of death
         I spy life peering, but I dare not say
         How near the tidings of our comfort is.
275 WILLOUGHBY   Nay, let us share thy thoughts, as thou dost ours.
ROSS   Be confident to speak, Northumberland.
         We three are but thyself, and speaking so,
         Thy words are but as thoughts: therefore be bold.
NORTHUMBERLAND   Then thus: I have from Port le Blanc, a bay
280   In Brittany, received intelligence
         That Harry Duke of Hereford, Rainold Lord Cobham,
         That late broke from the Duke of Exeter,
         His brother, Archbishop late of Canterbury,
         Sir Thomas Erpingham, Sir John Rainston,
285   Sir John Norbery, Sir Robert Waterton and Francis Quoint,
         All these well furnished by the Duke of Brittany
         With eight tall ships, three thousand men of war,
         Are making hither with all due expedience
         And shortly mean to touch our northern shore.
290   Perhaps they had ere this, but that they stay
         The first departing of the king for Ireland.
         If then we shall shake off our slavish yoke,
         Imp out our drooping country's broken wing,
         Redeem from broking pawn the blemished crown,
295   Wipe off the dust that hides our sceptre's gilt
         And make high majesty look like itself,
         Away with me in post to Ravenspurgh.

---

271 suffering enduring, permitting   **274 tidings** news   **281 Rainold . . . Exeter** in fact, it was
the young Earl of Arundel who escaped from Exeter's custody; it seems likely that a line is
missing here and many editors insert a line based on Shakespeare's source, Holinshed's
Chronicles: "Thomas, son and heir to th'Earl of Arundel"   **282 broke** escaped   **283 His** i.e.
the Earl of Arundel's   **286 furnished** equipped   **287 tall** large, grand   **288 expedience**
haste   **290 had ere this** would have done already   **stay** await   **293 Imp out** repair by
inserting new feathers (falconry term)   **294 broking pawn** being pledged to a pawnbroker
295 gilt gold (puns on "guilt")   **297 post** haste   **Ravenspurgh** a former Yorkshire port on the
River Humber

But if you faint, as fearing to do so,
Stay and be secret, and myself will go.
300 ROSS   To horse, to horse! Urge doubts to them that fear.
WILLOUGHBY Hold out my horse, and I will first be there.   *Exeunt*

Act 2 Scene 2   *running scene 6*

Enter Queen, Bushy and Bagot

BUSHY   Madam, your majesty is too much sad.
You promised, when you parted with the king,
To lay aside life-harming heaviness
And entertain a cheerful disposition.
5 QUEEN   To please the king I did. To please myself
I cannot do it. Yet I know no cause
Why I should welcome such a guest as grief,
Save bidding farewell to so sweet a guest
As my sweet Richard. Yet again, methinks,
10   Some unborn sorrow, ripe in fortune's womb,
Is coming towards me, and my inward soul
With nothing trembles. At something it grieves,
More than with parting from my lord the king.
BUSHY   Each substance of a grief hath twenty shadows,
15   Which shows like grief itself, but is not so.
For sorrow's eye, glazèd with blinding tears,
Divides one thing entire to many objects,
Like perspectives, which rightly gazed upon
Show nothing but confusion: eyed awry
20   Distinguish form. So your sweet majesty,
Looking awry upon your lord's departure,

298 faint lose heart, are nervous   301 Hold . . . horse as long as my horse holds out
2.2   *Location: the royal court*   3 heaviness sorrow   4 entertain maintain/receive
14 shadows mirrored reflections, insubstantial things   16 glazèd glassed over/covered with a
film   17 thing entire to complete thing into   18 perspectives optical devices incorporating
mirrors that produce distorted images/seemingly distorted paintings that only become clear
when viewed from a particular angle   rightly directly, from the front   19 awry obliquely,
from the side   20 Distinguish form make their shape clear, reveal order

Find shapes of grief, more than himself to wail,
Which, looked on as it is, is naught but shadows
Of what it is not. Then, thrice-gracious queen,
25   More than your lord's departure weep not. More's not seen;
Or if it be, 'tis with false sorrow's eye,
Which for things true weeps things imaginary.

QUEEN   It may be so, but yet my inward soul
Persuades me it is otherwise. Howe'er it be,
30   I cannot but be sad, so heavy sad
As though on thinking on no thought I think,
Makes me with heavy nothing faint and shrink.

BUSHY   'Tis nothing but conceit, my gracious lady.

QUEEN   'Tis nothing less. Conceit is still derived
35   From some forefather grief. Mine is not so,
For nothing hath begot my something grief,
Or something hath the nothing that I grieve.
'Tis in reversion that I do possess —
But what it is, that is not yet known — what
40   I cannot name. 'Tis nameless woe, I wot.

Enter Green

GREEN   Heaven save your majesty! And well met,
        gentlemen.
I hope the king is not yet shipped for Ireland.

QUEEN   Why hop'st thou so? 'Tis better hope he is,
For his designs crave haste, his haste good hope.
45   Then wherefore dost thou hope he is not shipped?

GREEN   That he, our hope, might have retired his power,
And driven into despair an enemy's hope,
Who strongly hath set footing in this land.

---

22 himself the original grief/Richard's departure   wail bewail, lament   25 More for more
27 for in place of/because of   30 heavy weightily/sorrowfully   31 on . . . think dwelling
anxiously on nothing, on the absence of thought   33 conceit imagination (the queen shifts
the sense to "thought, understanding")   34 nothing less i.e. far from it   still always
36 begot conceived, created   something substantial, actual   37 grieve grieve for, feel
sorrow over   38 in reversion i.e. as a legacy, not yet inherited   40 wot know, believe
45 wherefore why   46 retired pulled back (from Ireland)   48 strongly with a powerful
military force

The banished Bullingbrook repeals himself,
50   And with uplifted arms is safe arrived
At Ravenspurgh.

QUEEN   Now God in heaven forbid!

GREEN   O, madam, 'tis too true. And that is worse,
The Lord Northumberland, his son young Henry Percy,
55   The Lords of Ross, Beaumond and Willoughby,
With all their powerful friends, are fled to him.

BUSHY   Why have you not proclaimed Northumberland
And the rest of the revolted faction, traitors?

GREEN   We have: whereupon the Earl of Worcester
60   Hath broke his staff, resigned his stewardship,
And all the household servants fled with him
To Bullingbrook.

QUEEN   So, Green, thou art the midwife of my woe,
And Bullingbrook my sorrow's dismal heir.
65   Now hath my soul brought forth her prodigy,
And I, a gasping new-delivered mother,
Have woe to woe, sorrow to sorrow joined.

BUSHY   Despair not, madam.

QUEEN   Who shall hinder me?
70   I will despair, and be at enmity
With cozening hope; he is a flatterer,
A parasite, a keeper-back of death,
Who gently would dissolve the bands of life,
Which false hope lingers in extremity.

Enter York

75   GREEN   Here comes the Duke of York.

QUEEN   With signs of war about his agèd neck.
O, full of careful business are his looks!
Uncle, for heaven's sake, speak comfortable words.

---

49 repeals himself recalls himself from exile/revokes his sentence of banishment   **50 uplifted arms** arms raised in prayer/brandished weapons   **60 staff** i.e. the symbol of his role as Steward of the king's household   **61 household** i.e. royal establishment   **64 heir** child, offspring   **65 prodigy** portent/monster   **71 cozening** deceitful (may play on "cousin")   **73 bands** bonds   **74 lingers** draws out, causes to linger   **in extremity** to the very end/the final moments of life   **77 careful** anxious, care-filled   **78 comfortable** comforting

YORK   Comfort's in heaven, and we are on the earth,
80   Where nothing lives but crosses, care and grief.
      Your husband, he is gone to save far off,
      Whilst others come to make him lose at home.
      Here am I left to underprop his land,
      Who, weak with age, cannot support myself.
85   Now comes the sick hour that his surfeit made,
      Now shall he try his friends that flattered him.

Enter a Servant

SERVANT   My lord, your son was gone before I came.
YORK   He was? Why, so! Go all which way it will!
      The nobles they are fled, the commons they are cold,
90   And will, I fear, revolt on Hereford's side.
      Sirrah, get thee to Plashy, to my sister Gloucester:
      Bid her send me presently a thousand pound.
      Hold, take my ring.
SERVANT   My lord, I had forgot to tell your lordship:
95   Today as I came by, I callèd there —
      But I shall grieve you to report the rest.
YORK   What is't, knave?
SERVANT   An hour before I came, the duchess died.
YORK   Heav'n for his mercy! What a tide of woes
100   Come rushing on this woeful land at once!
      I know not what to do. I would to heaven —
      So my untruth had not provoked him to it —
      The king had cut off my head with my brother's.
      What, are there posts dispatched for Ireland?
105   How shall we do for money for these wars?
      Come, sister — cousin, I would say — pray, pardon   *To Queen*
          me.—
      Go, fellow, get thee home, provide some carts   *To Servant*

80 **crosses** obstacles   81 **save** protect (his rule in Ireland)   83 **underprop** support, prop up
85 **surfeit** excess, overindulgence   86 **try** put to the test   87 **son** i.e. the Duke of Aumerle
89 **cold** unenthusiastic/unmoved   91 **Sirrah** sir (used to an inferior)   **sister** sister-in-law
92 **presently** immediately   93 **take my ring** i.e. as a sign that the message is genuinely from
York   99 **Heav'n** i.e. I pray heaven (God)   101 **would** wish   102 **So** provided that   **untruth**
disloyalty   103 **brother's** i.e. the murdered Gloucester's   104 **posts** messengers   105 **do**
manage, provide

And bring away the armour that is there.—   [*Exit Servant*]
Gentlemen, will you muster men?
110 If I know how or which way to order these affairs
Thus disorderly thrust into my hands,
Never believe me. Both are my kinsmen.
Th'one is my sovereign, whom both my oath
And duty bids defend: th'other again
115 Is my kinsman, whom the king hath wronged,
Whom conscience and my kindred bids to right.
Well, somewhat we must do.— Come, cousin, I'll
Dispose of you.—
Gentlemen, go muster up your men,
120 And meet me presently at Berkeley Castle.
I should to Plashy too,
But time will not permit. All is uneven,
And everything is left at six and seven.

Exeunt [*York and Queen*]

BUSHY   The wind sits fair for news to go to Ireland,
125 But none returns. For us to levy power
Proportionable to th'enemy
Is all impossible.
GREEN   Besides, our nearness to the king in love
Is near the hate of those love not the king.
130 BAGOT   And that's the wavering commons, for their love
Lies in their purses, and whoso empties them,
By so much fills their hearts with deadly hate.
BUSHY   Wherein the king stands generally condemned.
BAGOT   If judgement lie in them, then so do we,
135 Because we have been ever near the king.
GREEN   Well, I will for refuge straight to Bristol Castle.
The Earl of Wiltshire is already there.

---

109 **muster** assemble in readiness for action   113 **oath** i.e. of allegiance   116 **kindred**
kinship, family bond   117 **somewhat** something   118 **Dispose of** make arrangements for
120 **Berkeley Castle** a castle in Gloucestershire, near Bristol   123 **at . . . seven** in chaos
124 **sits** i.e. blows   125 **power** troops   129 **those** those who   133 **generally** universally/by
the people   134 **judgement . . . we** they are to be judges, then our fate lies in their hands
136 **straight** (go) straightaway

BUSHY   Thither will I with you, for little office
             Will the hateful commons perform for us,
140   Except like curs to tear us all in pieces.
             Will you go along with us?   *To Bagot*
BAGOT   No, I will to Ireland to his majesty.
             Farewell. If heart's presages be not vain,
             We three here part that ne'er shall meet again.
145 BUSHY   That's as York thrives to beat back Bullingbrook.
GREEN   Alas, poor duke! The task he undertakes
             Is numb'ring sands and drinking oceans dry.
             Where one on his side fights, thousands will fly.
BUSHY   Farewell at once, for once, for all, and ever.
150   Well, we may meet again.
BAGOT   I fear me, never.   *Exeunt*

Act 2 Scene 3   *running scene 7*

Enter the Duke of Hereford [Bullingbrook] and Northumberland

BULLINGBROOK   How far is it, my lord, to Berkeley now?
NORTHUMBERLAND   Believe me, noble lord,
             I am a stranger here in Gloucestershire.
             These high wild hills and rough uneven ways
5   Draws out our miles, and makes them wearisome.
             And yet our fair discourse hath been as sugar,
             Making the hard way sweet and delectable.
             But I bethink me what a weary way
             From Ravenspurgh to Cottshold will be found
10   In Ross and Willoughby, wanting your company,
             Which, I protest, hath very much beguiled
             The tediousness and process of my travel.
             But theirs is sweetened with the hope to have

---

138 **office** service   139 **hateful** hate-filled   140 **curs** dogs   143 **presages** forebodings
vain wrong, in vain   145 **as** depends on how   **2.3** *Location: Gloucestershire*
9 **Cottshold** the Cotswolds, rural area covering part of Oxfordshire and Gloucestershire
10 **In** by   **wanting** lacking   11 **beguiled** whiled away   12 **tediousness and process** tedious
course

The present benefit that I possess;
15   And hope to joy is little less in joy
Than hope enjoyed. By this the weary lords
Shall make their way seem short, as mine hath done
By sight of what I have, your noble company.

BULLINGBROOK Of much less value is my company
20   Than your good words. But who comes here?

Enter Harry Percy

NORTHUMBERLAND It is my son, young Harry Percy,
Sent from my brother Worcester, whencesoever.—
Harry, how fares your uncle?

PERCY   I had thought, my lord, to have learned his health
of you.

25   NORTHUMBERLAND Why, is he not with the queen?

PERCY   No, my good lord. He hath forsook the court,
Broken his staff of office and dispersed
The household of the king.

NORTHUMBERLAND What was his reason?

30   He was not so resolved when we last spake together.

PERCY   Because your lordship was proclaimèd traitor.
But he, my lord, is gone to Ravenspurgh
To offer service to the Duke of Hereford,
And sent me over by Berkeley to discover
35   What power the Duke of York had levied there,
Then with direction to repair to Ravenspurgh.

NORTHUMBERLAND Have you forgot the Duke of Hereford, boy?

PERCY   No, my good lord, for that is not forgot
Which ne'er I did remember: to my knowledge,
40   I never in my life did look on him.

NORTHUMBERLAND Then learn to know him now: this is the duke.

PERCY   My gracious lord, I tender you my service,
Such as it is, being tender, raw and young,
Which elder days shall ripen and confirm
45   To more approvèd service and desert.

---

16 By this in this way/with this hope   **22 whencesoever** wherever he may be   **26 forsook**
abandoned, rejected   **35 levied** raised   **36 repair** go   **42 tender** offer (sense then shifts to
"youthful, inexperienced")   **45 approvèd** proven

BULLINGBROOK   I thank thee, gentle Percy, and be sure
I count myself in nothing else so happy
As in a soul rememb'ring my good friends.
And as my fortune ripens with thy love,
50   It shall be still thy true love's recompense.
My heart this covenant makes, my hand thus   *Gives Percy*
      seals it.   *his hand*
NORTHUMBERLAND   How far is it to Berkeley? And what stir
Keeps good old York there with his men of war?
PERCY   There stands the castle, by yond tuft of trees,
55   Manned with three hundred men, as I have heard.
And in it are the Lords of York, Berkeley and Seymour,
None else of name and noble estimate.

Enter Ross and Willoughby

NORTHUMBERLAND   Here come the Lords of Ross and Willoughby,
Bloody with spurring, fiery-red with haste.
60   BULLINGBROOK   Welcome, my lords. I wot your love pursues
A banished traitor. All my treasury
Is yet but unfelt thanks, which more enriched
Shall be your love and labour's recompense.
ROSS   Your presence makes us rich, most noble lord.
65   WILLOUGHBY   And far surmounts our labour to attain it.
BULLINGBROOK   Evermore thanks — th'exchequer of the poor,
Which, till my infant fortune comes to years,
Stands for my bounty. But who comes here?

Enter Berkeley

NORTHUMBERLAND   It is my Lord of Berkeley, as I guess.
70   BERKELEY   My Lord of Hereford, my message is to you.
BULLINGBROOK   My lord, my answer is — to Lancaster,
And I am come to seek that name in England.

---

46 **gentle** noble/courteous/kind   49 **fortune** success, luck/wealth   50 **still** always   52 **stir** events, activity   54 **yond** yonder, that   **tuft** clump   57 **estimate** repute   59 **spurring** i.e. the blood of the horses they have spurred on so hard   60 **wot** know   62 **unfelt** i.e. not yet expressed through material reward   **which** i.e. which treasury   66 **thanks . . . poor** i.e. gratitude is the only wealth the poor have   67 **comes to years** reaches the age of maturity   71 **my . . . Lancaster** Bullingbrook will respond only to his proper title (Duke of Lancaster), inherited from his father, John of Gaunt

And I must find that title in your tongue,
Before I make reply to aught you say.

75   BERKELEY   Mistake me not, my lord, 'tis not my meaning
To raze one title of your honour out.
To you, my lord, I come — what lord you will—
From the most glorious of this land,
The Duke of York, to know what pricks you on
80   To take advantage of the absent time
And fright our native peace with self-born arms.

Enter York [with Attendants]

BULLINGBROOK   I shall not need transport my words by you.
Here comes his grace in person.— My noble uncle!   *Kneels*

YORK   Show me thy humble heart, and not thy knee,
85   Whose duty is deceivable and false.

BULLINGBROOK   My gracious uncle—

YORK   Tut, tut! Grace me no grace, nor uncle me no uncle.
I am no traitor's uncle; and that word 'grace'
In an ungracious mouth is but profane.
90   Why have these banished and forbidden legs
Dared once to touch a dust of England's ground?
But then more 'why': why have they dared to march
So many miles upon her peaceful bosom,
Frighting her pale-faced villages with war
95   And ostentation of despisèd arms?
Com'st thou because th'anointed king is hence?
Why, foolish boy, the king is left behind,
And in my loyal bosom lies his power.
Were I but now the lord of such hot youth
100   As when brave Gaunt, thy father, and myself

---

74 aught anything   **76 raze** erase/scrape   **title** puns on "tittle," i.e. tiniest part
77 what . . . will whatever the title you wish me to use   **78 glorious** illustrious, important
79 pricks spurs   **80 absent time** i.e. time during which the king is absent   **81 native** natural,
inherent (with connotations of birth)   **self-born** originating with you, brandished for your
own cause (also "self-borne"—carried by yourself)   **85 deceivable** deceptive   **87 Grace . . .
grace** don't speak to me of "grace" (since your behavior is so **ungracious**)   **89 ungracious**
unmannerly/wicked/lacking in spiritual grace   **91 dust** particle of dust   **95 ostentation of
despisèd** display of despicable (because traitorous)

Rescued the Black Prince, that young Mars of men,
From forth the ranks of many thousand French,
O, then how quickly should this arm of mine,
Now prisoner to the palsy, chastise thee
105   And minister correction to thy fault!
BULLINGBROOK   My gracious uncle, let me know my fault.
On what condition stands it and wherein?
YORK   Even in condition of the worst degree,
In gross rebellion and detested treason.
110   Thou art a banished man, and here art come
Before th'expiration of thy time,
In braving arms against thy sovereign.
BULLINGBROOK   As I was banished, I was banished   *Stands*
    Hereford,
But as I come, I come for Lancaster.
115   And noble uncle, I beseech your grace
Look on my wrongs with an indifferent eye.
You are my father, for methinks in you
I see old Gaunt alive. O then, my father,
Will you permit that I shall stand condemned
120   A wand'ring vagabond; my rights and royalties
Plucked from my arms perforce and given away
To upstart unthrifts? Wherefore was I born?
If that my cousin king be King of England,
It must be granted I am Duke of Lancaster.
125   You have a son, Aumerle, my noble kinsman:
Had you first died, and he been thus trod down,
He should have found his uncle Gaunt a father
To rouse his wrongs and chase them to the bay.

---

101 Black Prince Edward, Richard's father and son of Edward III   **104 palsy** weakness of the body, accompanied at times with tremor   **107 On . . . wherein?** What point of law have I contravened and how?/What personal flaw am I deemed to have and how has it manifested itself?   **condition** legal stipulation/personal quality; York shifts the sense to "circumstances"   **112 braving** defiant, boastfully flaunted   **114 for** as/to claim the title of   **116 indifferent** impartial   **121 perforce** forcibly   **122 unthrifts** spendthrifts, wasteful people (with moral connotations)   **128 rouse** expose, chase from hiding (hunting term)   **bay** last stand (where the cornered animal turns on its hunters)

I am denied to sue my liv'ry here,

130 And yet my letters patents give me leave.

My father's goods are all distrained and sold,

And these and all are all amiss employed.

What would you have me do? I am a subject,

And challenge law. Attorneys are denied me;

135 And therefore personally I lay my claim

To my inheritance of free descent.

NORTHUMBERLAND The noble duke hath been too much abused.

ROSS   It stands your grace upon to do him right.

WILLOUGHBY Base men by his endowments are made great.

140 YORK   My lords of England, let me tell you this:

I have had feeling of my cousin's wrongs

And laboured all I could to do him right.

But in this kind to come, in braving arms,

Be his own carver and cut out his way,

145 To find out right with wrongs, it may not be,

And you that do abet him in this kind

Cherish rebellion and are rebels all.

NORTHUMBERLAND The noble duke hath sworn his coming is

But for his own; and for the right of that

150 We all have strongly sworn to give him aid.

And let him ne'er see joy that breaks that oath!

YORK   Well, well, I see the issue of these arms.

I cannot mend it, I must needs confess,

Because my power is weak and all ill left.

155 But if I could, by him that gave me life,

I would attach you all and make you stoop

Unto the sovereign mercy of the king.

But since I cannot, be it known to you

---

129 **denied . . . liv'ry** refused the right to legally claim my inheritance   130 **letters patents** documents signed by the king granting land or titles (Bullingbrook's have been revoked by Richard)   131 **distrained** confiscated by law   132 **amiss** wrongly   134 **challenge law** claim my legal rights   136 **of free descent** through legal succession   138 **stands . . . upon** is the responsibility of your grace   139 **endowments** i.e. wealth and property (that has now been given to others)   143 **kind** manner   144 **Be . . . way** i.e. act on his own authority, help himself (literally, carve his own piece of meat)   152 **issue** outcome   154 **power** army   **ill left** left in disordered, poor condition   156 **attach** arrest   **stoop** i.e. kneel for mercy

I do remain as neuter. So, fare you well,

160 Unless you please to enter in the castle
And there repose you for this night.

BULLINGBROOK   An offer, uncle, that we will accept.
But we must win your grace to go with us
To Bristol Castle, which they say is held

165 By Bushy, Bagot and their complices,
The caterpillars of the commonwealth,
Which I have sworn to weed and pluck away.

YORK   It may be I will go with you: but yet I'll pause,
For I am loath to break our country's laws.

170 Nor friends nor foes, to me welcome you are:
Things past redress are now with me past care.   *Exeunt*

Act 2 Scene 4   *running scene 9*

Enter Salisbury and a [Welsh] Captain

CAPTAIN   My lord of Salisbury, we have stayed ten days,
And hardly kept our countrymen together,
And yet we hear no tidings from the king;
Therefore we will disperse ourselves: farewell.

5 SALISBURY   Stay yet another day, thou trusty Welshman:
The king reposeth all his confidence in thee.

CAPTAIN   'Tis thought the king is dead: we will not stay.
The bay-trees in our country all are withered
And meteors fright the fixèd stars of heaven;

10 The pale-faced moon looks bloody on the earth
And lean-looked prophets whisper fearful change;
Rich men look sad and ruffians dance and leap,
The one in fear to lose what they enjoy,
The other to enjoy by rage and war.

15 These signs forerun the death of kings.

---

159 as neuter neutral   163 win persuade   166 caterpillars i.e. parasites   **2.4** *Location:*
Wales   1 stayed waited   2 hardly with difficulty   8 bay-trees bay leaves were associated
with victory and immortality   9 meteors regarded as bad omens   11 lean-looked gaunt,
lean-looking   13 The one i.e. rich men

Farewell. Our countrymen are gone and fled,
As well assured Richard their king is dead.   *Exit*
SALISBURY   Ah, Richard, with eyes of heavy mind
I see thy glory like a shooting star
20   Fall to the base earth from the firmament.
Thy sun sets weeping in the lowly west,
Witnessing storms to come, woe and unrest.
Thy friends are fled to wait upon thy foes,
And crossly to thy good all fortune goes.   *Exit*

Act 3 Scene 1   *running scene 9*

Enter Bullingbrook, York, Northumberland, Ross, Percy, Willoughby,
with Bushy and Green, prisoners

BULLINGBROOK   Bring forth these men.
Bushy and Green, I will not vex your souls —
Since presently your souls must part your bodies —
With too much urging your pernicious lives,
5   For 'twere no charity. Yet to wash your blood
From off my hands, here in the view of men
I will unfold some causes of your deaths.
You have misled a prince, a royal king,
A happy gentleman in blood and lineaments,
10   By you unhappied and disfigured clean.
You have in manner with your sinful hours
Made a divorce betwixt his queen and him,
Broke the possession of a royal bed
And stained the beauty of a fair queen's cheeks
15   With tears drawn from her eyes with your foul wrongs.

20 firmament sky   22 Witnessing betokening, indicating   23 wait upon offer allegiance to
24 crossly adversely   **3.1** *Location: Bristol*   3 presently immediately   part
depart from   4 urging insisting on, emphasizing   pernicious wicked, destructive
7 causes of legal reasons for   9 happy fortunate   10 unhappied made unfortunate, ruined
clean completely   11 in manner as it were, in a way   12 divorce breach, separation
13 Broke . . . bed i.e. interfered with marital union and happiness

Myself, a prince by fortune of my birth,
Near to the king in blood, and near in love
Till you did make him misinterpret me,
Have stooped my neck under your injuries,
20   And sighed my English breath in foreign clouds,
Eating the bitter bread of banishment;
While you have fed upon my signories,
Disparked my parks and felled my forest woods,
From mine own windows torn my household coat,
25   Razed out my imprese, leaving me no sign,
Save men's opinions and my living blood,
To show the world I am a gentleman.
This and much more, much more than twice all this,
Condemns you to the death.— See them delivered over
30   To execution and the hand of death

BUSHY   More welcome is the stroke of death to me
Than Bullingbrook to England.

GREEN   My comfort is that heaven will take our souls
And plague injustice with the pains of hell.

35   BULLINGBROOK   My Lord Northumberland, see them
          dispatched. —
[*Exeunt Northumberland and others, with the prisoners*]
Uncle, you say the queen is at your house:
For heaven's sake, fairly let her be entreated.
Tell her I send to her my kind commends;
Take special care my greetings be delivered.

40   YORK   A gentleman of mine I have dispatched
With letters of your love to her at large.

BULLINGBROOK   Thanks, gentle uncle.— Come, lords, away.
To fight with Glendower and his complices;
A while to work, and after holiday.   *Exeunt*

---

20 clouds mists of breath/climates, skies   22 signories estates   23 Disparked my parks
opened my enclosed hunting grounds for other uses   24 coat coat of arms (often emblazoned
on stained or painted windows)   25 imprese heraldic family emblem   29 death death
penalty (legal term)   35 dispatched dealt with/killed   37 entreated treated   38 commends
regards   41 at large (expressed) in full

Act 3 Scene 2

*Drums. Flourish and colours. Enter Richard, Aumerle, Carlisle and
Soldiers*

KING RICHARD   Barkloughly Castle call you this at hand?

AUMERLE   Yea, my lord. How brooks your grace the air,
After your late tossing on the breaking seas?

KING RICHARD   Needs must I like it well: I weep for joy

5   To stand upon my kingdom once again.
Dear earth, I do salute thee with my hand,
Though rebels wound thee with their horses' hoofs.
As a long-parted mother with her child
Plays fondly with her tears and smiles in meeting,

10   So, weeping, smiling, greet I thee, my earth,
And do thee favour with my royal hands.
Feed not thy sovereign's foe, my gentle earth,
Nor with thy sweets comfort his ravenous sense,
But let thy spiders, that suck up thy venom,

15   And heavy-gaited toads lie in their way,
Doing annoyance to the treacherous feet
Which with usurping steps do trample thee.
Yield stinging nettles to mine enemies;
And when they from thy bosom pluck a flower,

20   Guard it, I prithee, with a lurking adder
Whose double tongue may with a mortal touch
Throw death upon thy sovereign's enemies.
Mock not my senseless conjuration, lords:
This earth shall have a feeling and these stones

25   Prove armèd soldiers, ere her native king
Shall falter under foul rebellion's arms.

3.2   *Location: Barkloughly (Harlech) Castle, northern Wales   colours* military flags
(and those carrying them)   **1 Barkloughly Castle** actually Harlech Castle   **2 brooks** likes
(technically "tolerates")   **9 fondly** affectionately/foolishly   **13 sense** appetite   **14 spiders**
like **toads**, they were thought to be poisonous   **16 annoyance** harm   **20 Guard** protect/trim
with an ornamental border   **prithee** pray thee   **21 double** forked   **mortal** deadly
23 senseless conjuration appeal to the unfeeling earth/foolish entreaty   **25 native** rightful,
legitimately crowned

CARLISLE   Fear not, my lord. That power that made you king
　　　　Hath power to keep you king in spite of all.

AUMERLE   He means, my lord, that we are too remiss,
30　　　　Whilst Bullingbrook, through our security,
　　　　Grows strong and great in substance and in friends.

KING RICHARD   Discomfortable cousin! Know'st thou not
　　　　That when the searching eye of heaven is hid,
　　　　Behind the globe that lights the lower world,
35　　　　Then thieves and robbers range abroad unseen
　　　　In murders and in outrage bloody here;
　　　　But when from under this terrestrial ball
　　　　He fires the proud tops of the eastern pines
　　　　And darts his lightning through ev'ry guilty hole,
40　　　　Then murders, treasons and detested sins – –
　　　　The cloak of night being plucked from off their backs —
　　　　Stand bare and naked, trembling at themselves?
　　　　So when this thief, this traitor, Bullingbrook,
　　　　Who all this while hath revelled in the night,
45　　　　Shall see us rising in our throne, the east,
　　　　His treasons will sit blushing in his face,
　　　　Not able to endure the sight of day,
　　　　But, self-affrighted, tremble at his sin.
　　　　Not all the water in the rough rude sea
50　　　　Can wash the balm from an anointed king;
　　　　The breath of worldly men cannot depose
　　　　The deputy elected by the Lord.
　　　　For every man that Bullingbrook hath pressed
　　　　To lift shrewd steel against our golden crown,
55　　　　Heaven for his Richard hath in heavenly pay
　　　　A glorious angel. Then, if angels fight,
　　　　Weak men must fall, for heaven still guards the right.

---

30 security overconfidence　32 Discomfortable discouraging　33 eye . . . world when, to
us, the sun is hidden beneath the earth, lighting the underside of the world　49 rude
turbulent　50 balm consecrating oil, used to anoint a king at his coronation　53 pressed
conscripted　54 shrewd sharp, biting　steel sword　56 angel puns on the sense of "gold
coin"

Enter Salisbury

Welcome, my lord. How far off lies your power?

SALISBURY   Nor near nor farther off, my gracious lord,

60   Than this weak arm. Discomfort guides my tongue

And bids me speak of nothing but despair.

One day too late, I fear, my noble lord,

Hath clouded all thy happy days on earth.

O, call back yesterday, bid time return,

65   And thou shalt have twelve thousand fighting men!

Today, today, unhappy day too late,

O'erthrows thy joys, friends, fortune and thy state;

For all the Welshmen, hearing thou wert dead,

Are gone to Bullingbrook, dispersed and fled.

70   AUMERLE   Comfort, my liege. Why looks your grace so pale?

KING RICHARD   But now the blood of twenty thousand men

Did triumph in my face, and they are fled.

And till so much blood thither come again,

Have I not reason to look pale and dead?

75   All souls that will be safe fly from my side,

For time hath set a blot upon my pride.

AUMERLE   Comfort, my liege. Remember who you are.

KING RICHARD   I had forgot myself. Am I not king?

Awake, thou sluggard majesty, thou sleepest.

80   Is not the king's name forty thousand names?

Arm, arm, my name! A puny subject strikes

At thy great glory. Look not to the ground,

Ye favourites of a king. Are we not high?

High be our thoughts. I know my uncle York

85   Hath power enough to serve our turn. But who comes here?

Enter Scroop

SCROOP   More health and happiness betide my liege

Than can my care-tuned tongue deliver him!

---

59 Nor near no nearer   60 Discomfort sorrow/discouragement   63 happy fortunate
67 state kingship, power   71 But now only a moment ago   72 triumph rejoice, exult
83 high noble in rank (sense then shifts to "proud, ambitious")   85 power . . . turn sufficient
troops for our needs   86 betide befall, come to   87 care-tuned tuned by sorrow/tuned to a
sorrowful key   deliver report to

KING RICHARD   Mine ear is open and my heart prepared.
The worst is worldly loss thou canst unfold.
90   Say, is my kingdom lost? Why, 'twas my care,
And what loss is it to be rid of care?
Strives Bullingbrook to be as great as we?
Greater he shall not be. If he serve God,
We'll serve him too and be his fellow so.
95   Revolt our subjects? That we cannot mend.
They break their faith to God as well as us.
Cry woe, destruction, ruin, loss, decay.
The worst is death, and death will have his day.

SCROOP   Glad am I that your highness is so armed
100   To bear the tidings of calamity.
Like an unseasonable stormy day,
Which makes the silver rivers drown their shores,
As if the world were all dissolved to tears,
So high above his limits swells the rage
105   Of Bullingbrook, covering your fearful land
With hard bright steel and hearts harder than steel.
Whitebeards have armed their thin and hairless scalps
Against thy majesty, and boys with women's voices
Strive to speak big and clap their female joints
110   In stiff unwieldy arms against thy crown.
Thy very beadsmen learn to bend their bows
Of double-fatal yew against thy state.
Yea, distaff-women manage rusty bills
Against thy seat. Both young and old rebel,
115   And all goes worse than I have power to tell.

KING RICHARD   Too well, too well thou tell'st a tale so ill.
Where is the Earl of Wiltshire? Where is Bagot?

---

90 **care** burden, source of anxiety   94 **fellow** equal/servant   95 **mend** remedy   104 **his** applies both to **rage** and to **Bullingbrook**   105 **Bullingbrook** probably puns on "brook" **fearful** frightened   107 **Whitebeards** i.e. old men   109 **big** with deep voices (like men)   **clap** place, thrust   **female** feminine, i.e. youthful   110 **arms** armor   111 **beadsmen** almsmen who were paid to pray on behalf of another   112 **double-fatal** doubly deadly (the wood of the yew was used to make bows; its leaves and berries were poisonous)   113 **distaff-women** women occupied in spinning (a distaff was a staff used to hold wool)   **bills** long-handled weapons with blades at the ends   114 **seat** throne

What is become of Bushy, where is Green,
That they have let the dangerous enemy
120   Measure our confines with such peaceful steps?
If we prevail, their heads shall pay for it.
I warrant they have made peace with Bullingbrook.

SCROOP   Peace have they made with him indeed, my lord.

KING RICHARD O, villains, vipers, damned without redemption!
125   Dogs, easily won to fawn on any man!
Snakes, in my heart-blood warmed, that sting my heart!
Three Judases, each one thrice worse than Judas!
Would they make peace? Terrible hell make war
Upon their spotted souls for this offence!

130   SCROOP   Sweet love, I see, changing his property,
Turns to the sourest and most deadly hate.
Again uncurse their souls; their peace is made
With heads, and not with hands: those whom you curse
Have felt the worst of death's destroying hand
135   And lie full low, graved in the hollow ground.

AUMERLE   Is Bushy, Green and the Earl of Wiltshire dead?

SCROOP   Yea, all of them at Bristol lost their heads.

AUMERLE   Where is the duke my father with his power?

KING RICHARD   No matter where; of comfort no man speak.
140   Let's talk of graves, of worms, and epitaphs,
Make dust our paper and with rainy eyes
Write sorrow on the bosom of the earth.
Let's choose executors and talk of wills.
And yet not so; for what can we bequeath
145   Save our deposèd bodies to the ground?
Our lands, our lives and all are Bullingbrook's,
And nothing can we call our own but death
And that small model of the barren earth
Which serves as paste and cover to our bones.

---

120 **Measure our confines** travel over our territories   **peaceful** i.e. unopposed
122 **I warrant** I'm sure, I'll guarantee   127 **Judas** the disciple who betrayed Jesus Christ
129 **spotted** stained (with sin)   130 **property** essence, own nature   133 **hands** used to sign a
document or swear an oath   135 **graved** buried   148 **model** microcosm, replica/mold
149 **paste and cover** pastry covering/pie crust

150   For heaven's sake let us sit upon the ground
       And tell sad stories of the death of kings:
       How some have been deposed, some slain in war,
       Some haunted by the ghosts they have deposed,
       Some poisoned by their wives, some sleeping killed,
155   All murdered. For within the hollow crown
       That rounds the mortal temples of a king
       Keeps Death his court and there the antic sits,
       Scoffing his state and grinning at his pomp,
       Allowing him a breath, a little scene,
160   To monarchize, be feared and kill with looks,
       Infusing him with self and vain conceit,
       As if this flesh which walls about our life,
       Were brass impregnable. And humoured thus,
       Comes at the last and with a little pin
165   Bores through his castle walls, and farewell king!
       Cover your heads and mock not flesh and blood
       With solemn reverence. Throw away respect,
       Tradition, form and ceremonious duty,
       For you have but mistook me all this while:
170   I live with bread like you, feel want,
       Taste grief, need friends. Subjected thus,
       How can you say to me, I am a king?
       CARLISLE   My lord, wise men ne'er wail their present woes,
       But presently prevent the ways to wail.
175   To fear the foe, since fear oppresseth strength,
       Gives in your weakness strength unto your foe,
       And so your follies fight against yourself.
       Fear and be slain. No worse can come to fight.

---

151 sad solemn/sorrowful   stories historical narratives   156 rounds encircles   mortal
human/destined for death   157 antic grotesque buffoon   158 his state at the king's regality
160 monarchize act the monarch   161 self self-made/self-centered   conceit imaginings,
concept (of himself)   163 humoured thus Death having amused himself in this way/Death,
being so inclined/Death, having allowed the king to indulge himself in this way
171 Subjected under the dominion of grief/turned into a mere subject (rather than being a
king)   174 presently immediately   prevent . . . wail seek to forestall the routes to (or sources
of) grief   177 And . . . yourself this line is omitted in Folio, seemingly as a printer's error
rather than a deliberate cut   178 No . . . fight nothing worse (than being slain) can come
from fighting

And fight and die is death destroying death,
180   Where fearing dying pays death servile breath.
AUMERLE   My father hath a power. Enquire of him
And learn to make a body of a limb.
KING RICHARD   Thou chid'st me well. Proud Bullingbrook, I come
To change blows with thee for our day of doom:
185   This ague fit of fear is over-blown,
An easy task it is to win our own.
Say, Scroop, where lies our uncle with his power?
Speak sweetly, man, although thy looks be sour.
SCROOP   Men judge by the complexion of the sky
190   The state and inclination of the day;
So may you by my dull and heavy eye,
My tongue hath but a heavier tale to say.
I play the torturer, by small and small
To lengthen out the worst that must be spoken.
195   Your uncle York is joined with Bullingbrook,
And all your northern castles yielded up,
And all your southern gentlemen in arms
Upon his faction.
KING RICHARD   Thou hast said enough.
200   Beshrew thee, cousin, which didst lead me forth   *To Aumerle*
Of that sweet way I was in to despair!
What say you now? What comfort have we now?
By heaven, I'll hate him everlastingly
That bids me be of comfort any more.
205   Go to Flint Castle: there I'll pine away.
A king, woe's slave, shall kingly woe obey.
That power I have, discharge, and let 'em go

---

179 **death destroying death** i.e. defying death by dying nobly (and, perhaps, being
remembered in such a way)/by conquering death's power to make one afraid   182 **a . . . limb**
i.e. a great fighting force out of a small number of soldiers   183 **chid'st** reprove, upbraid
184 **change** exchange   **doom** destiny   185 **ague** acute or violent fever/fit of shaking or
shivering   **over-blown** blown over   191 **heavy** gloomy, sorrowful   193 **by . . . small** by
increments, little by little   200 **Beshrew** curse   **forth Of** out of   205 **Flint Castle** situated in
northeast Wales   207 **power** forces, troops   **discharge** dismiss

To ear the land that hath some hope to grow,
For I have none. Let no man speak again
210   To alter this, for counsel is but vain.

AUMERLE   My liege, one word.

KING RICHARD   He does me double wrong
That wounds me with the flatteries of his tongue.
Discharge my followers. Let them hence away,
215   From Richard's night to Bullingbrook's fair day.   *Exeunt*

Act 3 Scene 3   *running scene 11*

*Enter, with Drum and Colours, Bullingbrook, York, Northumberland
[and] Attendants*

BULLINGBROOK   So that by this intelligence we learn
The Welshmen are dispersed, and Salisbury
Is gone to meet the king, who lately landed
With some few private friends upon this coast.

5   NORTHUMBERLAND   The news is very fair and good, my lord.
Richard not far from hence hath hid his head.

YORK   It would beseem the Lord Northumberland
To say 'King Richard'. Alack the heavy day
When such a sacred king should hide his head.

10   NORTHUMBERLAND   Your grace mistakes. Only to be brief
Left I his title out.

YORK   The time hath been,
Would you have been so brief with him, he would
Have been so brief with you to shorten you,
15   For taking so the head, your whole head's length.

BULLINGBROOK   Mistake not, uncle, further than you should.

YORK   Take not, good cousin, further than you should,
Lest you mistake the heavens are o'er your head.

---

208 ear plow, cultivate   **3.3**   ***Location: outside Flint Castle***   1 So that Bullingbrook
enters in mid-conversation   **7 beseem** befit   **14 to** as to   **15 taking . . . head** treating the
head of state in such a manner/being headstrong/omitting the king's title   **your** by your
16 Mistake misunderstand (puns on "mis-take")   **17 Take** seize/presume   **18 mistake** fail to
understand that

BULLINGBROOK   I know it, uncle, and oppose not myself
20   Against their will. But who comes here?
Enter Percy
        Welcome, Harry. What, will not this castle yield?
PERCY   The castle royally is manned, my lord,
        Against thy entrance.
BULLINGBROOK   Royally? Why, it contains no king?
25   PERCY   Yes, my good lord,
        It doth contain a king: King Richard lies
        Within the limits of yond lime and stone,
        And with him the Lord Aumerle, Lord Salisbury,
        Sir Stephen Scroop, besides a clergyman
30   Of holy reverence, who, I cannot learn.
NORTHUMBERLAND   O, belike it is the Bishop of Carlisle.
BULLINGBROOK   Noble lord,
        Go to the rude ribs of that ancient castle.
        Through brazen trumpet send the breath of parle
35   Into his ruined ears, and thus deliver:
        Henry Bullingbrook
        Upon his knees doth kiss King Richard's hand
        And sends allegiance and true faith of heart
        To his most royal person, hither come
40   Even at his feet to lay my arms and power
        Provided that my banishment repealed
        And lands restored again be freely granted.
        If not, I'll use th'advantage of my power
        And lay the summer's dust with showers of blood
45   Rained from the wounds of slaughtered Englishmen;
        The which, how far off from the mind of Bullingbrook
        It is, such crimson tempest should bedrench
        The fresh green lap of fair King Richard's land,

---

26 lies dwells, is   **30 who** i.e. who he is   **31 belike** probably   **33 rude** rough, rugged   **ribs**
i.e. walls   **34 brazen** brass (plays on the sense of "audacious, shameless")   **parle** parley,
negotiation between enemy forces (or the trumpet call signifying this)   **35 his** its (the castle's,
but possibly also referring to Richard)   **ruined** battered   **41 my . . . again** the revoking of my
banishment and restoration of my lands   **43 th'advantage . . . power** the superiority of my
military force   **44 lay** flatten, subdue   **47 such** that such a   **bedrench** drench thoroughly,
soak

My stooping duty tenderly shall show.
50   Go signify as much, while here we march
Upon the grassy carpet of this plain.
Let's march without the noise of threat'ning drum,
That from this castle's tattered battlements
Our fair appointments may be well perused.
55   Methinks King Richard and myself should meet
With no less terror than the elements
Of fire and water, when their thund'ring smoke
At meeting tears the cloudy cheeks of heaven.
Be he the fire, I'll be the yielding water;
60   The rage be his, while on the earth I rain
My waters on the earth, and not on him.
March on, and mark King Richard how he looks.

Parley without, and answer within. Then a flourish. Enter on the
walls, Richard, Carlisle, Aumerle, Scroop [and] Salisbury

See, see, King Richard doth himself appear,
As doth the blushing discontented sun
65   From out the fiery portal of the east,
When he perceives the envious clouds are bent
To dim his glory and to stain the tract
Of his bright passage to the occident.
YORK   Yet looks he like a king. Behold, his eye,
70   As bright as is the eagle's, lightens forth
Controlling majesty. Alack, alack, for woe,
That any harm should stain so fair a show!
KING RICHARD   We are amazed; and thus long have we   *To*
        stood   *Northumberland*
To watch the fearful bending of thy knee
75   Because we thought ourself thy lawful king.
And if we be, how dare thy joints forget
To pay their awful duty to our presence?

---

49 **tenderly** gently, peacefully/lovingly   53 **tattered** battered, old/jagged   54 **fair**
appointments fine military provision   57 **fire and water** i.e. lightning and rain   60 **rain** puns
on "reign"   62 **mark** note, observe   *Parley* trumpet summons to negotiation   64 **blushing**
i.e. in anger   66 **envious** hostile   67 **stain** obscure, dim   **tract** course   68 **occident** west
(where the sun sets)   70 **lightens forth** flashes out, like lightning   73 **amazed** astounded,
bewildered   74 **watch** expect, wait for   **fearful** full of reverence   77 **awful** full of awe

If we be not, show us the hand of God
That hath dismissed us from our stewardship,
80   For well we know, no hand of blood and bone
Can grip the sacred handle of our sceptre,
Unless he do profane, steal, or usurp.
And though you think that all, as you have done,
Have torn their souls by turning them from us,
85   And we are barren and bereft of friends,
Yet know, my master, God omnipotent,
Is must'ring in his clouds on our behalf
Armies of pestilence, and they shall strike
Your children yet unborn and unbegot,
90   That lift your vassal hands against my head
And threat the glory of my precious crown.
Tell Bullingbrook — for yond methinks he is —
That every stride he makes upon my land
Is dangerous treason. He is come to ope
95   The purple testament of bleeding war;
But ere the crown he looks for live in peace,
Ten thousand bloody crowns of mothers' sons
Shall ill become the flower of England's face,
Change the complexion of her maid-pale peace
100   To scarlet indignation and bedew
Her pastor's grass with faithful English blood.
NORTHUMBERLAND   The king of heaven forbid our lord the king
Should so with civil and uncivil arms
Be rushed upon! Thy thrice-noble cousin,
105   Harry Bullingbrook, doth humbly kiss thy hand.
And by the honourable tomb he swears,
That stands upon your royal grandsire's bones,
And by the royalties of both your bloods —

---

78 hand sign/signature   82 profane sin, commit sacrilege   84 torn i.e. ruined, damned
turning . . . us i.e. betraying me   88 strike blight, afflict with plague (pestilence)   89 unbegot
not yet conceived   90 That of you who   vassal servile, slavish   94 ope open   95 purple
testament bloody legacy   97 crowns heads (plays on crown in the previous line)   99 maid-
pale virgin white, pale as a young girl   101 pastor's shepherd's, i.e. Richard, England's
shepherd or spiritual protector   103 civil domestic, used in civil war   uncivil violent,
barbarous

Currents that spring from one most gracious head —
110   And by the buried hand of warlike Gaunt,
And by the worth and honour of himself,
Comprising all that may be sworn or said,
His coming hither hath no further scope
Than for his lineal royalties and to beg
115   Enfranchisement immediate on his knees,
Which on thy royal party granted once,
His glittering arms he will commend to rust,
His barbèd steeds to stables, and his heart
To faithful service of your majesty.
120   This swears he, as he is a prince, is just:
And, as I am a gentleman, I credit him.
    KING RICHARD   Northumberland, say thus the king returns.
His noble cousin is right welcome hither,
And all the number of his fair demands
125   Shall be accomplished without contradiction.
With all the gracious utterance thou hast,
Speak to his gentle hearing kind commends.—
We do debase ourself, cousin, do we not,   *To Aumerle*
To look so poorly and to speak so fair?
130   Shall we call back Northumberland, and send
Defiance to the traitor, and so die?
    AUMERLE   No, good my lord, let's fight with gentle words
Till time lend friends and friends their helpful swords.
    KING RICHARD   O God, O God, that e'er this tongue of mine,
135   That laid the sentence of dread banishment
On yond proud man, should take it off again
With words of sooth! O, that I were as great
As is my grief, or lesser than my name!

---

109 **head** source   113 **scope** aim   114 **lineal royalties** hereditary rights as one with royal blood   115 **Enfranchisement** freedom (from banishment), restoration of rights   116 **party** part   117 **commend** commit   118 **barbèd** armored with barbs (metal protectors)   120 **is** and is   121 **credit** believe   122 **returns** replies   125 **accomplished** carried out   126 **gracious** courteous, elegant   127 **commends** greetings, regards   129 **poorly** abject, lowly   134 **e'er** ever   136 **yond** yonder, i.e. at some distance but within sight   137 **sooth** smooth words, appeasing terms

Or that I could forget what I have been,
140 Or not remember what I must be now!
Swell'st thou, proud heart? I'll give thee scope to beat,
Since foes have scope to beat both thee and me.

AUMERLE   Northumberland comes back from Bullingbrook.

KING RICHARD   What must the king do now? Must he submit?
145 The king shall do it. Must he be deposed?
The king shall be contented. Must he lose
The name of king? O'God's name, let it go.
I'll give my jewels for a set of beads,
My gorgeous palace for a hermitage,
150 My gay apparel for an almsman's gown,
My figured goblets for a dish of wood,
My sceptre for a palmer's walking staff,
My subjects for a pair of carvèd saints,
And my large kingdom for a little grave,
155 A little little grave, an obscure grave.
Or I'll be buried in the king's highway,
Some way of common trade, where subjects' feet
May hourly trample on their sovereign's head,
For on my heart they tread now whilst I live,
160 And buried once, why not upon my head?—
Aumerle, thou weep'st, my tender-hearted cousin!
We'll make foul weather with despisèd tears,
Our sighs and they shall lodge the summer corn,
And make a dearth in this revolting land.
165 Or shall we play the wantons with our woes,
And make some pretty match with shedding tears?
As thus, to drop them still upon one place,
Till they have fretted us a pair of graves

---

141 scope room, freedom/a purpose   142 beat conquer, strike (plays on the sense of a heart
beating)   146 be contented i.e. submit, agree   148 set of beads rosary   150 almsman
recipient of charity   151 figured embossed, ornamented   152 palmer pilgrim   157 trade
commerce/tread   160 buried once once I am buried   162 despisèd despicable/to be
scorned/unimportant   163 lodge flatten   164 dearth famine   revolting rebellious   165 play
the wantons trifle, frolic   166 make devise   pretty match ingenious game   167 still always
168 fretted us eroded for us (fretted puns on the sense of "been distressed, complained")

Within the earth, and, therein laid — there lies
170   Two kinsmen digged their graves with weeping eyes.
Would not this ill do well?— Well, well, I see
I talk but idly, and you mock at me.—
Most mighty prince, my lord Northumberland,
What says King Bullingbrook? Will his majesty
175   Give Richard leave to live till Richard die?
You make a leg, and Bullingbrook says 'Ay'.

NORTHUMBERLAND   My lord, in the base court he doth attend
To speak with you. May it please you to come down?

KING RICHARD   Down, down I come, like glist'ring Phaethon,
180   Wanting the manage of unruly jades.
In the base court? Base court where kings grow base,
To come at traitors' calls and do them grace.
In the base court, come down: down court, down king,
For night-owls shriek where mounting larks should
        sing.   [Exeunt from above]
185   BULLINGBROOK   What says his majesty?

NORTHUMBERLAND   Sorrow and grief of heart
Makes him speak fondly, like a frantic man
Yet he is come.
[Enter King Richard and his Attendants below]

BULLINGBROOK   Stand all apart,
190   And show fair duty to his majesty.
My gracious lord—   Kneels

KING RICHARD   Fair cousin, you debase your princely knee
To make the base earth proud with kissing it.
Me rather had my heart might feel your love
195   Than my unpleased eye see your courtesy.

---

171 ill affliction   176 make a leg bow   177 base court lower or servants' court   attend
wait   179 glist'ring glistening, glittering   Phaethon in Greek mythology, the son of Apollo,
the sun god; he was unable to control his father's horse-drawn sun chariot, burned part of the
earth and was felled with a thunderbolt hurled by Zeus   180 manage control   jades
worthless horses   182 do them grace bow to them courteously/grant them favor
184 night-owls shriek considered a bad omen   187 fondly foolishly   frantic mad, frenzied
189 apart aside   192 debase continues the earlier wordplay on base   194 Me rather had
I had rather   195 courtesy curtsy, i.e. bow

Up, cousin, up! Your heart is up, I know,
Thus high at least, although your knee be low.

BULLINGBROOK   My gracious lord, I come but for mine own.

KING RICHARD   Your own is yours, and I am yours, and all.

200   BULLINGBROOK   So far be mine, my most redoubted lord,
As my true service shall deserve your love.

KING RICHARD   Well you deserved. They well deserve to have,
That know the strong'st and surest way to   *Bullingbrook*
        get.—   *rises*
Uncle, give me your hand: nay, dry your eyes.   *To York*
205   Tears show their love, but want their remedies.—
Cousin, I am too young to be your father,   *To Bullingbrook*
Though you are old enough to be my heir.
What you will have, I'll give, and willing too,
For do we must what force will have us do.
210   Set on towards London, cousin, is it so?

BULLINGBROOK   Yea, my good lord.

KING RICHARD   Then I must not say no.   *Flourish. Exeunt*

Act 3 Scene 4   *running scene 12*

Enter the Queen and two Ladies

QUEEN   What sport shall we devise here in this garden,
To drive away the heavy thought of care?

LADY   Madam, we'll play at bowls.

QUEEN   'Twill make me think the world is full of rubs,
5   And that my fortune runs against the bias.

LADY   Madam, we'll dance.

QUEEN   My legs can keep no measure in delight
When my poor heart no measure keeps in grief:
Therefore, no dancing, girl, some other sport.

---

196 up i.e. proud, ambitious/rebellious   200 redoubted dreaded, revered   205 want their
remedies lack remedies for what caused them   208 willing willingly   **3.4** *Location: the*
Duke of York's garden   2 heavy burdensome/sad   4 rubs hindrances (technically,
impediments that interrupt the course of a bowling ball)   5 against the bias contrary to the
desired course (a **bias** is the weight in the ball that enables it to be bowled in a curve)
7 measure due proportion/stately dance step   8 measure limit

10	LADY	Madam, we'll tell tales.
	QUEEN	Of sorrow or of joy?
	LADY	Of either, madam.
	QUEEN	Of neither, girl.

For if of joy, being altogether wanting,
15 It doth remember me the more of sorrow.
Or if of grief, being altogether had,
It adds more sorrow to my want of joy.
For what I have I need not to repeat,
And what I want it boots not to complain.

20	LADY	Madam, I'll sing.
	QUEEN	'Tis well that thou hast cause,

But thou shouldst please me better, wouldst thou weep.

LADY   I could weep, madam, would it do you good.

QUEEN   And I could sing, would weeping do me good,
25 And never borrow any tear of thee.

Enter a Gardener and two Servants

But stay, here come the gardeners.
Let's step into the shadow of these trees.
My wretchedness unto a row of pins,
They'll talk of state, for everyone doth so
30 Against a change; woe is forerun with woe.   *Queen and Ladies*

GARDENER   Go bind thou up yond dangling apricocks,   *stand aside*
Which, like unruly children, make their sire
Stoop with oppression of their prodigal weight.
Give some supportance to the bending twigs.
35 Go thou, and like an executioner,
Cut off the heads of too fast-growing sprays,
That look too lofty in our commonwealth:

---

14 **wanting** lacking   15 **remember** remind   16 **being altogether had** as I am entirely
possessed by it   17 **want** lack   19 **boots not** is useless   **complain** lament   21 'Tis . . .
cause i.e. it is a good thing that you are happy enough to do so   28 **My** I'll wager my   **row of
pins** i.e. insignificant items   29 **state affairs** of state, politics   30 **Against** in anticipation of
forerun with heralded by   31 **apricocks** apricots   32 **sire** father, i.e. tree that bears them
33 **oppression** burden   **prodigal** excessive   34 **supportance** support   36 **sprays** shoots
37 **lofty** tall/proud, ambitious

All must be even in our government.
You thus employed, I will go root away
40 The noisome weeds, that without profit suck
The soil's fertility from wholesome flowers.
SERVANT   Why should we in the compass of a pale
Keep law and form and due proportion,
Showing, as in a model, our firm estate,
45 When our sea-wallèd garden, the whole land,
Is full of weeds, her fairest flowers choked up,
Her fruit-trees all unpruned, her hedges ruined,
Her knots disordered and her wholesome herbs
Swarming with caterpillars?
50 GARDENER   Hold thy peace.
He that hath suffered this disordered spring
Hath now himself met with the fall of leaf.
The weeds that his broad-spreading leaves did shelter,
That seemed in eating him to hold him up,
55 Are pulled up root and all by Bullingbrook —
I mean the Earl of Wiltshire, Bushy, Green.
SERVANT   What, are they dead?
GARDENER   They are. And Bullingbrook
Hath seized the wasteful king. O, what pity is it
60 That he had not so trimmed and dressed his land
As we this garden: we at time of year
Do wound the bark, the skin of our fruit-trees,
Lest, being over-proud with sap and blood,
With too much riches it confound itself.
65 Had he done so to great and growing men,
They might have lived to bear and he to taste
Their fruits of duty. Superfluous branches

---

38 **even** equal   40 **noisome** noxious, harmful   41 **wholesome** healthy   42 **compass**
limits   **pale** fenced area, enclosure   44 **model** copy in miniature   **firm estate** settled
situation/secure kingdom   48 **knots** intricately designed flower beds   51 **suffered**
permitted/undergone   52 **fall of leaf** i.e. autumn   59 **seized** taken into custody
60 **trimmed** adorned   61 **at time of year** in season   63 **over-proud** too swollen
64 **confound** ruin

We lop away, that bearing boughs may live.
Had he done so, himself had borne the crown,
70   Which waste and idle hours hath quite thrown down.

SERVANT   What, think you the king shall be deposed?

GARDENER   Depressed he is already, and deposed
'Tis doubted he will be. Letters came last night
To a dear friend of the Duke of York's,
75   That tell black tidings.

QUEEN   O, I am pressed to death through want   *Comes forward*
of speaking!
Thou, old Adam's likeness, set to dress this garden,
How dares thy harsh rude tongue sound this unpleasing
    news?
What Eve, what serpent, hath suggested thee
80   To make a second fall of cursèd man?
Why dost thou say King Richard is deposed?
Dar'st thou, thou little better thing than earth,
Divine his downfall? Say, where, when, and how,
Cam'st thou by this ill tidings? Speak, thou wretch.

85   GARDENER   Pardon me, madam. Little joy have I
To breathe these news; yet what I say is true.
King Richard, he is in the mighty hold
Of Bullingbrook. Their fortunes both are weighed:
In your lord's scale is nothing but himself,
90   And some few vanities that make him light.
But in the balance of great Bullingbrook,
Besides himself, are all the English peers,
And with that odds he weighs King Richard down.

---

68 **bearing** fertile, fruit-bearing   69 **crown** king's crown/leafy head of a tree   72 **Depressed** humbled, lowered in fortune   73 **doubted** feared   76 **pressed to death** a punishment that involved pressing suspects with heavy weights until they pleaded innocent or guilty, or died   77 **Adam** in the Bible, the first man; he was in charge of cultivating the Garden of Eden until he was tempted into sin by Eve, who had been tricked by the devil in the guise of a **serpent**   79 **suggested** tempted   83 **Divine** prophesy   87 **hold** grasp/custody   90 **vanities** follies **light** of little weight/frivolous   93 **odds** advantage

Post you to London, and you'll find it so,
95   I speak no more than everyone doth know.
QUEEN   Nimble mischance, that art so light of foot,
Doth not thy embassage belong to me,
And am I last that knows it? O, thou think'st
To serve me last, that I may longest keep
100   Thy sorrow in my breast. Come, ladies, go
To meet at London London's king in woe.
What, was I born to this, that my sad look
Should grace the triumph of great Bullingbrook?
Gard'ner, for telling me this news of woe,
105   I would the plants thou graft'st may never grow.   *Exeunt*
        [*Queen and Ladies*]
GARDENER   Poor queen, so that thy state might be no worse,
I would my skill were subject to thy curse.
Here did she drop a tear. Here in this place
I'll set a bank of rue, sour herb of grace.
110   Rue, e'en for ruth, here shortly shall be seen,
In the remembrance of a weeping queen.   *Exeunt*

Act 4 Scene 1   *running scene 13*

Enter, as to the Parliament, Bullingbrook, Aumerle, Northumberland,
Percy, Fitzwaters, Surrey, Carlisle, Abbot of Westminister, Herald,
Officers and Bagot

BULLINGBROOK   Call forth Bagot.—   *Bagot is brought forward*
Now, Bagot, freely speak thy mind,
What thou dost know of noble Gloucester's death,
Who wrought it with the king, and who performed
5   The bloody office of his timeless end.
BAGOT   Then set before my face the lord Aumerle.

---

94 Post hasten   97 embassage message/errand   belong to i.e. concern   103 triumph
public festivity, triumphal procession   106 so provided   state situation/royal status
109 rue herb symbolizing repentance and grace   sour bitter, sad   110 e'en for ruth for sheer
pity   **4.1   *Location: Westminster Hall, London***   4 wrought worked/arranged   5 office
task/duty   timeless untimely/everlasting

BULLINGBROOK   Cousin, stand forth, and look upon   *To Aumerle*
    that man.

BAGOT   My lord Aumerle, I know your daring tongue
    Scorns to unsay what it hath once delivered.

10   In that dead time when Gloucester's death was plotted,
    I heard you say, 'Is not my arm of length,
    That reacheth from the restful English court
    As far as Calais, to my uncle's head?'
    Amongst much other talk, that very time,

15   I heard you say that you had rather refuse
    The offer of an hundred thousand crowns
    Than Bullingbrook's return to England;
    Adding withal how blest this land would be
    In this your cousin's death.

20 AUMERLE   Princes and noble lords,
    What answer shall I make to this base man?
    Shall I so much dishonour my fair stars,
    On equal terms to give him chastisement?
    Either I must, or have mine honour soiled

25   With th'attainder of his sland'rous lips.—   *Throws down his gage*
    There is my gage, the manual seal of death
    That marks thee out for hell. I say thou liest,
    And will maintain what thou hast said is false
    In thy heart-blood, though being all too base

30   To stain the temper of my knightly sword.

BULLINGBROOK   Bagot, forbear. Thou shalt not take it up.

AUMERLE   Excepting one, I would he were the best
    In all this presence that hath moved me so.

FITZWATERS   If that thy valour stand on sympathy,   *To Aumerle*

35   There is my gage, Aumerle, in gage to thine.   *Throws down his gage*

---

9 unsay deny, retract   **10 dead** fatal, deadly/secret, dark/past   **11 of length** long
16 crowns gold coins   **17 Than** than have   **18 withal** besides   **21 base** contemptible/low-
born   **22 stars** birth, rank/destiny   **23 On . . . chastisement?** To correct/punish him as if we
were equals?   **25 th'attainder** the dishonorable slur, accusation   **26 manual . . . death**
gauntlet (glove thrown down as a **gage**)/death warrant sealed by my hand   **30 temper** steely
firmness/condition   **31 forbear** stop   **32 one** i.e. Bullingbrook   **33 moved** roused, angered
34 stand insist   **sympathy** equal rank (in an opponent)   **35 in gage** engaged

By that fair sun that shows me where thou stand'st,
I heard thee say, and vauntingly thou spak'st it,
That thou wert cause of noble Gloucester's death.
If thou deniest it twenty times, thou liest,
40   And I will turn thy falsehood to thy heart,
Where it was forgèd, with my rapier's point.

AUMERLE   Thou dar'st not, coward, live to see the day.

FITZWATERS   Now by my soul, I would it were this hour.

AUMERLE   Fitzwaters, thou art damned to hell for this.

45 PERCY   Aumerle, thou liest: his honour is as true
In this appeal as thou art all unjust.
And that thou art so, there I throw my gage,
To prove it on thee to th'extremest point   *Throws down his gage*
Of mortal breathing. Seize it, if thou dar'st.

50 AUMERLE   An if I do not, may my hands rot off   *Picks up the gage*
And never brandish more revengeful steel
Over the glittering helmet of my foe!

SURREY   My lord Fitzwaters, I do remember well
The very time Aumerle and you did talk.

55 FITZWATERS   My lord, 'tis very true. You were in presence then
And you can witness with me this is true.

SURREY   As false, by heaven, as heaven itself is true.

FITZWATERS   Surrey, thou liest.

SURREY   Dishonourable boy!
60   That lie shall lie so heavy on my sword
That it shall render vengeance and revenge
Till thou the lie-giver and that lie do lie
In earth as quiet as thy father's skull,
In proof whereof, there is mine honour's pawn.   *Throws down*
65   Engage it to the trial, if thou dar'st.   *his gage*

FITZWATERS   How fondly dost thou spur a forward horse!
If I dare eat, or drink, or breathe, or live,

---

37 vauntingly boastfully   **39 deniest** two syllables ("deny'st")   **40 turn** return   **46 appeal**
accusation   **48 th'extremest . . . breathing** i.e. the death   **50 An** if if   **51 more** again
55 in presence present   **61 render** return   **65 Engage . . . trial** accept it and thus pledge
yourself to combat (**trial**)   **66 fondly** foolishly   **forward** eager

I dare meet Surrey in a wilderness,
And spit upon him, whilst I say he lies,
70   And lies, and lies. There is my bond of faith,   *Throws down his gage*
To tie thee to my strong correction.
As I intend to thrive in this new world,
Aumerle is guilty of my true appeal.
Besides, I heard the banished Norfolk say
75   That thou, Aumerle, didst send two of thy men
To execute the noble duke at Calais.

AUMERLE   Some honest Christian trust me with a gage.   *Borrows*
That Norfolk lies, here do I throw down this,   *a gage, then*
If he may be repealed, to try his honour.   *throws it down*
80   BULLINGBROOK   These differences shall all rest under gage
Till Norfolk be repealed. Repealed he shall be,
And, though mine enemy, restored again
To all his lands and signories. When he's returned,
Against Aumerle we will enforce his trial.
85   CARLISLE   That honourable day shall ne'er be seen.
Many a time hath banished Norfolk fought
For Jesu Christ in glorious Christian field,
Streaming the ensign of the Christian cross
Against black pagans, Turks and Saracens,
90   And toiled with works of war, retired himself
To Italy, and there at Venice gave
His body to that pleasant country's earth,
And his pure soul unto his captain Christ,
Under whose colours he had fought so long.
95   BULLINGBROOK   Why, bishop, is Norfolk dead?
CARLISLE   As sure as I live, my lord.
BULLINGBROOK   Sweet peace conduct his sweet soul to the bosom
Of good old Abraham! Lords appellants,

---

68 wilderness i.e. even somewhere remote or where no help is available   **71 tie** bind
correction punishment, rebuke   **78 That** to assert that   **79 repealed** called back from exile
try test in combat   **80 differences** disputes   **rest under gage** remain challenges
83 signories estates   **84 enforce his trial** make sure that the combat takes place   **87 field**
i.e. battle   **88 Streaming the ensign** flying the banner   **90 toiled** exhausted   **94 colours**
battle flags   **97 bosom . . . Abraham** i.e. heaven   **98 appellants** who have made formal
accusations

Your differences shall all rest under gage
100   Till we assign you to your days of trial.

Enter York

YORK   Great Duke of Lancaster, I come to thee
From plume-plucked Richard, who with willing soul
Adopts thee heir, and his high sceptre yields
To the possession of thy royal hand.
105   Ascend his throne, descending now from him,
And long live Henry, of that name the fourth!

BULLINGBROOK   In God's name, I'll ascend the regal throne.

CARLISLE   Marry, heaven forbid!
Worst in this royal presence may I speak,
110   Yet best beseeming me to speak the truth.
Would God that any in this noble presence
Were enough noble to be upright judge
Of noble Richard! Then true noblesse would
Learn him forbearance from so foul a wrong.
115   What subject can give sentence on his king?
And who sits here that is not Richard's subject?
Thieves are not judged but they are by to hear,
Although apparent guilt be seen in them.
And shall the figure of God's majesty,
120   His captain, steward, deputy-elect,
Anointed, crownèd, planted many years,
Be judged by subject and inferior breath,
And he himself not present? O, forbid it, God,
That in a Christian climate souls refined
125   Should show so heinous, black, obscene a deed.
I speak to subjects, and a subject speaks,
Stirred up by heaven, thus boldly for his king.
My lord of Hereford here, whom you call king,
Is a foul traitor to proud Hereford's king.

---

102 **plume-plucked** humbled, stripped of his glory   105 **descending** i.e. being passed to an heir   108 **Marry** by the Virgin Mary   109 **Worst** of lowest rank   110 **beseeming** befitting (as he is a clergyman)   113 **noblesse** nobility   114 **Learn** teach   117 **by** present 118 **apparent** obvious   119 **figure** image   122 **subject** i.e. of a subject   125 **heinous** grave/wicked   **obscene** repulsive, foul

130 And if you crown him, let me prophesy
The blood of English shall manure the ground,
And future ages groan for his foul act.
Peace shall go sleep with Turks and infidels,
And in this seat of peace tumultuous wars
135 Shall kin with kin and kind with kind confound.
Disorder, horror, fear and mutiny
Shall here inhabit, and this land be called
The field of Golgotha and dead men's skulls.
O, if you rear this house against this house,
140 It will the woefullest division prove
That ever fell upon this cursèd earth.
Prevent it, resist it, and let it not be so,
Lest child, child's children, cry against you 'Woe!'

NORTHUMBERLAND Well have you argued, sir. And for your pains,
145 Of capital treason we arrest you here.
My lord of Westminster, be it your charge
To keep him safely till his day of trial.
May it please you, lords, to grant the commons' suit?

BULLINGBROOK Fetch hither Richard, that in common view
150 He may surrender, so we shall proceed
Without suspicion.

YORK   I will be his conduct.   *Exit*

BULLINGBROOK Lords, you that here are under our arrest,
Procure your sureties for your days of answer.
155 Little are we beholding to your love,
And little looked for at your helping hands.

Enter Richard and York [with Officers bearing the regalia]

KING RICHARD Alack, why am I sent for to a king,
Before I have shook off the regal thoughts

---

131 manure fertilize (after being spilled)   135 kind countrymen   confound bring to ruin
138 field battlefield   Golgotha Calvary (called "the place of skulls"), the hill outside Jerusalem
where Christ was crucified   139 house royal family/Parliament   148 suit request (that the
terms of Richard's abdication be declared publicly to Parliament)   150 surrender abdicate
152 conduct escort   154 sureties guarantors (who will vouch for your appearance)   answer
trial   155 beholding indebted   156 little looked for little expected your love   *regalia* crown
and scepter

Wherewith I reigned? I hardly yet have learned
160   To insinuate, flatter, bow, and bend my knee.
Give sorrow leave awhile to tutor me
To this submission. Yet I well remember
The favours of these men: were they not mine?
Did they not sometime cry, 'All hail!' to me?
165   So Judas did to Christ, but he in twelve
Found truth in all but one; I, in twelve thousand, none.
God save the king! Will no man say 'Amen'?
Am I both priest and clerk? Well then, amen.
God save the king, although I be not he.
170   And yet, amen, if heaven do think him me.
To do what service am I sent for hither?
YORK   To do that office of thine own good will
Which tired majesty did make thee offer:
The resignation of thy state and crown
175   To Henry Bullingbrook.
KING RICHARD   Give me the crown.— Here, cousin,   *Takes the crown*
        seize the crown: *and offers it to Bullingbrook*
Here cousin, on this side my hand, on that side thine.
Now is this golden crown like a deep well
That owes two buckets, filling one another,
180   The emptier ever dancing in the air,
The other down, unseen and full of water:
That bucket down and full of tears am I,
Drinking my griefs, whilst you mount up on high.
BULLINGBROOK   I thought you had been willing to resign.
185   KING RICHARD   My crown I am, but still my griefs are mine.
You may my glories and my state depose,
But not my griefs; still am I king of those.
BULLINGBROOK   Part of your cares you give me with your crown.

---

160 **insinuate** ingratiate myself   163 **favours** faces/support, kindness/gifts   164 **sometime** formerly   165 **twelve** i.e. the twelve disciples   168 **priest and clerk** in church services the priest said prayers to which the clerk responded "Amen"   171 **service** puns on the sense of "church service"   173 **tired majesty** exhausted, weary dignity/sovereign power   176 **seize** grasp/take legal possession of/arrest   179 **owes** owns, possesses   **filling one another** the rising of the full bucket causes the other to be lowered and filled

KING RICHARD Your cares set up do not pluck my cares down.

190   My care is loss of care, by old care done:
       Your care is gain of care, by new care won.
       The cares I give I have, though given away,
       They tend the crown, yet still with me they stay.

BULLINGBROOK Are you contented to resign the crown?

195 KING RICHARD Ay, no; no, ay, for I must nothing be:
       Therefore no 'no', for I resign to thee.
       Now mark me how I will undo myself:
       I give this heavy weight from off my head,   *Bullingbrook accepts*

                                                        crown

       And this unwieldy sceptre from my hand,   *Bullingbrook*
200   The pride of kingly sway from out my heart.   *accepts sceptre*
       With mine own tears I wash away my balm,
       With mine own hands I give away my crown,
       With mine own tongue deny my sacred state,
       With mine own breath release all duteous oaths.
206   All pomp and majesty I do forswear:
       My manors, rents, revenues I forgo:
       My acts, decrees, and statutes I deny.
       God pardon all oaths that are broke to me,
       God keep all vows unbroke are made to thee.
210   Make me, that nothing have, with nothing grieved,
       And thou with all pleased, that hast all achieved.
       Long mayst thou live in Richard's seat to sit,
       And soon lie Richard in an earthy pit!
       'God save King Henry', unkinged Richard says,
215   'And send him many years of sunshine days!' —
       What more remains?

NORTHUMBERLAND No more, but that you read   *Gives a paper*
       These accusations and these grievous crimes

---

189 Your . . . down your assumption of the anxieties and obligations of kingship does not
detract from my grief; in the following lines Richard plays on several senses of **care**: kingly
responsibility/personal grief/concern   190 by . . . done caused by my former inadequate
responsibility   193 tend attend, follow   195 Ay puns on "I"   no puns on "know"
197 mark me note   undo bring to naught, destroy, unmake   200 sway rule
204 release . . . oaths release my subjects from their oaths of allegiance to me   205 forswear
reject   210 with nothing grieved not grieved at all/grieved with the fact that I have nothing

Committed by your person and your followers
220   Against the state and profit of this land,
That, by confessing them, the souls of men
May deem that you are worthily deposed.

KING RICHARD   Must I do so? And must I ravel out
My weaved-up follies? Gentle Northumberland,
225   If thy offences were upon record,
Would it not shame thee in so fair a troop
To read a lecture of them? If thou wouldst,
There shouldst thou find one heinous article,
Containing the deposing of a king
230   And cracking the strong warrant of an oath,
Marked with a blot, damned in the book of heaven.
Nay, all of you that stand and look upon me,
Whilst that my wretchedness doth bait myself,
Though some of you with Pilate wash your hands
235   Showing an outward pity, yet you Pilates
Have here delivered me to my sour cross,
And water cannot wash away your sin.

NORTHUMBERLAND   My lord, dispatch. Read o'er these articles.

KING RICHARD   Mine eyes are full of tears, I cannot see.
240   And yet salt water blinds them not so much
But they can see a sort of traitors here.
Nay, if I turn mine eyes upon myself,
I find myself a traitor with the rest,
For I have given here my soul's consent
245   T'undeck the pompous body of a king;
Made glory base and sovereignty a slave,
Proud majesty a subject, state a peasant.

NORTHUMBERLAND   My lord—

---

223 **ravel out** unravel   224 **Gentle** noble/kind   226 **troop** company   227 **read a lecture** read out an account (as though preaching a lesson)   228 **article** item forming part of an accusation   230 **warrant** guarantee   233 **bait** harass, torment (like a bear being baited for sport)   234 **Pilate** Pontius Pilate, Roman governor of Judaea involved in the crucifixion of Christ, but who washed his hands before the discontented crowd as a means of exonerating himself from blame   236 **sour** bitter, harsh   238 **dispatch** make haste, get on with it   241 **sort** pack, gang   245 **T'undeck** to undress, to strip of ornament   **pompous** splendid, ceremonially dressed

KING RICHARD   No lord of thine, thou haught insulting man,
250   No, nor no man's lord.— I have no name, no title;
      No, not that name was given me at the font,
      But 'tis usurped. Alack the heavy day,
      That I have worn so many winters out,
      And know not now what name to call myself.
255   O, that I were a mockery king of snow,
      Standing before the sun of Bullingbrook,
      To melt myself away in water-drops!
      Good king, great king — and yet not greatly good —
      An if my word be sterling yet in England,
260   Let it command a mirror hither straight,
      That it may show me what a face I have,
      Since it is bankrupt of his majesty.
BULLINGBROOK   Go some of you and fetch a looking-glass.
                                                [Exit an Attendant]
NORTHUMBERLAND   Read o'er this paper while the glass doth
      come.
265   KING RICHARD   Fiend, thou torments me ere I come to hell!
BULLINGBROOK   Urge it no more, my lord Northumberland.
NORTHUMBERLAND   The commons will not then be satisfied.
KING RICHARD   They shall be satisfied. I'll read enough,
      When I do see the very book indeed
270   Where all my sins are writ, and that's myself.
Enter one, with a glass
      Give me that glass, and therein will I read.   *Takes the mirror*
      No deeper wrinkles yet? Hath sorrow struck
      So many blows upon this face of mine,
      And made no deeper wounds? O flatt'ring glass,
275   Like to my followers in prosperity,
      Thou dost beguile me! Was this face the face
      That every day under his household roof
      Did keep ten thousand men? Was this the face

---

249 **haught** haughty, arrogant   251 **at the font** i.e. at my christening   255 **mockery**
imitation/subject of ridicule   259 **An if** if   **sterling** valid currency   261 **what** what kind of
262 **his** its   263 **some** i.e. one   *glass* mirror   276 **beguile** deceive   278 **keep** maintain

That like the sun did make beholders wink?
280   Is this the face which faced so many follies,
That was at last out-faced by Bullingbrook?
A brittle glory shineth in this face,
As brittle as the glory is the face.   *Throws the mirror down*
For there it is, cracked in an hundred shivers.   *against the ground*
285   Mark, silent king, the moral of this sport,
How soon my sorrow hath destroyed my face.

BULLINGBROOK The shadow of your sorrow hath destroyed
The shadow of your face.

KING RICHARD Say that again.
290   The shadow of my sorrow? Ha? Let's see,
'Tis very true, my grief lies all within,
And these external manner of laments
Are merely shadows to the unseen grief
That swells with silence in the tortured soul.
295   There lies the substance: and I thank thee, king,
For thy great bounty, that not only giv'st
Me cause to wail, but teachest me the way
How to lament the cause. I'll beg one boon,
And then be gone and trouble you no more.
300   Shall I obtain it?

BULLINGBROOK Name it, fair cousin.

KING RICHARD 'Fair cousin'? I am greater than a king,
For when I was a king, my flatterers
Were then but subjects; being now a subject,
305   I have a king here to my flatterer.
Being so great, I have no need to beg.

BULLINGBROOK Yet ask.

KING RICHARD And shall I have?

BULLINGBROOK You shall.

310   KING RICHARD Then give me leave to go.

---

279 **wink** blink, shut their eyes   280 **faced** covered over/countenanced, sanctioned
281 **out-faced** defied, challenged/replaced by   284 **shivers** shards, fragments   285 **moral**
significance, true meaning   287 **shadow** reflection/dark, gloomy shade (Richard develops
the sense to include delusive semblance, "thing without substance")   292 **manner** forms
298 **boon** favor   305 **to** as

BULLINGBROOK Whither?

KING RICHARD Whither you will, so I were from your sights.

BULLINGBROOK Go, some of you convey him to the Tower.

KING RICHARD O, good! 'Convey'? Conveyers are you all,

315   That rise thus nimbly by a true king's fall.

[*Exeunt Richard, some Lords and a Guard*]

BULLINGBROOK On Wednesday next we solemnly set down

Our coronation. Lords, prepare yourselves.

Exeunt [all except Carlisle, the Abbot and Aumerle]

ABBOT   A woeful pageant have we here beheld.

CARLISLE   The woe's to come. The children yet unborn

320   Shall feel this day as sharp to them as thorn.

AUMERLE   You holy clergymen, is there no plot

To rid the realm of this pernicious blot?

ABBOT   Before I freely speak my mind herein,

You shall not only take the sacrament

325   To bury mine intents, but also to effect

Whatever I shall happen to devise.

I see your brows are full of discontent,

Your heart of sorrow and your eyes of tears.

Come home with me to supper. I'll lay

330   A plot shall show us all a merry day.   *Exeunt*

Act 5 Scene 1   *running scene 14*

Enter Queen and Ladies

QUEEN   This way the king will come. This is the way

To Julius Caesar's ill-erected tower,

To whose flint bosom my condemnèd lord

Is doomed a prisoner by proud Bullingbrook.

---

313 **convey** escort (Richard goes on to play on the sense of "steal")   316 **set down** appoint
the time for   322 **pernicious** destructive   324 **take the sacrament** receive Holy Communion
(as a means of confirming your word)   325 **bury** conceal   **5.1** *Location: London, near
the Tower*   2 **Julius Caesar** it was a popular notion that the Roman emperor built the Tower of
London; in fact, it was erected by William the Conqueror   **ill-erected** built for wicked ends and
with evil consequences   3 **flint** i.e. hard   4 **doomed** judged/consigned to some adverse fate

5   Here let us rest, if this rebellious earth
           Have any resting for her true king's queen.

Enter Richard and Guard

           But soft, but see, or rather do not see,
           My fair rose wither. Yet look up, behold,
           That you in pity may dissolve to dew,
10   And wash him fresh again with true-love tears.
           Ah, thou, the model where old Troy did stand,
           Thou map of honour, thou King Richard's tomb,
           And not King Richard. Thou most beauteous inn,
           Why should hard-favoured grief be lodged in thee,
15   When triumph is become an ale-house guest?

KING RICHARD   Join not with grief, fair woman, do not so,
           To make my end too sudden. Learn, good soul,
           To think our former state a happy dream;
           From which awaked, the truth of what we are
20   Shows us but this. I am sworn brother, sweet,
           To grim Necessity, and he and I
           Will keep a league till death. Hie thee to France
           And cloister thee in some religious house.
           Our holy lives must win a new world's crown,
25   Which our profane hours here have stricken down.

QUEEN   What, is my Richard both in shape and mind
           Transformed and weakened? Hath Bullingbrook deposed
           Thine intellect? Hath he been in thy heart?
           The lion dying thrusteth forth his paw,
30   And wounds the earth, if nothing else, with rage
           To be o'erpowered. And wilt thou, pupil-like,
           Take thy correction mildly, kiss the rod,

---

11 **model** ground plan, outline   **Troy** supposedly founded by the Trojan Brutus, London was often referred to as the New Troy   12 **map** outline, image   13 **inn** house/place of temporary lodging   14 **hard-favoured** ugly   15 **ale-house** cheap, lowly place of lodging   18 **state** situation/kingship   20 **sworn brother** the devoted, loyal friend   22 **league** bond of friendship, allegiance   **Hie** hurry   23 **cloister** seclude, conceal   **religious house** convent   24 **new world's** i.e. heaven's   26 **shape** physical appearance   31 **To be** at being   32 **rod** punishment cane

And fawn on rage with base humility,
Which art a lion and a king of beasts?

35   KING RICHARD   A king of beasts, indeed. If aught but beasts,
I had been still a happy king of men.
Good sometime queen, prepare thee hence for France:
Think I am dead and that even here thou tak'st,
As from my death-bed, thy last living leave.

40   In winter's tedious nights sit by the fire
With good old folks and let them tell thee tales
Of woeful ages long ago betid.
And ere thou bid good night, to quit their grief,
Tell thou the lamentable fall of me

45   And send the hearers weeping to their beds.
For why the senseless brands will sympathize
The heavy accent of thy moving tongue
And in compassion weep the fire out,
And some will mourn in ashes, some coal-black,

50   For the deposing of a rightful king.

Enter Northumberland [and others]

NORTHUMBERLAND   My lord, the mind of Bullingbrook is changed.
You must to Pomfret, not unto the Tower.—
And, madam, there is order ta'en for you: *To the Queen*
With all swift speed you must away to France.

55   KING RICHARD   Northumberland, thou ladder wherewithal
The mounting Bullingbrook ascends my throne,
The time shall not be many hours of age
More than it is ere foul sin, gathering head,
Shall break into corruption. Thou shalt think,

---

35 **beasts** beastly men   **aught but** anything other than   36 **still** yet/always   **happy**
fortunate   37 **sometime** former   42 **long ago betid** that happened long ago   43 **quit**
requite, repay   **grief** i.e. mournful **tales**   46 **why** this cause   **brands** burning logs
sympathize feel for, respond to   47 **heavy accent** sorrowful tone   **moving** talking/affecting,
stirring to sorrow   48 **weep** literally, exude resin as they burn   49 **some** i.e. of the firewood
(**brands**)   52 **Pomfret** Pontefract Castle, in Yorkshire   53 **order ta'en** instructions issued,
arrangements made   55 **wherewithal** by means of which   57 **many . . . age** i.e. older
58 **head** to a head (of a boil, with play on the sense of "insurrection")   59 **corruption** pus
(plays on the sense of "sin, destruction")

60   Though he divide the realm and give thee half,
        It is too little, helping him to all.
        He shall think that thou, which know'st the way
        To plant unrightful kings, wilt know again,
        Being ne'er so little urged, another way
65   To pluck him headlong from th'usurpèd throne.
        The love of wicked friends converts to fear;
        That fear to hate, and hate turns one or both
        To worthy danger and deservèd death.
NORTHUMBERLAND   My guilt be on my head, and there an end.
70   Take leave and part, for you must part forthwith.
KING RICHARD   Doubly divorced? Bad men, ye violate
        A twofold marriage, 'twixt my crown and me
        And then betwixt me and my married wife.—
        Let me unkiss the oath 'twixt thee and me;   *To Queen*
75   And yet not so, for with a kiss 'twas made.—
        Part us, Northumberland. I towards the north,
        Where shivering cold and sickness pines the clime.
        My queen to France, from whence, set forth in pomp,
        She came adornèd hither like sweet May,
80   Sent back like Hallowmas or short'st of day.
    QUEEN   And must we be divided? Must we part?
    KING RICHARD   Ay, hand from hand, my love, and heart from
            heart.
    QUEEN   Banish us both and send the king with me.
    NORTHUMBERLAND   That were some love but little policy.
85 QUEEN   Then whither he goes, thither let me go.
    KING RICHARD   So two, together weeping, make one woe.
        Weep thou for me in France, I for thee here.
        Better far off than, near, be ne'er the near.
        Go, count thy way with sighs; I mine with groans.

60 Though he even if he were to   61 helping you having helped   62 which who
63 unrightful illegitimate   67 one or both i.e. either usurping king or his collaborator
68 worthy well-deserved   70 part separate (from the queen; sense then shifts to "depart")
72 'twixt betwixt, between   74 unkiss annul with a kiss   77 pines afflicts, wastes away
78 from whence from where; Isabel was daughter to the French king   80 Hallowmas
November 1, All Saints' Day   short'st of day the winter solstice, shortest day of the year
84 were would show   88 be . . . near not being together   near nearer

90 QUEEN   So longest way shall have the longest moans.

KING RICHARD   Twice for one step I'll groan, the way being short,

And piece the way out with a heavy heart.

Come, come, in wooing sorrow let's be brief,

Since, wedding it, there is such length in grief.

95 One kiss shall stop our mouths, and dumbly part;   *They kiss*

Thus give I mine, and thus take I thy heart.

QUEEN   Give me mine own again. 'Twere no good part

To take on me to keep and kill thy heart.   *They kiss*

So, now I have mine own again, be gone,

100 That I may strive to kill it with a groan.

KING RICHARD   We make woe wanton with this fond delay.

Once more, adieu; the rest let sorrow say.   *Exeunt*

Act 5 Scene 2

running scene 15

Enter York and his Duchess

DUCHESS OF YORK   My lord, you told me you would tell the rest,

When weeping made you break the story off,

Of our two cousins coming into London.

YORK   Where did I leave?

5 DUCHESS OF YORK   At that sad stop, my lord,

Where rude misgoverned hands from windows' tops

Threw dust and rubbish on King Richard's head.

YORK   Then, as I said, the duke, great Bullingbrook,

Mounted upon a hot and fiery steed

10 Which his aspiring rider seemed to know,

With slow but stately pace kept on his course,

While all tongues cried 'God save thee, Bullingbrook!'

You would have thought the very windows spake,

---

92 **piece . . . out** lengthen the journey   95 **stop** stop up, silence   97 **'Twere . . . me** it
would do no good to take it upon myself (**part** plays on the sense of "parting" and "body part,
organ")   98 **kill** i.e. with sorrow   101 **wanton** playful, unrestrained, self-indulgent   **fond**
foolish/doting   102 **adieu** goodbye   **5.2** *Location: the Duke of York's house*
3 **cousins** kinsmen, i.e. Richard and Bullingbrook; York was their uncle   4 **leave** break off
6 **rude** unkind, uncivilized, rough   **misgoverned** unruly, unrestrained   **windows' tops**
upper windows   10 **Which** i.e. which horse   **aspiring** ambitious

So many greedy looks of young and old
15 Through casements darted their desiring eyes
Upon his visage, and that all the walls
With painted imagery had said at once
'Jesu preserve thee! Welcome, Bullingbrook!'
Whilst he, from one side to the other turning,
20 Bareheaded, lower than his proud steed's neck,
Bespake them thus: 'I thank you, countrymen',
And thus still doing, thus he passed along.

DUCHESS OF YORK   Alas, poor Richard! Where rides he the whilst?

YORK   As in a theatre, the eyes of men,
25 After a well-graced actor leaves the stage,
Are idly bent on him that enters next,
Thinking his prattle to be tedious,
Even so, or with much more contempt, men's eyes
Did scowl on Richard. No man cried 'God save him',
30 No joyful tongue gave him his welcome home,
But dust was thrown upon his sacred head,
Which with such gentle sorrow he shook off,
His face still combating with tears and smiles,
The badges of his grief and patience,
35 That had not God, for some strong purpose, steeled
The hearts of men, they must perforce have melted
And barbarism itself have pitied him.
But heaven hath a hand in these events,
To whose high will we bound our calm contents.
40 To Bullingbrook are we sworn subjects now,
Whose state and honour I for aye allow.

Enter Aumerle

DUCHESS OF YORK   Here comes my son Aumerle.

YORK   Aumerle that was,

---

15 **casements** windows   17 **painted imagery** the people, or speaking figures in painted wall-coverings   20 **Bareheaded** removing one's hat was a sign of respect or deference
21 **Bespake** addressed   22 **still** continually   23 **the whilst** during this   25 **well-graced** attractive/skilled/well-regarded, favored   26 **idly** unenthusiastically/inattentively
33 **combating with** fighting between   34 **badges** signs/livery   36 **perforce** of necessity
39 **bound** bind/limit, confine   **contents** contentment   41 **state** regality, kingship   **aye** ever, i.e. fully

But that is lost for being Richard's friend.
45   And, madam, you must call him Rutland now.
I am in parliament pledge for his truth
And lasting fealty to the new-made king.
DUCHESS OF YORK   Welcome, my son. Who are the violets now
That strew the green lap of the new come spring?
50   AUMERLE   Madam, I know not, nor I greatly care not.
God knows I had as lief be none as one.
YORK   Well, bear you well in this new spring of time,
Lest you be cropped before you come to prime.
What news from Oxford? Hold those jousts and triumphs?
55   AUMERLE   For aught I know, my lord, they do.
YORK   You will be there, I know.
AUMERLE   If God prevent not, I purpose so.
YORK   What seal is that, that hangs without thy bosom?
Yea, look'st thou pale? Let me see the writing.
60   AUMERLE   My lord, 'tis nothing.
YORK   No matter, then, who sees it.
I will be satisfied. Let me see the writing.
AUMERLE   I do beseech your grace to pardon me.
It is a matter of small consequence,
65   Which for some reasons I would not have seen.
YORK   Which for some reasons, sir, I mean to see.
I fear, I fear—
DUCHESS OF YORK   What should you fear?
'Tis nothing but some bond that he is entered into
70   For gay apparel against the triumph.
YORK   Bound to himself? What doth he with a bond
That he is bound to? Wife, thou art a fool.
Boy, let me see the writing.

---

45 **Rutland** for his support of Richard, Aumerle lost his status as duke, though he retained the title Earl of Rutland   46 **pledge . . . truth** guarantor of his loyalty   47 **fealty** allegiance   48 **violets** i.e. court favorites   49 **spring** i.e. Bullingbrook's kingship   51 **as lief** as soon, rather   52 **bear you** conduct yourself   53 **cropped** cut down/beheaded   54 **Hold** go ahead   **triumphs** public festivities   58 **seal** i.e. seal attached to the bottom of a document (which Aumerle apparently carries in his doublet or jacket)   69 **bond** financial agreement (retained by the creditor)   70 **against** in preparation for

AUMERLE   I do beseech you pardon me. I may not show it.

75   YORK   I will be satisfied. Let me see it, I say.   *Snatches it*

Treason, foul treason! Villain, traitor, slave!

DUCHESS OF YORK   What's the matter, my lord?

YORK   Ho! Who's within there?

[*Enter a Servant*]

Saddle my horse.

80   Heaven for his mercy, what treachery is here!

DUCHESS OF YORK   Why, what is't, my lord?

YORK   Give me my boots, I say. Saddle my horse.—

[*Exit Servant*]

Now, by my honour, my life, my troth,

I will appeach the villain.

85   DUCHESS OF YORK   What is the matter?

YORK   Peace, foolish woman.

DUCHESS OF YORK   I will not peace. What is the matter, son?

AUMERLE   Good mother, be content. It is no more

Than my poor life must answer.

90   DUCHESS OF YORK   Thy life answer?

Enter Servant with boots

YORK   Bring me my boots. I will unto the king.

DUCHESS OF YORK   Strike him, Aumerle. Poor boy, thou art
        amazed.—

Hence, villain! Never more come in my sight.   *To Servant*

YORK   Give me my boots, I say.

95   DUCHESS OF YORK   Why, York, what wilt thou do?

Wilt thou not hide the trespass of thine own?

Have we more sons? Or are we like to have?

Is not my teeming date drunk up with time?

And wilt thou pluck my fair son from mine age,

100   And rob me of a happy mother's name?

Is he not like thee? Is he not thine own?

YORK   Thou fond mad woman,

Wilt thou conceal this dark conspiracy?

---

84 appeach denounce, inform against   **89 answer** answer for   **92 amazed** stunned, confused   **93 villain** rogue/servant   **96 own** i.e. own child   **98 teeming date** time for childbearing   **102 fond** foolish/doting

A dozen of them here have ta'en the sacrament,
105   And interchangeably set down their hands,
To kill the king at Oxford.

DUCHESS OF YORK   He shall be none.
We'll keep him here. Then what is that to him?

YORK   Away, fond woman! Were he twenty times my son,
110   I would appeach him.

DUCHESS OF YORK   Hadst thou groaned for him
As I have done, thou wouldst be more pitiful.
But now I know thy mind; thou dost suspect
That I have been disloyal to thy bed,
115   And that he is a bastard, not thy son.
Sweet York, sweet husband, be not of that mind:
He is as like thee as a man may be,
Not like to me, nor any of my kin,
And yet I love him.

120   YORK   Make way, unruly woman!   *Exit*

DUCHESS OF YORK   After, Aumerle! Mount thee upon his horse.
Spur post, and get before him to the king,
And beg thy pardon ere he do accuse thee.
I'll not be long behind. Though I be old,
125   I doubt not but to ride as fast as York:
And never will I rise up from the ground
Till Bullingbrook have pardoned thee. Away, begone!   *Exeunt*

Act 5 Scene 3   *running scene 16*

Enter Bullingbrook, Percy and other Lords

BULLINGBROOK   Can no man tell of my unthrifty son?
'Tis full three months since I did see him last.
If any plague hang over us, 'tis he.

---

105 **interchangeably** reciprocally (so each of the conspirators has a copy of the agreement)
107 **be none** not be one of them   108 **that** i.e. the plot/the actions of the conspirators
111 **groaned** i.e. in labor   121 **his horse** i.e. grab his saddled horse and ride out first
122 **post** speedily   126 **the ground** i.e. kneeling   **5.3** *Location: the royal court*
1 **unthrifty** extravagant, dissolute   **son** Prince Hal, later Henry V

I would to heaven, my lords, he might be found.
5   Enquire at London, 'mongst the taverns there,
For there, they say, he daily doth frequent,
With unrestrainèd loose companions,
Even such, they say, as stand in narrow lanes,
And rob our watch, and beat our passengers,
10   Which he, young wanton and effeminate boy,
Takes on the point of honour to support
So dissolute a crew.

PERCY   My lord, some two days since I saw the prince,
And told him of these triumphs held at Oxford.

15   BULLINGBROOK   And what said the gallant?

PERCY   His answer was, he would unto the stews,
And from the common'st creature pluck a glove,
And wear it as a favour, and with that
He would unhorse the lustiest challenger.

20   BULLINGBROOK   As dissolute as desp'rate. Yet through both
I see some sparks of better hope, which elder days
May happily bring forth. But who comes here?

Enter Aumerle

AUMERLE   Where is the king?

BULLINGBROOK   What means our cousin, that he stares and
looks so wildly?

25   AUMERLE   God save your grace! I do beseech your majesty,
To have some conference with your grace alone.

BULLINGBROOK   Withdraw yourselves, and leave us here alone.

[*Exeunt Henry Percy and Lords*]

What is the matter with our cousin now?

---

7 **loose** immoral, wasteful   9 **watch** night watchmen   **passengers** travelers   10 **effeminate**
frivolous, self-indulgent, immature   11 **Takes on the** undertakes as a   15 **gallant** fashionable
young man/fine fellow   16 **stews** brothels/part of a city occupied by houses of ill fame
17 **common'st** most whorish, promiscuous   **creature** prostitute   **glove** with vaginal
connotations   18 **favour** love token (worn by knights in jousts)   **with that** wearing the token
19 **unhorse** plays on the sense of "deprive of a whore"   **lustiest** most vigorous (plays on the
sense of "most licentious")   20 **desp'rate** reckless   **both** i.e. both flaws   22 **happily** with
favorable destiny/with a happy result   24 **stares** gapes, looks horrorstruck

AUMERLE   Forever may my knees grow to the earth,
30   My tongue cleave to my roof within my mouth
         Unless a pardon ere I rise or speak.
BULLINGBROOK   Intended or committed was this fault?
         If on the first, how heinous e'er it be,
         To win thy after-love I pardon thee.
35 AUMERLE   Then give me leave that I may turn the key,
         That no man enter till my tale be done.
BULLINGBROOK   Have thy desire.   *Aumerle locks door*
YORK   (*Within*) My liege, beware! Look to thyself:
         Thou hast a traitor in thy presence there.
40 BULLINGBROOK   Villain, I'll make thee safe.   *Draws his sword*
AUMERLE   Stay thy revengeful hand, thou hast no cause to
              fear.
YORK   (*Within*) Open the door, secure, foolhardy king:
         Shall I for love speak treason to thy face?
         Open the door, or I will break it open.   *Bullingbrook unlocks door*
Enter York
45 BULLINGBROOK   What is the matter, uncle? Speak,
         Recover breath, tell us how near is danger,
         That we may arm us to encounter it.
YORK   Peruse this writing here, and thou shalt know
         The reason that my haste forbids me show.   *Presents paper*
50 AUMERLE   Remember, as thou read'st, thy promise passed.
         I do repent me: read not my name there
         My heart is not confederate with my hand.
YORK   It was, villain, ere thy hand did set it down.
         I tore it from the traitor's bosom, king.
55   Fear, and not love, begets his penitence;
         Forget to pity him, lest thy pity prove
         A serpent that will sting thee to the heart.

---

29 grow i.e. be fixed   **31 a pardon** i.e. I am granted a pardon   **34 after-love** future loyalty
40 safe harmless, i.e. dead   **41 Stay** withhold   **42 secure** overconfident   **43 speak treason**
i.e. by having to use such disrespectful terms   **49 haste** i.e. breathlessness   **50 passed** just
made   **52 hand** signature

BULLINGBROOK   O, heinous, strong and bold conspiracy!
    O loyal father of a treacherous son!
60   Thou sheer, immaculate and silver fountain,
    From whence this stream through muddy passages
    Hath held his current and defiled himself!
    Thy overflow of good converts to bad,
    And thy abundant goodness shall excuse
65   This deadly blot in thy digressing son.
YORK   So shall my virtue be his vice's bawd,
    And he shall spend mine honour with his shame,
    As thriftless sons their scraping fathers' gold.
    Mine honour lives when his dishonour dies,
70   Or my shamed life in his dishonour lies.
    Thou kill'st me in his life: giving him breath,
    The traitor lives, the true man's put to death.
DUCHESS OF YORK   (*Within*) What ho, my liege! For heaven's sake,
    let me in.
BULLINGBROOK   What shrill-voiced suppliant makes this eager
    cry?
75 DUCHESS OF YORK   (*Within*) A woman, and thine aunt, great
    king. 'Tis I.
    Speak with me, pity me, open the door:
    A beggar begs that never begged before.
BULLINGBROOK   Our scene is altered from a serious thing,
    And now changed to 'The Beggar and the King'.—
80   My dangerous cousin, let your mother in.
    I know she's come to pray for your foul sin.
YORK   If thou do pardon, whosoever pray,
    More sins for this forgiveness prosper may.

---

58 **strong** flagrant/significant, dangerous   60 **sheer** pure, clear   **fountain** spring   62 **held his current** taken its course   65 **deadly blot** fatal sin/ink signature   **digressing** deviating from its course/transgressing morally   66 **bawd** pimp, procurer   67 **spend** waste/may play on the sense of "ejaculate"   68 **scraping** money-saving   72 **true** loyal   79 'The . . . King' probably refers to a ballad telling the popular tale of King Cophetua and the beggar maid he fell in love with   83 **for** as a result of

This festered joint cut off, the rest rests sound:

85   This let alone will all the rest confound.

Enter Duchess

DUCHESS OF YORK   O king, believe not this hard-hearted man!

Love loving not itself none other can.

YORK   Thou frantic woman, what dost thou make here?

Shall thy old dugs once more a traitor rear?

90   DUCHESS OF YORK   Sweet York, be patient. Hear me,   *Kneels*

gentle liege.

BULLINGBROOK   Rise up, good aunt.

DUCHESS OF YORK   Not yet, I thee beseech.

Forever will I kneel upon my knees,

And never see day that the happy sees,

95   Till thou give joy, until thou bid me joy,

By pardoning Rutland, my transgressing boy.

AUMERLE   Unto my mother's prayers I bend my knee.   *Kneels*

YORK   Against them both my true joints bended be.   *Kneels*

DUCHESS OF YORK   Pleads he in earnest? Look upon his face:

100   His eyes do drop no tears, his prayers are in jest:

His words come from his mouth, ours from our breast.

He prays but faintly and would be denied:

We pray with heart and soul and all beside.

His weary joints would gladly rise, I know:

105   Our knees shall kneel till to the ground they grow.

His prayers are full of false hypocrisy,

Ours of true zeal and deep integrity.

Our prayers do out-pray his: then let them have

That mercy which true prayers ought to have.

110   BULLINGBROOK   Good aunt, stand up.

DUCHESS OF YORK   Nay, do not say, 'stand up'.

But, 'pardon' first, and afterwards 'stand up'.

And if I were thy nurse, thy tongue to teach,

---

84 **festered** corrupt/diseased   85 **let alone** left untreated   **confound** destroy   87 **itself** i.e. its own flesh and blood, one's son   88 **frantic** mad   89 **dugs** breasts   94 **happy** happy/fortunate person   98 **true** loyal   100 **in jest** pretend   102 **would** wishes to

'Pardon' should be the first word of thy speech.
115   I never longed to hear a word till now:
Say 'pardon', king, let pity teach thee how.
The word is short, but not so short as sweet:
No word like 'pardon' for kings' mouths so meet.

YORK   Speak it in French, king: say, '*pardonnez-moi*'.
120   DUCHESS OF YORK   Dost thou teach pardon pardon to destroy?
Ah, my sour husband, my hard-hearted lord,
That sets the word itself against the word!—
Speak 'pardon' as 'tis current in our land: *To Bullingbrook*
The chopping French we do not understand.
125   Thine eye begins to speak, set thy tongue there,
Or in thy piteous heart plant thou thine ear,
That hearing how our plaints and prayers do pierce,
Pity may move thee 'pardon' to rehearse.

BULLINGBROOK   Good aunt, stand up.
130   DUCHESS OF YORK   I do not sue to stand:
Pardon is all the suit I have in hand.

BULLINGBROOK   I pardon him, as heaven shall pardon me.

DUCHESS OF YORK   O, happy vantage of a kneeling knee!
Yet am I sick for fear: speak it again,
135   Twice saying 'pardon' doth not pardon twain,
But makes one pardon strong.

BULLINGBROOK   I pardon him with all my heart.

DUCHESS OF YORK   A god on earth thou art.   *York, Duchess and*

BULLINGBROOK   But for our trusty brother-in-law, the   *Aumerle rise*
abbot,
140   With all the rest of that consorted crew,
Destruction straight shall dog them at the heels.
Good uncle, help to order several powers
To Oxford, or where'er these traitors are:

---

118 meet fitting   119 '*pardonnez-moi*' French for "pardon me," i.e. excuse me for refusing
your request   124 chopping meaning-shifting, logic-chopping/affected   127 plaints laments
128 rehearse pronounce/repeat   130 sue beg   131 suit request (puns on the sense of "suit
of cards," an image maintained in hand)   133 happy joyous/fortunate   vantage profit,
gain/advantageous position   135 twain divide in two   139 for as for   brother-in-law i.e. the
Duke of Exeter   the i.e. and the   140 consorted conspiring   142 several separate, various

They shall not live within this world, I swear,

145   But I will have them, if I once know where.

Uncle, farewell, and, cousin, adieu:

Your mother well hath prayed, and prove you true.

DUCHESS OF YORK   Come, my old son. I pray heaven make thee

new.   *Exeunt*

[Act 5 Scene 4]   *running scene 16 continues*

Enter Exton and Servants

EXTON   Didst thou not mark the king, what words he

spake —

'Have I no friend will rid me of this living fear?'

Was it not so?

SERVANT   Those were his very words.

5   EXTON   'Have I no friend?' quoth he; he spake it twice,

And urged it twice together, did he not?

SERVANT   He did.

EXTON   And speaking it, he wistly looked on me,

As who should say, 'I would thou wert the man

10   That would divorce this terror from my heart',

Meaning the king at Pomfret. Come, let's go:

I am the king's friend, and will rid his foe.   *Exeunt*

Act 5 Scene [5]   *running scene 17*

Enter Richard

KING RICHARD   I have been studying how to compare

This prison where I live unto the world.

And for because the world is populous

And here is not a creature but myself,

5   I cannot do it. Yet I'll hammer't out.

My brain I'll prove the female to my soul,

---

147 prove i.e. make sure you prove   **5.4   8 wistly** intently, meaningfully   **9 As** as one
5.5   *Location: Pomfret (Pontefract) Castle*   1 studying thinking about, dwelling on
3 for because because

My soul the father, and these two beget
A generation of still-breeding thoughts;
And these same thoughts people this little world,
In humours like the people of this world,
For no thought is contented. The better sort,
As thoughts of things divine, are intermixed
With scruples and do set the faith itself
Against the faith: as thus, 'Come, little ones',
And then again:
'It is as hard to come as for a camel
To thread the postern of a needle's eye.'
Thoughts tending to ambition, they do plot
Unlikely wonders; how these vain weak nails
May tear a passage through the flinty ribs
Of this hard world, my ragged prison walls,
And, for they cannot, die in their own pride.
Thoughts tending to content flatter themselves
That they are not the first of fortune's slaves,
Nor shall not be the last, like silly beggars
Who sitting in the stocks refuge their shame,
That many have and others must sit there;
And in this thought they find a kind of ease,
Bearing their own misfortune on the back
Of such as have before endured the like.
Thus play I in one prison many people,
And none contented. Sometimes am I king;
Then treason makes me wish myself a beggar,
And so I am. Then crushing penury

10
15
20
25
30

---

7 beget conceive   **8 still-breeding** constantly reproducing   **10 humours** dispositions, moods
12 As such as   **13 scruples** doubts   **faith** i.e. religious belief, as manifested through Scripture
14 'Come, little ones' from the Bible (Luke 18:16; also Matthew 19:14)   **16 'It . . . eye'**
biblical (Luke 18:25; also Matthew 19:24 and Mark 10:25)   **17 postern** back or side gate
21 ragged rough, rugged   **22 for** because   **pride** prime/arrogance   **23 content** acceptance
25 silly simple/lowly/helpless   **26 stocks** contraption for public punishment in which the
arms or legs were confined   **refuge** take refuge from, reduce   **27 That** with the thought that
31 prison most editions follow Quarto's "person," but Folio's "prison" seems to be a purposeful
alteration, not a printer's error   **33 treason** thoughts of treason   **34 penury** poverty

35   Persuades me I was better when a king.
      Then am I kinged again, and by and by
      Think that I am unkinged by Bullingbrook,
      And straight am nothing. But whate'er I am,   *Music*
      Nor I nor any man that but man is
40   With nothing shall be pleased, till he be eased
      With being nothing. Music do I hear?
      Ha, ha! Keep time. How sour sweet music is
      When time is broke and no proportion kept!
      So is it in the music of men's lives.
45   And here have I the daintiness of ear
      To hear time broke in a disordered string,
      But for the concord of my state and time
      Had not an ear to hear my true time broke.
      I wasted time, and now doth time waste me,
50   For now hath time made me his numb'ring clock.
      My thoughts are minutes; and with sighs they jar
      Their watches on unto mine eyes, the outward watch,
      Whereto my finger, like a dial's point,
      Is pointing still, in cleansing them from tears.
55   Now sir, the sound that tells what hour it is
      Are clamorous groans, that strike upon my heart,
      Which is the bell. So sighs and tears and groans
      Show minutes, hours and times. But my time
      Runs posting on in Bullingbrook's proud joy,
60   While I stand fooling here, his Jack o'th'clock.
      This music mads me. Let it sound no more,   ↓*Music stops*↓

---

36 by and by soon   **38 straight** straightaway   **39 but man is** is merely mortal   **40 nothing**
anything   **41 nothing** i.e. dead   **43 proportion** musical time, rhythm   **45 daintiness**
sensitivity   **46 string** individual string/musical instrument   **47 concord** harmony
49 waste decay   **50 numb'ring clock** clock with hours marked on it (i.e. not an hourglass)
51 jar . . . on tick on, jump forward (**jar** plays on the sense of "make discordant")   **52 watches**
intervals between minutes/wakeful periods   **watch** clockface (plays on the sense of
"sentry/wakeful person")   **53 dial's point** clock's hand   **54 still** continuously (plays on the
sense of "motionless")   **55 tells** counts out/reveals   **56 strike** beat, pound/toll   **58 times**
marks on the dial, i.e. quarter or half hours   **time** lifetime, time on earth   **59 posting**
hurrying   **60 Jack o'th'clock** figure of a man that strikes a bell on the outside of some types
of clock   **61 mads** maddens

For though it have holp madmen to their wits,
In me it seems it will make wise men mad.
Yet blessing on his heart that gives it me,
65   For 'tis a sign of love, and love to Richard
Is a strange brooch in this all-hating world.

Enter Groom

GROOM   Hail, royal prince!

KING RICHARD   Thanks, noble peer.
The cheapest of us is ten groats too dear.
70   What art thou? And how com'st thou hither
Where no man ever comes but that sad dog
That brings me food to make misfortune live?

GROOM   I was a poor groom of thy stable, king,
When thou wert king, who, travelling towards York,
75   With much ado, at length have gotten leave
To look upon my sometimes royal master's face.
O, how it yearned my heart when I beheld
In London streets, that coronation-day,
When Bullingbrook rode on roan Barbary,
80   That horse that thou so often hast bestrid,
That horse that I so carefully have dressed!

KING RICHARD   Rode he on Barbary? Tell me, gentle friend,
How went he under him?

GROOM   So proudly as if he had disdained the ground.

85   KING RICHARD   So proud that Bullingbrook was on his back?
That jade hath eat bread from my royal hand,
This hand hath made him proud with clapping him.
Would he not stumble? Would he not fall down,

---

62 holp . . . wits music was thought to assist the recovery of the insane   holp helped
65 to for   66 strange brooch rare jewel   68 peer equal/nobleman   69 The . . . us i.e. the
imprisoned Richard   ten groats Richard plays on the financial senses of royal and noble
(types of gold coin): a royal was worth ten groats more than a noble, so the Groom has
overvalued the royal prince by that amount (Richard identifies himself and the Groom as
nobles)   groat coin worth four old pence   71 sad dismal, unsmiling   72 misfortune i.e.
Richard   75 ado trouble, fuss   76 sometimes formerly   77 yearned grieved, moved
79 roan horse with a coat in which the prevailing color is interspersed with some other
Barbary the horse's name, suggesting that it was imported from the Barbary coast of northern
Africa, whose horses were noted for great speed and endurance   80 bestrid straddled, ridden
82 gentle noble   86 jade worthless old horse   87 clapping patting

Since pride must have a fall, and break the neck
90   Of that proud man that did usurp his back?
Forgiveness, horse. Why do I rail on thee,
Since thou, created to be awed by man,
Wast born to bear? I was not made a horse,
And yet I bear a burden like an ass,
95   Spurred, galled and tired by jauncing Bullingbrook.

Enter Keeper, with a dish

KEEPER   Fellow, give place. Here is no longer stay.

KING RICHARD   If thou love me, 'tis time thou wert away.   *To Groom*

GROOM   What my tongue dares not, that my heart
shall say.   *Exit*

KEEPER   My lord, will't please you to fall to?

100   KING RICHARD   Taste of it first, as thou wert wont to do.

KEEPER   My lord, I dare not. Sir Pierce of Exton, who
Lately came from th'king, commands the contrary.

KING RICHARD   The devil take Henry of Lancaster and thee!
Patience is stale, and I am weary of it.   *Beats him*

105   KEEPER   Help, help, help!

Enter Exton and Servants [armed]

KING RICHARD   How now? What means death in this rude
assault?
Villain, thine own hand yields thy death's instrument.—

Takes a weapon from one man and kills him with it

Go thou, and fill another room in hell.—   *Kills another man*

Exton strikes him down

That hand shall burn in never-quenching fire
110   That staggers thus my person. Exton, thy fierce hand
Hath with the king's blood stained the king's own land.
Mount, mount, my soul! Thy seat is up on high,
Whilst my gross flesh sinks downward, here to die.   *Dies*

---

91 rail on abuse   92 awed controlled, subdued   95 galled made sore   jauncing hard-riding
96 Fellow servant   give place move, withdraw/defer to me   99 fall to begin eating
100 wont accustomed   106 rude rough, violent   108 room empty space   110 staggers
makes stagger   my person my royal person   112 seat royal throne/place in heaven
113 gross earthly, fleshy, lowly

EXTON   As full of valour as of royal blood.

115   Both have I spilled. O, would the deed were good!
    For now the devil that told me I did well
    Says that this deed is chronicled in hell.
    This dead king to the living king I'll bear.—
    Take hence the rest, and give them burial here.   *Exeunt*

Act 5 Scene [6]   *running scene 18*

Flourish. Enter Bullingbrook, York, with other Lords and Attendants

BULLINGBROOK   Kind uncle York, the latest news we hear
    Is that the rebels have consumed with fire
    Our town of Cicester in Gloucestershire,
    But whether they be ta'en or slain we hear not.
Enter Northumberland
5   Welcome, my lord. What is the news?
NORTHUMBERLAND   First, to thy sacred state wish I all happiness.
    The next news is, I have to London sent
    The heads of Salisbury, Spencer, Blunt and Kent.
    The manner of their taking may appear
10   At large discoursèd in this paper here.   *Gives a paper*
BULLINGBROOK   We thank thee, gentle Percy, for thy pains,
    And to thy worth will add right worthy gains.
Enter Fitzwaters
FITZWATERS   My lord, I have from Oxford sent to London
    The heads of Brocas and Sir Bennet Seely,
15   Two of the dangerous consorted traitors
    That sought at Oxford thy dire overthrow.
BULLINGBROOK   Thy pains, Fitzwaters, shall not be forgot.
    Right noble is thy merit, well I wot.
Enter Percy and Carlisle

5.6   *Location: the royal court*   3 Cicester Cirencester   **4 ta'en** taken, captured   **7 next**
most pressing   **9 taking** capture   **10 at large discoursèd** related in full   **12 worthy** well-
deserved/valuable   **16 dire** dangerous, dreadful   **18 wot** know

PERCY   The grand conspirator, Abbot of Westminster,
20   With clog of conscience and sour melancholy
        Hath yielded up his body to the grave,
        But here is Carlisle living, to abide
        Thy kingly doom and sentence of his pride.
BULLINGBROOK   Carlisle, this is your doom:
25   Choose out some secret place, some reverend room,
        More than thou hast, and with it joy thy life.
        So as thou liv'st in peace, die free from strife:
        For though mine enemy thou hast ever been,
        High sparks of honour in thee have I seen.
Enter Exton, with [Attendants carrying] a coffin
30   EXTON   Great king, within this coffin I present
        Thy buried fear. Herein all breathless lies
        The mightiest of thy greatest enemies,
        Richard of Bordeaux, by me hither brought
BULLINGBROOK   Exton, I thank thee not, for thou hast wrought
35   A deed of slaughter with thy fatal hand
        Upon my head and all this famous land.
        EXTON   From your own mouth, my lord, did I this deed.
        BULLINGBROOK   They love not poison that do poison need,
        Nor do I thee. Though I did wish him dead,
40   I hate the murd'rer, love him murderèd.
        The guilt of conscience take thou for thy labour,
        But neither my good word nor princely favour.
        With Cain go wander through the shade of night,
        And never show thy head by day nor light.
45   Lords, I protest, my soul is full of woe
        That blood should sprinkle me to make me grow.
        Come, mourn with me for that I do lament,

---

19 grand chief   **20 clog** burden   **22 abide** await   **23 doom** judgment, punishment
25 reverend room holy place (i.e. monastery)   **26 More** i.e. more worthy of reverence/larger
than your prison cell   **joy** enjoy   **29 High** noble   **33 Bordeaux** Richard's birthplace
34 wrought created, fashioned   **40 love . . . murderèd** love him who has been murdered/love
the fact that he has been murdered   **43 Cain** in the Bible, the world's first murderer

And put on sullen black incontinent.
I'll make a voyage to the Holy Land,
50   To wash this blood off from my guilty hand.
March sadly after: grace my mourning here,
In weeping after this untimely bier.   *Exeunt*

---

48 **sullen** mournful, somber   **incontinent** immediately   49 **Holy Land** i.e. Jerusalem
51 **sadly** solemnly/sorrowfully   **grace** dignify   52 **after** as you follow   **bier** stretcher-like
structure on which a corpse is carried to the grave

TEXTUAL NOTES

Q = First Quarto text of 1597
F = First Folio text of 1623
F2 = a correction introduced in the Second Folio text of 1632
Ed = a correction introduced by a later editor

List of parts = Ed

1.1.127 duly = Q. *Not in* F **163 Obedience bids** = Ed. F *erroneously prints the words twice* **203 we shall** = Q. F = you shall
1.2.20 faded *spelled* vaded *in* F **43 to** = F. Q = and **62 my** – F. Q = thy
1.3.28 plated = Q. F = placed **29 formally** = Q. F = formerly **76 furbish** = Q. F = furnish **86 King** = Q. F = Kings **256 as foil** = Q. F = a soyle **266 never** = Q. F = euer
1.4.7 blew = Q. F = grew **22 Bagot here** = Q. F = heere *Bagot* **27 smiles** = Q. F = soules
2.1.18 found = Q. F = sound **118 chasing** = Q. F = chafing **191 grip** *spelled* gripe *in* F **234 thou wouldst** = Q. F = thou'dst **286 Brittany** = Ed. F = *Britaine*
2.2.3 life-harming = Q. F = selfe-harming **27 weeps** = Q. F = weepe **54 son young** = Q. F = yong sonne **74 hope lingers** = Q. F = hopes linger **95 as . . . callèd** = Q. F = I came by,and call'd
2.3.87 nor uncle me no uncle = Ed. F = nor Unckle me **92 then more** = Q. F = more then
3.2.26 rebellion's = Q. F = Rebellious **102 makes** = Q. F = make **107 White-beards** = Q. F = White Beares **177 And . . . yourself** = Q. *Not in* F
3.3.39 most royal = Q. F = Royall *(F's lineation is also aberrant in these lines)*
3.4.11 joy = Ed. F = Griefe **26 come** = Q. F = comes **61 we at** = Ed. F = at **62 Do** = Q. F = And **70 and** = F. Q = of
4.1.27 I say thou = Q. F = Thou **34 sympathy** = Q. F = sympathize **113 noblesse** = Q. F = noblenesse **132 his** = F. Q = this **139 rear** = F. Q = raise
5.1.39 thy = Q. F = my
5.3.36 be = Q. F = me **49 reason** = F. Q = treason **62 held** = Q. F = had **93 kneel** = F. Q = walke
5.5 [Scene 5] = Ed. F = *Scoena Quarta (i.e. numbered 5.4, since previous scene break is not noted)* **31 prison** = F. Q = person **95 Spurred, galled** = Q. F = Spur-gall'd
5.6 [Scene 6] = Ed. F = *Scoena Quinta*

QUARTO PASSAGES THAT DO NOT APPEAR IN THE FOLIO

Following 1.3.127:
> And for we think the eagle-wingèd pride
> Of sky-aspiring and ambitious thoughts,
> With rival-hating envy, set on you
> To wake our peace, which in our country's cradle
> Draws the sweet infant breath of gentle sleep;

Following 1.3.232:
> O, had it been a stranger, not my child,
> To smooth his fault I should have been more mild:
> A partial slander sought I to avoid,
> And in the sentence my own life destroyed.

Following 1.3.257:
> BULLINGBROOK   Nay, rather, every tedious stride I make
> Will but remember me what a deal of world
> I wander from the jewels that I love.
> Must I not serve a long apprenticehood
> To foreign passages, and in the end,
> Having my freedom, boast of nothing else
> But that I was a journeyman to grief?
> GAUNT   All places that the eye of heaven visits
> Are to a wise man ports and happy havens.
> Teach thy necessity to reason thus;
> There is no virtue like necessity.
> Think not the king did banish thee,
> But thou the king. Woe doth the heavier sit,
> Where it perceives it is but faintly borne.
> Go, say I sent thee forth to purchase honour
> And not the king exiled thee; or suppose
> Devouring pestilence hangs in our air
> And thou art flying to a fresher clime:

Look what thy soul holds dear, imagine it
To lie that way thou go'st, not whence thou comest:
Suppose the singing birds musicians,
The grass whereon thou tread'st the presence strewed,
The flowers fair ladies, and thy steps no more
Than a delightful measure or a dance;
For gnarling sorrow hath less power to bite
The man that mocks at it and sets it light.

Following 3.2.28:

The means that heaven yields must be embraced,
And not neglected; else, if heaven would,
And we will not, heaven's offer we refuse,
The proffered means of succour and redress.

Following 4.1.52:

LORD   I task the earth to the like, forsworn Aumerle;
And spur thee on with full as many lies
As may be holloaed in thy treacherous ear
From sun to sun: there is my honour's pawn;
Engage it to the trial, if thou darest.

AUMERLE   Who sets me else? By heaven, I'll throw at all:
I have a thousand spirits in one breast,
To answer twenty thousand such as you.

OATHS FROM THE QUARTO

The following oaths were altered in the Folio text as a result of the Parliamentary Act to Restrain the Abuses of Players (spelling has been modernized in this list):

	1597 QUARTO	FOLIO
1.1.188	O God defend my soul	O, heaven defend my soul
1.2.37	God's is the quarrel for God's substitute	Heaven's is the quarrel, for heaven's substitute
1.2.43	To God the widow's champion	To heaven, the widow's champion
1.3.18	(Which God defend . . .)	Which heaven defend
1.3.37	To prove by God's grace,	To prove, by heaven's grace
1.3.78	God, in thy good cause	Heaven in thy good cause
1.3.85	How ever God or Fortune	However, heaven or fortune
1.3.101	. . . and God defend the right	And heaven defend thy right!
1.3.174	that y'owe to God,	that you owe to heaven
1.3.177	so help you truth and God	so help you truth and heaven
1.3.198	But what thou art, God, thou, and I, do know	But what thou art heaven, thou, and I, do know

1.4.58	Now put it (God) in the physician's mind	Now put it, heaven, in his physician's mind
1.4.63	Pray God we may make haste	Pray heaven we may make haste
2.1.240	Now afore God	Now, afore heaven,
2.2.41	God save your majesty,	Heaven save your majesty!
2.2.78	Uncle, for God's sake	Uncle, for heaven's sake,
2.2.99	God for his mercy	Heav'n for his mercy!
2.2.101	I would to God,	I would to heaven—
3.1.37	For God's sake fairly	For heaven's sake, fairly
3.2.55	God for his Ric[hard]:	Heaven for his Richard
3.2.150	For God's sake let us	For heaven's sake let us
3.4.108	Pray God the plants	I would the plants
4.1.8	Marry God forbid	Marry, heaven forbid!
4.1.127	Stirred up by God	Stirred up by heaven
5.2.80	God for his mercy!	Heaven for his mercy,
5.3.4	I would to God	I would to heaven,
5.3.73	. . . for God's sake let me in	For heaven's sake, let me in
5.3.132	I pardon him as God shall pardon me	I pardon him as heaven shall pardon me
5.3.148	I pray God make thee new	I pray heaven make thee new

SCENE-BY-SCENE ANALYSIS

ACT 1 SCENE 1

The scene begins in medias res, emphasizing that the events of the play are part of a much wider span of English history, also shown by many references to the past, present, and future.

Lines 1–151: Gaunt has brought his son, Henry Bullingbrook, Duke of Hereford, to court to make his accusations against Thomas Mowbray, Duke of Norfolk. Richard has the two men called "Face to face / And frowning brow to brow," introducing recurrent themes of opposition/conflict and "mirroring." Bullingbrook and Mowbray greet the king formally, emphasizing the importance of status and ceremony, but Richard responds that one of them merely "flatters" him, drawing attention to the secrecy and plotting under the surface. Bullingbrook calls Mowbray a "traitor and a miscreant," an accusation he claims his "divine soul" will answer "in heaven," establishing the religious aspect of Bullingbrook's characterization and the play's Christian framework. The furious Mowbray calls him a "slanderous coward," at which Bullingbrook throws down his gage as a challenge to personal combat, and Mowbray accepts by picking it up.

Bullingbrook outlines three charges. First, Mowbray spent money intended for paying Richard's soldiers on "lewd employment." Second, he has instigated "all the treasons" against Richard for the last "eighteen years." Third, he is implicated in the Duke of Gloucester's murder. Bullingbrook repeatedly refers to "blood," a key motif in the play signifying both violence and lineage. His comparison between Gloucester's blood and "sacrificing Abel's," however, perhaps implicates a family member, a hint at Richard's involvement. Mowbray denies everything, although his arguments are ambiguous. He, too, throws down his gage.

Lines 152–206: Richard tries to command peace, declaring "Lions make leopards tame," revealing his awareness of the power and importance of the king. He fails to reconcile them, however, reluctantly recognizing that their dispute can only be resolved through personal combat.

ACT 1 SCENE 2

Gaunt is visited by his sister-in-law, Gloucester's widow. He assures her that he grieves for Gloucester, but is unable to do anything, believing "correction lieth in those hands / Which made the fault," a reference to Richard's part in the murder. He says that they will have to place their faith in "the will of heaven." The duchess argues that this is not enough and urges him to take action, reminding him of the ties of kinship through the metaphor of a tree, part of the play's natural imagery. Gaunt argues though that "Heaven's is the quarrel" and that Richard is heaven's "deputy anointed on earth," establishing the concept of the "divine right of kings" that is central to the play. Despite believing that Richard "Hath caused his death," Gaunt will not avenge Gloucester since it would become an act of treason, introducing a recurring tension between personal feelings and traditional codes and duties.

ACT 1 SCENE 3

Lines 1–137: The ceremony and formal language emphasize the protocols of the court that conceal the personal emotions beneath. Richard commands the Lord Marshal to ask "yonder champion / The cause of his arrival." Mowbray declares his identity and cause: to defend his "loyalty and truth." Bullingbrook in turn declares that he is there "To prove, by heaven's grace," that Mowbray is a traitor. Bullingbrook and Mowbray are given lances, but, as the charge is sounded, Richard stops proceedings. His motives are not entirely clear, although he argues that he does not wish blood to soil the "kingdom's earth." He announces that Bullingbrook is to be banished for a period of ten years while Mowbray is banished forever.

Lines 138–201: Bullingbrook seems to accept his fate, taking comfort from the fact that the same sun that shines on England will "gild" his banishment. The sun, a recurring image in the play, is usually associated with kingship and juxtaposed with images of night/darkness. Mowbray complains at being sent where he may not use his "native English," claiming that Richard has "enjailed" his tongue, implying that he has been banished to ensure his silence. Bullingbrook urges Mowbray to confess his "treasons" before he goes, but Mowbray continues to proclaim his innocence and warns that what Bullingbrook is, "heaven, thou and I do know," and that "all too soon" the king will "rue."

Lines 202–273: Seeing Gaunt's "sad aspect," Richard shortens Bullingbrook's banishment to six years, but Gaunt knows he will die before then. He tries to encourage his son to look upon his banishment as "a travel" that he takes "for pleasure," but Bullingbrook, sad and angry, refuses to be comforted. He bids "farewell" to England's "sweet soil," establishing the sentimental, nationalistic representations of the country, apparent in Bullingbrook's reference to England as his "mother" and "nurse."

ACT 1 SCENE 4

Aumerle describes Bullingbrook's emotional departure to Richard, adding that he himself was unmoved. Richard complains about Bullingbrook's popularity with "the common people," describing how he showed the English people "humble and familiar courtesy." Richard shows his own attitude to his people and the contrasts between the cousins when he describes this as a "reverence . . . throw[n] away on slaves." Green reassures Richard that Bullingbrook "is gone" and urges him to think about the Irish rebels instead. Richard decides to go "in person" to war in Ireland, but realizes that he will need more money as the excesses of his court mean his coffers "are grown somewhat light." He intends to "farm [his] royal realm" to raise the money, or to demand it through enforced loans. Both this and his departure to Ireland emphasize Richard's greed and neglect as a king. Bushy brings news that Gaunt is "very sick." Callously, Richard hopes that Gaunt will die so that he can appropriate his wealth "for these Irish wars."

ACT 2 SCENE 1

Lines 1–68: York warns Gaunt that it is useless to "counsel" Richard, arguing that he is deaf to anything but the "flatt'ring sounds" that are poured like "venom" into his ears, one of many images of poison and decay. Gaunt, however, regards himself as a "prophet" who will "foretell" that Richard's "rash fierce blaze of riot cannot last," setting out a series of prophecies and forebodings. In a well-known speech that epitomizes images of England throughout the play, Gaunt laments the effects of Richard's kingship. Using a series of strong but often opposing images that evoke both pride and defensiveness, he describes England's power and majesty, "this seat of Mars," "This fortress" and "This precious stone," but balances them with a simultaneous series of more intimate, domestic images of a "little world," comparable to "a house" or a "plot." This last image of a "plot" evokes the natural imagery associated with England, perceived as an idyllic, pastoral space: "This other Eden," as Gaunt calls it. Gaunt places his description in a strongly Christian context, seeing the kingdom as synonymous with the people: "This happy breed of men." England is also gendered as female: like Bullingbrook at the end of Act 1 Scene 3, he refers to England as a mother and a nurse and concludes by lamenting the fact that England is "now leased out" by Richard, "Like to a tenement or pelting farm," echoing the king's own words in the previous scene.

Lines 69–138: York warns Gaunt to "Deal mildly" with Richard, but Gaunt accuses him of being England's "landlord" rather than its king. Reminding us of the play's place in history, he claims that if Richard's "grandsire" (Edward III) could have seen what he would do to the country, he would depose him. With a final, direct accusation against Richard concerning Gloucester's death, Gaunt is carried away.

Lines 139–225: Northumberland brings news of Gaunt's death, but Richard shows no emotion, merely commenting, "So much for that," and seizing Gaunt's estate to finance his Irish wars. York, whose "tender duty" to Richard has so far prevented him from commenting on his wrongs, is finally moved to speak out. He reminds

Richard of Bullingbrook's claims, arguing that if Richard denies this fundamental right of lineage and inheritance then he is challenging divinely ordained order and potentially denying his own right to be king: "For how art thou a king / But by fair sequence and succession?" He warns Richard that his actions will make him unpopular, and leaves. Richard announces his intention to go to Ireland the next day, leaving York as "Governor of England."

Lines 226–301: Northumberland, Ross, and Willoughby discuss Richard, commenting that he is "basely led / By flatterers." They are cautious, aware that Richard's spies will inform on them, but they agree that Bullingbrook is wronged and that Richard has lost the hearts of the commoners through taxation and the nobles through enforced loans. Northumberland reveals that Bullingbrook and several other noblemen have gathered an army and mean to land in the north once Richard has left for Ireland. They agree to join him.

ACT 2 SCENE 2

Lines 1–74: Bushy attempts to comfort the queen, but she refuses to be reassured, disturbed by a vague sense of foreboding: "Some unborn sorrow, ripe in fortune's womb." Bushy argues that her grief at the king's departure is influencing her perspective, that sorrow "Divides one thing entire into many objects," and his references to sight, "perspectives," and "shadows" reinforce the theme of fragmentation (personal and national). Green brings news of Bullingbrook's arrival at Ravenspurgh and reports that Northumberland "and the rest" have been declared traitors, which has prompted Worcester to join them. The queen tells Green he is "the midwife" of her woe, reinforcing her earlier metaphor.

Lines 75–151: York arrives, distressed and uncertain. He has been left to "underprop" Richard in his absence, but is "weak with age." His unhappiness is compounded by news of the Duchess of Gloucester's death. He knows that the current situation is Richard's fault: "the sick hour that his surfeit made," and he is torn between loyalty to his two nephews, the king and Bullingbrook. Despite the fact that his "oath / And duty" mean that he must defend Richard, his "conscience" favors Bullingbrook. His declaration that "All is uneven" emphasizes the literal and metaphorical disorder in the kingdom. Bushy, Bagot, and Green, followers and favorites of Richard, agree that they are in danger and leave; Bushy and Green to Bristol Castle, and Bagot to join Richard.

ACT 2 SCENE 3

Lines 1–81: Bullingbrook and Northumberland head for Berkeley Castle, where they are met by Harry Percy, Northumberland's son. Percy explains that Worcester has defected from Richard, and Northumberland introduces Percy to Bullingbrook. This formal presentation of the two Henrics again introduces the themes of opposition and mirroring, reinforced by their shared name. Additionally, it compounds awareness of the play as part of a wider series of events: although Percy swears allegiance to Bullingbrook now, he is to become the opposition to his kingship in the future, playing the role that Bullingbrook currently plays to Richard (see *Henry IV, Part I* and *Part II*). Ross and Willoughby arrive.

Lines 82–171: York berates Bullingbrook for daring to return from his banishment, and for marching upon England's "peaceful bosom" in Richard's absence. He points out that he is Richard's representative, but acknowledges that he is too old to fight as he once did. York is again divided between duty to Richard and sympathy for Bullingbrook, who reminds York of the wrongs Richard has done him. Bullingbrook shows his command over language as he skillfully uses rhetorical devices, claiming that he sees Gaunt "alive" in York, and addressing him as "my father." Torn, York decides that he will remain neutral, but his sympathy with Bullingbrook is evident as he offers him shelter for the night. Bullingbrook announces that they are going to Bristol Castle to capture Bushy and other "caterpillars of the commonwealth," reinforcing the image of England as an Eden threatened by decay.

ACT 2 SCENE 4

Richard's Welsh army disperses, convinced he is dead. Salisbury comments that Richard's glory, "like a shooting star," has fallen "to base earth."

ACT 3 SCENE 1

Bullingbrook sentences Bushy and Green to death for misleading Richard, causing a rift between Richard and the queen, and his own banishment by making Richard "misinterpret" him. Bushy and Green remain defiant. Bullingbrook sends York with a gentle message to the queen and leads his followers to fight Glendower.

ACT 3 SCENE 2

Lines 1–85: Richard lands and "salutes" his kingdom, comparing himself to "a long-parted mother with her child," an inversion of Bullingbrook's image at the end of Act 1 Scene 3. Richard invokes the poisonous elements of his land—"spiders," "toads," and "adders"—against Bullingbrook, emphasizing the link between himself and the land as its "native king." Carlisle reinforces this with his reference to Richard's divine right to the throne, the "power that made you king." Richard takes this theme and develops it in a speech that shows a poetic eloquence equal to Bullingbrook's. Returning to the motif of the sun, Richard describes how, "rising in our throne, the east," he will shed light on Bullingbrook's treasons "in the night" and cause him to "tremble at his sin." Salisbury brings Richard the news that his Welsh armies have defected. Aumerle comforts him, but Richard's demand, "Am I not king?," seems more uncertain than defiant.

Lines 86–215: Scroop brings news that Richard's subjects, from old men to "distaff-women," have joined Bullingbrook. Richard inquires after his loyal followers and, misunderstanding Scroop's euphemistic reply that they have "made peace with Bullingbrook," believes that they have betrayed him. Scroop hastens to explain that they have, in fact, been executed. Richard is plunged into despair, his temporary defiance over, and muses on his own mortality and the fragility of kingship, the "hollow" nature of his crown. Aumerle and Carlisle try to rally him, and he returns to a temporary defiance, before being told by Scroop that "York is joined with Bullingbrook." Richard bitterly refuses any more comfort and gives instructions for his followers to be discharged "From Richard's night, to Bullingbrook's fair day," inverting the images of light and dark from his earlier speech.

ACT 3 SCENE 3

Lines 1–72: Outside Flint Castle, Bullingbrook and Northumberland discuss events. Percy confirms that Richard is inside, and Bullingbrook sends a message that he will "kiss King Richard's hand" and lay his "arms and power" at his feet if Richard will repeal his banishment and restore his inheritance. If not, he threatens to "lay the summer's dust with showers of blood." He offers to meet Richard, but before the message can be delivered, Richard appears on the castle walls. At this point, Bullingbrook is careful to emphasize that Richard is king, implying that he has no aspirations beyond his restored inheritance.

Lines 73–212: Richard demands to know why they have not knelt before their "lawful" king. He invokes his divine right, claiming that "the hand of God" has not dismissed him, and that "no hand of blood and bone / Can grip the sacred handle of our sceptre, / Unless he do profane, steal, or usurp." Northumberland reiterates Bullingbrook's claim that he merely wants his lawful inheritance, and assures him of Bullingbrook's loyalty. Richard agrees, remaining formal and regal, but his aside to Aumerle reveals that he feels that he has no choice and that he is debasing himself. He bitterly regrets that he cannot "forget" what he has been, again showing his confusion over his identity, which is intrinsically bound up with being king. Kingship is more than the title and trappings that attend it, it is a fundamental part of him: if he is not king, he is not himself. He knows that Bullingbrook will not let him remain king and, seeing Aumerle weeping, says they will "fret" themselves two graves with their tears. He agrees to come down, aware of the way in which this literal descent reflects his metaphorical one. Bullingbrook kneels before him, but Richard is unconvinced by his show of loyalty.

ACT 3 SCENE 4

Walking in the Duke of York's garden, the queen and her ladies overhear the gardener and his servants discussing the state of the country and Richard's poor management. Using the image of the garden as a metaphor, they emphasize the pastoral representation of England, describing how the "sea-wallèd garden" is "full of weeds," "unpruned" and "swarming with caterpillars," an image that echoes Bullingbrook's words in Act 2 Scene 3. The gardener comments that "Bullingbrook / Hath seized the wasteful king." Unable to bear it, the queen rushes forward and demands to know if this is true. He apologetically confirms it, revealing the view of the common people in his description of Richard's "vanities that make him light" and Bullingbrook "great."

ACT 4 SCENE 1

A long scene that forms the whole of the fourth act, emphasizing the swift and irreversible nature of events. Once again, ceremony is important, establishing the court setting and reinforcing the official nature of Bullingbrook's new power, but also echoing Act 1 Scene 3, forcing parallels and comparisons between Bullingbrook and Richard.

Lines 1–156: Bullingbrook summons Bagot for questioning about the Duke of Gloucester's death. Bagot accuses Aumerle of involvement, but he denies it and throws down his gage. Bullingbrook refuses to allow Bagot to accept the challenge, but Fitzwaters and Percy also accuse Aumerle and throw their gages down. Aumerle damns Fitzwaters, but takes up Percy's gage. Surrey then steps in, accusing Fitzwaters of complicity with Aumerle, and challenges him. Fitzwaters throws down a gage in return, claiming that the banished Mowbray implicated Aumerle in the plot. Aumerle is forced to borrow a gage to throw down in response to this. This sequence reflects the complicated nature of the court's politics. Bullingbrook commands that Mowbray be returned from banishment, but learns that he is dead.

York arrives from "plume-plucked" Richard with the message that he is yielding his throne to Bullingbrook, who accepts, but Carlisle intervenes, insisting that Richard is king by divine right, and that if Bullingbrook accepts the crown, there will be civil war, and that the "blood of English shall manure the ground / And future ages groan for his foul act," echoing Gaunt's prophecies against Richard in Act 2 Scene 1. Northumberland arrests Carlisle for treason and Bullingbrook summons Richard to come and surrender publicly. Bullingbrook's desire to "proceed / Without suspicion" contrasts with the secrecy that surrounded Richard's court.

Lines 157–330: Richard arrives, comparing himself to Christ betrayed by Judas. His declaration, "God save the king, although I be not he, / And yet, amen, if heaven do think him me," emphasizes the confusion over the nature of kingship: whether "king" is merely a title, or an innate, God-given identity. This question of what denotes a "king" is emphasized as Richard offers his crown (the external symbol of his role) to Bullingbrook. As he does so, he uses the image of a mirror, saying: "on this side my hand, on that side thine." Bullingbrook asks if Richard is "contented" to "resign the crown." Richard's uncertainty is clear, but he eventually formally relinquishes the crown and scepter as well as all "pomp and majesty" together with his "manors, rents" and "revenues," in a reverse ceremony of coronation. Richard presents a pitiful figure, but when Northumberland demands that he read a confession of his "grievous crimes" against his country, and thus acknowledge that he is "worthily deposed," he refuses, arguing that none of them are innocent. He asks for a mirror and, when it is brought, examines his own face. He claims that the glass "flatters" him like his followers, and throws it to the ground, where it is "cracked in an hundred shivers," symbolizing the fragmentation of his identity. He asks to be allowed to leave, and Bullingbrook has him "conveyed" to the Tower, before designating the following Wednesday for his own coronation. The Abbot, Carlisle, and Aumerle begin to plot against Bullingbrook.

ACT 5 SCENE 1

The queen waits on the route to the Tower, so that she may see Richard. Resigned to "grim Necessity," he urges her to join a convent in France. The queen hates to see him "Transformed and weakened" and reminds him that even "the lion dying . . . wounds the earth," an ironic echo of Richard's own image of himself in Act 1 Scene 1. Northumberland brings news that Bullingbrook has changed his mind: Richard is to go to Pomfret Castle. The queen is to be sent to France. Richard warns Northumberland that he and Bullingbrook will eventually turn against each other. His says goodbye to the queen in a tender, personal exchange that reveals a different, more sympathetic, side to his character.

ACT 5 SCENE 2

Distressed, York tells his duchess about the contrast between the arrival in London of Richard and Bullingbrook. He describes how the crowds "Threw dust and rubbish" on Richard's head. Bullingbrook, however, rode on a "fiery steed" while crowds cheered him. In a moment of meta-theater, York compares the two men to actors, one leaving the stage while the audience are "idly bent on him that enters next." Aumerle arrives and York reminds the duchess that their son is now called "Rutland," having been stripped of his title for loyalty to Richard, although York himself has pledged Aumerle's "fealty to the new-made king." However, he finds a letter concealed by his son that shows he is involved in a conspiracy to kill Bullingbrook. He prepares to ride to tell the new king, despite his wife's pleas that Aumerle is their only son. York leaves, and the duchess tells Aumerle that he must reach the king first and beg for pardon.

ACT 5 SCENE 3

Bullingbrook is worrying about his own dissolute, "unthrifty son," Prince Henry, when he is interrupted by Aumerle. He begs to see Bullingbrook alone, kneels, and demands to be pardoned before he will either rise or speak. York arrives, shouting to Bullingbrook that he has "a traitor" in his presence. Aumerle assures Bullingbrook that he has nothing to fear, but York gives him the letter incriminating his son. Emphasizing the rising thematic importance of father–son relationships, Bullingbrook comments that York is a "loyal father of a treacherous son," whose lineage is tainted like a "muddy" stream from an "immaculate" fountain. The Duchess of York arrives, calling for admission to the king's presence. She kneels and begs for her son's life, but is mirrored by York, who kneels and pleads against her. Eventually, Bullingbrook pardons Aumerle, but orders the execution of his fellow conspirators.

ACT 5 SCENE 4

Believing that Bullingbrook wishes him to kill Richard, Exton heads to Pomfret.

ACT 5 SCENE 5

Alone in prison, Richard delivers a metaphysical soliloquy as he seeks to counter his loneliness by creating thoughts with which to "people the world," imagining them as the "children" of his brain and soul. He perceives that his body is the "prison" for his soul and acknowledges the fragmented nature of his identity, commenting that "Thus play I in one prison many people." A former groom, still loyal, visits him and tells Richard how Bullingbrook rode his favorite horse to his coronation, a final image of betrayal. The keeper brings Richard's food, but under Exton's orders, refuses to taste it for him. Richard beats the keeper and Exton and his servants rush in, armed. Richard kills both servants but is struck down by Exton. Commending his soul to heaven, he dies. Exton recognizes Richard's "valour" and, already regretting his actions, goes to tell Bullingbrook.

ACT 5 SCENE 6

The new king learns of the fate of the various conspirators. Carlisle is brought before him and is ordered to "Choose out some secret place" and remain there. Exton arrives, bearing the coffin of Richard and claiming that he acted on Bullingbrook's instructions. In ambiguous language, which echoes that surrounding Gloucester's death at the beginning of the play, Bullingbrook admits that he wished Richard dead, but neither denies nor confirms that he ordered his death: "I hate the murd'rer, love him murderèd." He banishes Exton, comparing him to "Cain," reflecting his own references to Abel in Act 1 Scene 1 and reinforcing the sense of the cyclical nature of historical events. He vows to mourn for Richard and to undertake a penitential "voyage to the Holy Land," and the play ends with this image of the future, reminding the audience of its place within a wider historical narrative.

RICHARD II IN PERFORMANCE: THE RSC AND BEYOND

The best way to understand a Shakespeare play is to see it or ideally to participate in it. By examining a range of productions, we may gain a sense of the extraordinary variety of approaches and interpretations that are possible—a variety that gives Shakespeare his unique capacity to be reinvented and made "our contemporary" four centuries after his death.

We begin with a brief overview of the play's theatrical and cinematic life, offering historical perspectives on how it has been performed. We then analyze in more detail a series of productions staged over the last half century by the Royal Shakespeare Company. The sense of dialogue between productions that can only occur when a company is dedicated to the revival and investigation of the Shakespeare canon over a long period, together with the uniquely comprehensive archival resource of promptbooks, program notes, reviews, and interviews held on behalf of the RSC at the Shakespeare Birthplace Trust in Stratford-upon-Avon, allows an "RSC stage history" to become a crucible in which the chemistry of the play can be explored.

We then go to the horse's mouth. Modern theater is dominated by the figure of the director. He or she must hold together the whole play, whereas the actor must concentrate on his or her part. The director's viewpoint is therefore especially valuable. Shakespeare's plasticity is wonderfully revealed when we hear the directors of two highly successful productions answering the same questions in very different ways. And in a play where the central character so dominates the dialogue, it is fitting that we also hear the voice of an actor who has played him. We offer the especially interesting angle of that actor being Fiona Shaw, a woman playing a man (an inversion of the condition of the original Shakespearean stage upon which men played women).

FOUR CENTURIES OF *RICHARD II*: AN OVERVIEW

Tim Carroll describes a moment during his 2003 original-practices production (i.e. an attempt to reproduce the techniques of the Elizabethan theater) of *Richard II* at Shakespeare's Globe in which, as John of Gaunt "talked about the betrayal of the country he loved, he made the audience for a while the whole of England. It was not a very comfortable experience."[1] Questioning, provoking, accusing: *Richard II* has, for four centuries, been confronting its audiences with difficult questions and challenges that, even in its own time, led to its becoming perhaps the most dangerous of all Shakespeare's plays to reach the stage, as shown by the performance specially commissioned by the followers of the Earl of Essex in February 1601, discussed in the introduction, above.

Significantly, the scene depicting Richard's deposition was not included in any printed version of the play until the Fourth Quarto of 1608, implying that this scene may not have been performed during Elizabeth's reign.

The play would first have been performed at The Theatre, with the 1601 revival taking place at the Globe. The play itself presents staging requirements that suggest full use of the different levels of these large open-air amphitheaters, such as the entrance of Richard and his attendants on the walls of Flint Castle (Act 3 Scene 3). Richard Burbage undoubtedly played the title character, though other casting details are only conjectural. There is no obvious part for the company clown, although a long-standing stage tradition turns the sober gardener of Act 3 Scene 4 into a comic part.

While there may have been some continuity of casting into *Henry IV Part I*, there are no records of the history plays being performed in sequence until Frank Benson's "Week of Kings" at Stratford-upon-Avon in 1901. Perhaps more interestingly, the play with the earliest connection to *Richard II* is *Hamlet*: records of the East India Company ship *Dragon* show that the ship's crew performed the play off the coast of Sierra Leone on September 30, 1607 for an audience of Portuguese visitors, a few days after one of the first recorded performances of *Hamlet*.

Unsurprisingly, in the immediate wake of the Restoration of Charles II in 1660, it would have been dangerously inappropriate to attempt a revival of *Richard II* in its Shakespearean form, the political climate still being too sensitive to tolerate even a distant depiction of regicide. Nahum Tate attempted to get around the problem through geography, resituating the play in Sicily with the title *The Sicilian Usurper* in December 1680. The play lasted for two performances before being banned, and an attempt the following month to revive the play as *The Tyrant of Sicily* met a similar fate. Despite Tate's claims that "My Design was to engage the pitty of the Audience for him in his Distresses" and that he shows his King Oswald "Preferring the Good of his Subjects to his own private Pleasure,"[2] the plot still resonated too nearly with recent events. The political power of *Richard II*, even in adapted form, continued to render the play dangerous.

This bias against the play continued into the eighteenth century. Only two productions of *Richard II* are recorded in London during the century:[3] an adaptation by Lewis Theobald in 1719 and John Rich's production of the original at Covent Garden in 1738–39. Theobald's Preface to this "Orphan Child of *Shakespear*" sets out his agenda:

> The many scatter'd Beauties, which I have long admir'd in His Life and Death of K. Richard the II, induced me to think they would have stronger Charms, if they were interwoven in a regular Fable.[4]

Interestingly, Theobald's most powerful intervention was to bolster the character of Aumerle, turning him into a sentimental tragic hero who ultimately dies for his king. The play's finale becomes a bloodbath in which Richard is killed by Exton but survives long enough to tell Bullingbrook that "all thy Fears with me ly bury'd: / Unrival'd, wear the crown"[5] before crying out for Isabella, who witnesses his death. Lady Piercy, another of Theobald's additions, commits suicide for Aumerle's sake, and even York dies of a broken heart upon seeing Richard's body. The buildup of tragic pathos is symptomatic of the period's tastes, and the play was evidently briefly popular: a 1720 promptbook survives for performances at Dublin's Smock Alley Theatre.

Rich's production was the first since the Restoration to revive Shakespeare's text in something nearing a complete form. The testimony of Thomas Davies suggests political intent behind the production, with one particular addition greeted rapturously by the audience,

> who applied almost every line that was spoken to the occurrences of the time, and to the measures and character of the ministry . . . when Ross said "The earl of Wiltshire hath the state in farm" it was immediately applied to Walpole, with the loudest shouts and huzzas I ever heard.[6]

During the previous decade, the prime minister, Robert Walpole, had been attacked viciously on stage and in the press for perceived attempts to censor both. The London audience, experienced in recognizing satirical portraits, evidently responded well to the employment of Shakespeare's text in the continuing war of words. Over a century after the Essex rebellion, *Richard II* continued to be read by spectators as a commentary on the ruling classes.

While failing to establish the play as a regular repertory piece in their own century, both Theobald's and Rich's versions of the play laid the groundwork for future revivals. Most influentially, Rich's production foregrounded spectacle. Sketches from the promptbook show highly formal compositions for the lists and deposition scenes, supporting Davies' assertion that "the ancient ceremony which belonged to the single combat was very accurately observed."[7] This tendency toward spectacle and historical accuracy would continue into the next century.

The first major production of the nineteenth century was an adaptation by Richard Wroughton conceived as a star vehicle for Edmund Kean, performed at Drury Lane in 1814–15, and which later served as the basis for the first North American production of the play in 1819.[8] Kean's performance, predictably, was the center of attention, and William Hazlitt notes the general consensus that "It has been supposed that this is his finest part," though he goes on to give his personal opinion that this is "a total misrepresentation."[9] A natural successor to Theobald's adaptation, Wroughton aimed for similar sentimental and pathetic effect, but chose to do so through increased focus on Richard himself; thus, where Theobald had expanded the Aumerle conspiracy, here it is cut altogether. In editing his play, Wroughton "makes his hero more decisive, less prone to lament his condition, less culpable and less pettily vicious."[10] Isabella is again present in the final scene, and her death concludes the action, with King Lear's dying speeches transferred to her lips.

The success of Kean's production established the play's potential as a star vehicle, and the move toward pathos and spectacle additionally served to distance it from the troubling political appropriations of previous centuries. The stage was set for a full-blown Victorian spectacular, which Kean's son Charles provided in 1857 at London's Princess's Theatre. Theodor Fontane's description of one moment shows the production's scale:

> Between the third and fourth acts is an interlude devised by Kean: Bolingbroke is treated like a god as he enters London. Behind him is Richard, greeted by the people first with silence, then with muttering and curses . . . the representation (for good or ill) is a masterpiece. It is no exaggeration to say that the whole effect is that of a part of a street brought onstage, with the genuine London life and bustle.[11]

Kean's interest in antiquarianism and full-scale reproduction led to jokes that even the playbills were printed on "fly-leaves from old folio editions of the History of England."[12] In 1902, Herbert Beerbohm Tree followed in Kean's footsteps with the inclusion of a triumphant entry into London for Richard on a real horse.

Following Kean, the play fell again into obscurity until Frank Benson's revival in 1896 for the Stratford-upon-Avon festival. While the sets of Benson's production followed in the grand tradition of the Victorian spectacular, the production was more notable for remaking Richard II himself as a star part:

1. Charles Kean's large-scale antiquarian production at the London Princess's Theatre, 1857.

Mr Benson's Richard is a figure not to be looked upon without commiseration and pity. The Nemesis of his own folly has brought him so utterly low, his fantastic nature is so acutely sensitive, his will so impotent, his dejection so complete, that sympathy turns against the more manly Bolingbroke, and perhaps does him wrong.[13]

As well as establishing the role of Richard II as a key showcase for major actors, the production's revival in 1901 as part of Stratford's "Week of Kings" reestablished the play as part of a historical sequence. Benson's performances in the role continued until 1915.

John Gielgud dominated both role and play on the early twentieth-century London stage. From his first performance, directed by Harcourt Williams at the Old Vic in 1929, "Gielgud focused on superb delivery of verse, perhaps emphasising Richard as pathetic, and certainly a man unfitted for the demanding duties of a ruler."[14] However, other aspects of the production impressed less. *The Times* remarked that "many of the parts, and many far above the rank of the grooms and servants, are played badly and, what is worse, listlessly," singling out Brember Wills' Gaunt: "let us have stillness sometimes: let us have firmness and splendour, not the nervous, bubbling senility of a dotard."[15] Gielgud performed and directed at the Queen's in 1937, and in 1953 directed Paul Scofield at the Lyric Hammersmith, in a performance "strangely different from the others we have seen . . . the actor presents to us a mask of celestial composure in which two half-closed eyes glitter with inscrutable menace."[16]

If Gielgud dominated the play in London, in Stratford-upon-Avon it was the property of W. Bridges Adams. Between 1920 and 1930 Adams moved through a succession of Richards, culminating in George Hayes (1929). Adams' medieval costumes were singled out for praise, and the combination of modest historical spectacle with strong ensemble performances contributed to the growing appreciation of the play. Hayes continued to play Richard for Tyrone Guthrie (1933, "an inherently dull play"[17]), B. Iden Payne (1941, with Richard's "uncanny dignity"[18] foremost) and Robert Atkins (1944), in which a "vision scene"[19] at Richard's death was particularly praised, the dungeon wall dissolving behind the body as a choir sang to reveal Bullingbrook as the new king.

Hal Burton's direction of Robert Harris in 1947 was praised for reviving the quality of the artist in Richard that Benson had emphasized, although some reviewers still worked from Victorian criteria: "It achieves distinction because of its dignity, its pageantry, its beauty of outline and of detail and its admirably controlled lighting."[20] Far more influential was Michael Redgrave's performance in 1951 under the direction of Anthony Quayle, who directed the entire second tetralogy as part of Stratford's contribution to the Festival of Britain. Redgrave's performance in the role, remembered by Laurence Olivier as an "out-and-out pussy queer,"[21] was greeted with mixed reviews by critics unable—or unwilling—to acknowledge the character's homosexuality, and confused by a mixture of lyricism and cruelty. Alan Dent suggested that "we found ourselves watching the excellent Bolingbroke (Harry Andrews), instead of the King, for in this Bolingbroke's eyes lurked an infinity of contemptuous patience while he heeded Richard's elaborately fanciful speeches."[22] The challenges of *Richard II* here shifted from the politics of state to the politics of sexuality, with lasting effect; by the time Ian McKellen performed both Richard II and Edward II to great acclaim for the Prospect Theatre Company in 1968–69, critics read a homosexual agenda into the play even though, as Margaret Shewring suggests, this was not actually intended by the company.[23]

2. A queenly king? Michael Redgrave (left) with Harry Andrews as Bullingbrook in Anthony Quayle's 1951 production.

Despite its early African performance, *Richard II* is not among the most successful international exports in the Shakespearean canon. An exception is Germany, where the play was first staged in the 1770s, and where its potential as political commentary has been fully utilized. The fiercely anti-Nazi Jürgen Fehling directed the play in 1939 at Berlin's Staatstheater, using abstract sets that acted to separate the profligate Richard and his court from the distant problems of their people. Claus Peymann directed a "death-obsessed"[24] Beckettian production in Braunschweig in 1969, which emphasized "Richard's reflections on man's existential exposure and separateness."[25] Three decades later, Peymann directed a far more political interpretation of the play for the Berliner Ensemble, which toured to the RSC Complete Works Festival in 2006. Achim Freyer's starkly white abstract set became a blank canvas on which history wrote its impact in dirt and blood, most strikingly as invisible hands hurled piles of mud at Richard upon his return to London. While Michael Maertens' "charismatic" Richard was praised, the production allowed other parts to shine: Bullingbrook was a "repressed bureaucrat [who] was more comfortable with his bowler hat than with the crown," while Northumberland became "the true Machiavel of this piece."[26]

On the late twentieth century stage, a fascination with Richard's performativity was emerging. David William's production of 1972 marked the first performance of any of Shakespeare's history plays by the new National Theatre Company. Despite one view that "this Richard was not only unmoving, he was fatally uninteresting,"[27] others found Ronald Pickup's performance enlightening: "Surrounded by ceremonies and flattery he has complete belief in his authority. But as soon as the externals start crumbling, so does his inner conviction."[28]

Increasingly, the play was produced as part of a sequence. David Giles' 1978 televised *Richard II*, one of the strongest productions in the BBC Shakespeare series, featured Derek Jacobi in the title role supported by Jon Finch (Bullingbrook) and John Gielgud (Gaunt), while the casting of Charles Gray and Dame Wendy Hiller as the Yorks "brings alive a whole subplot"[29] often previously cut in performance. The camerawork prioritized actors over spectacle, exploiting the possibilities of television for Richard's soliloquy of Act 5

Scene 5, which was shot in several sections, drawing out his ruminations over an extended period of incarceration. The English Shakespeare Company's *The Wars of the Roses* (1986–89), a seven-play adaptation of the two tetralogies which was also later filmed for television, began with a *Richard II* which adapted a "Regency style, Beau Brummell dandyism"[30] that director Michael Bogdanov confessed would probably not have been their first choice for a stand-alone production. In such a large context, "the victim of production was invariably *Richard II* . . . the guinea pig that opened the sequence,"[31] and both Bogdanov and his Richard, Michael Pennington, expressed disappointment in the result.

Internationally, interest in the formal aspects of the play and its pageantry have continued to stimulate directorial interest, though often unsuccessfully. At the Stratford Ontario Festival in Canada, Stuart Burge's 1964 production ran over four hours when it debuted, losing the favor of many critics. However, it continued a twentieth-century trend to paint Northumberland as the piece's key mover, with Leo Cicery's Bullingbrook "a genuinely bewildered man caught up in a situation which he could not comprehend."[32] Zoe Caldwell's 1979 production was felt by many to be overly gimmick-led, with three different actors for both Richard and Bullingbrook, no doubt in an attempt to replicate the success of the RSC's Pasco/Richardson pairing six years earlier. Critics were bored, however, by the pageant-like blocking of all three versions, with a central staircase creating "a rigid formality on the playing space that is reflected, with a vengeance, in the performances."[33] More successful was Ariane Mnouchkine's production in 1982 for Théâtre du Soleil in Vincennes. Inspired by Japanese kabuki theater, the production ran for over five hours, and drew critical praise for its precise choreography through which "the formality of the play's constructions is revealed. The argument develops like a terrific algebra."[34]

In the last two decades, two major London productions have shown that the play has lost none of its power to cause controversy. In 1995, Deborah Warner's production for the National Theatre caused a stir with its casting of Fiona Shaw in the title role. Shaw's performance deeply divided critics, prompting Paul Taylor to mount a defense in the *Independent*:

Fiona Shaw's dazzlingly discomforting impersonation of Richard is so integral to the thinking behind Deborah Warner's gripping, lucidly felt production that it would only make sense to like neither or both . . . her portrayal of the monarch as an anguishedly insecure, clowningly exhibitionist man-child— mirrors more than subliminally the psychological confusions caused by the identity crisis of a King's dual nature.[35]

As Shewring argues, "it is not the fact that the King is played by a woman that is significant; it is that the presentation of kingship is, in itself, an elaborate theatrical charade."[36]

Trevor Nunn's 2005 production for the Old Vic brought the play right up to date in a modern-dress production that used video to display footage of the decline of Britain, emphasizing both the impact of Richard's ineffectual rule and his isolation from those effects, "the split between inner and outer, public and private."[37] Starring Kevin Spacey in the lead role, combining authority with "a really terrifying temper,"[38] it was nevertheless the play's contemporary resonances that once again commanded critical attention. The play's cynical commentary on the interaction between the public and the ruling classes was made uncomfortably clear in Genevieve O'Reilly's Queen Isabel, "interrupted in the middle of a Diana-style photo session,"[39] and Charles Spencer compared Spacey's "self-dramatising" Richard and Ben Miles' "humourless, sharp-suited Bolingbroke" to Tony Blair and Gordon Brown.[40] While perhaps not as directly dangerous as the Star Chamber of 1601 once deemed it to be, it is clear that *Richard II* remains a timelessly political tool for directors wishing to hold up Richard's own mirror to today's leaders.

AT THE RSC

Shakespeare's history is always about the "now" of Elizabethan England.[41]

Queen Elizabeth I: "I am Richard II, know ye not that?"[42]

Richard II is a play that can stand alone, but directors also position it first in an epic cycle, as the catalyst for the bloody action that Shakespeare unfolds in his dramatic sweep of English history. In an interesting departure, Michael Boyd's *The Histories* (2008) produced *Richard II*, not only as first in a chronological ordering of history but in a distinctly separate cycle, based on the order of their composition. The *first* cycle begins with Shakespeare's earlier (written) plays, *Henry VI Part 1*, *Part 2*, and *Part 3*, and *Richard III*, and charts the playwright's developing relationship with the politics of Elizabethan England, culminating in his dissection of kingship in *Richard II*, the strategies of king-making in *Henry IV Part 1* and *Part 2*, and the disturbingly modern account of Henry V's decision to wage war with France through an appeal to the value of an English "nation." The *second* complete cycle of eight plays charts "over a century of turbulent English history, from the usurpation of Richard II and Henry V's glorious battle at Agincourt, to the bloody chaos of the Wars of the Roses and their brutal climax on Bosworth Field."[43]

For actors and directors there are distinct challenges in what Stuart Hampton-Reeves refers to as "the totalising notions of 'tetralogy thinking,' " or seeing the plays as episodes in a national epic.[44] The yoking together of four or eight plays can exert a particular pressure on the chronologically first play, *Richard II*, to begin a political history of England, worked through the performed cycle. Anthony Quayle's *The Cycle of the Historical Plays 1951* at the Memorial Theatre in Stratford marked the Festival of Britain by treating the four plays, beginning with *Richard II*, as "one great play."[45] Richard (Michael Redgrave) was to be viewed as "the last of the old line of mediaeval kings, the last ruler by hereditary right, unbroken, undisputed since the Conqueror," but the "true hero" of "the whole play" was to be King Henry V, "the ideal King: brave, warlike, generous, just" (played by Richard Burton). Michael Hattaway argues that Tanya Moiseiwitsch's sets, fashioned in an "Elizabethan style," created "a kind of illusion that turned politics back into romanticized history."[46] This "history" owed much to the spirit of E. M. W. Tillyard's *Shakespeare's History Plays* (1944), which offers an account of the working through of divine providence, from the sinful deposition of Richard II to the expiation of a curse on the House of Lancaster. Such an approach in the theater risks idealizing Richard and pushing the play's politics back into an older world of medieval kingship

to be contrasted with the more modern and secular kingship, por-
trayed in *Henry V*. This treatment downplays the modern political
resonance of *Richard II* for Shakespeare and his Elizabethan theater-
goers in the context of an impending succession crisis.

It is possible to perform the plays as a historical cycle but to attend
carefully to the *differences* within each play in order to resist the
temptation of trying to make seamless connections that totalize the
experience for an audience. Where the play is performed on its own,
there may be an opportunity to place more emphasis on personal
aspects of kingship, particularly the idea of the Divine Right of
Kings, rather than political history. However, the political realities of
the Elizabethan context are clearly illustrated in the Queen's com-
ment, "I am Richard II, know ye not that?" She was apparently
responding some months later to an attempt by the Essex conspirators to stage a play, about King Richard's deposition, on the eve of
their rebellion in 1601.

Peter Hall, John Barton, and Clifford Williams (1964)

Modern power politics lies at the heart of the landmark production
of seven plays in 1964, directed by Peter Hall, John Barton, and
Clifford Williams. The production celebrated the four hundredth
anniversary of Shakespeare's birth at a moment of political uncer-
tainties just two years after the Cuban missile crisis of 1962. Jan Kott
wrote in *Shakespeare Our Contemporary* (1964) that "the great abdication scene in *Richard II*, the scene omitted in all editions published
in the Queen Elizabeth's lifetime," revealed "the working of the Grand
Mechanism."[47] He explained this was "the very moment when power
was changing hands."

The throne of England was given center place in John Bury's
model set of steel-clad walls and metallic stage, conveying the stark,
cold reality of a brutal power politics. The tetralogy of *Richard II,
Henry IV Part I* and *Part 2*, and *Henry V* was added to *The Wars of the
Roses* (1963), which comprised a two-part adaptation of the three
Henry VI plays (*Henry VI* and *Edward IV*), followed by *Richard III*. In
this earlier production the central image was a great steel council
table that alienated the action in Brechtian fashion, revealing the
strategies of the self-serving opportunists who grouped around it, as

they jostled for position and power. Hall and Bury banished romanticized pageantry by creating costumes attuned to their metallic setting. Colin Chambers describes some of Bury's experiments to
achieve texture: "Glue crystals, marble chippings, chicken grit and
stone gravel swept up from tennis courts in Southern Lane were all
thrown onto the 'gunked' costumes while still wet."[48]

Margaret Shewring commented of the whole cycle: "John Bury's
stage picture provided a sustained visual image" that helped to link
the tetralogy and trilogy.[49] One reviewer observed:

> John Bury's settings for *Richard II* are an impressive part of the
> production, and allow scene changes to be made with maxi-
> mum smoothness.
>
> Heavy armour-plated walls have a coppery tint and can
> quickly be revolved to bring something fresh into the exciting
> pictures created on the stage.
>
> For many scenes there is a background of trees, woven
> together like some delicate tracery. Mellow, autumnal colours
> are used at one point—suggesting the beginnings of decay
> which Richard's mismanagement has brought about.[50]

David Warner played the saintly but weak and ineffectual King
Henry VI in the earlier trilogy, and brought a corresponding impression of weakness to his role as King Richard II. The critic J. C. Trewin
observed:

> It is the gilded throne of England that one sees first on entering
> the theatre. Even so, one hardly observes Richard's entrance.
> In this production, he is deliberately insignificant, the vain
> indulgent weakling—strange offspring of the Black Prince,
> that Mars of men—who, like one of his forerunners, dies for
> the sweet fruition of an earthly crown.[51]

Shewring felt that the impression of weakness was a reading that
"could be accommodated in *Richard II* played as part of a full cycle,
but would, perhaps, have been less appropriate had the play stood on
its own."[52] However, Harold Hobson took an opposing view:

If one sees *Richard II* alone, even in the unsurpassed performance of Sir John Gielgud, one sees only the sad downfall of a
tragic poet who is overthrown by a rebellious and dynamic
subject. But in Mr Hall's programme *Richard II*, placed in its
proper sequence, takes on a more cataclysmic significance. The
deposition of Richard is seen, not as in any way excused by the
tyrannical vagaries of his rule, but, quite simply and unforgiv-
ably, as a crime against God.[53]

However, the king's downfall could not be romanticized. One
reviewer commented that Richard's actions were "firmly anchored
in the world of practical politics," for example, in the Mowbray-
Lancaster quarrel, where the king could be seen "meting out subtly
different degrees of intimacy to his kinsmen and his favourites."[54]
Eric Porter played Bullingbrook as a strong-willed opportunist, dis-
playing "just the right amount of blended patience and impatience
with the weak king he manages to depose."[55] The theater program
suggests that Bullingbrook be viewed as "the new man, the coming
man of integrity" who "becomes a rebel almost against his will."
This idea was borne out in performance, one reviewer remarking on
Eric Porter's "fine study" in "restrained but ruthless ambition," a
portrayal that suggested "an underlying hint of unease and guilt at
having deposed the king."[56]

John Barton (1973)

In 1971, Richard Pasco played King Richard in the touring production by Theatregoround which took the company's work to theaters, schools, colleges, and community centers throughout Great
Britain. The production served as the "prototype" for his exciting
and innovative "mirror image" version in 1973 with Pasco and Ian
Richardson alternating the roles of King Richard and Bullingbrook.
Irving Wardle remarked on the need to break with the history cycle
mentality:

For nearly 10 years the Royal Shakespeare Company have lived
in the shadow of *The Wars of the Roses*. Apart from an erratic
revival of *Richard III* they have left the English histories

severely alone. Now, at last, they are laying the ghost starting with the first play in the cycle which John Barton (a co-director of *The Wars of the Roses*) has cast in a determinedly fresh optique. The last production was the cornerstone of an epic; the new one is a work in itself.[57]

As Robert Shaughnessy relates, apart from "a poorly received" production of *Richard III*, directed by Terry Hands in 1970, Barton's *Richard II* (1973) "was the first major production of a mainstream history play since *The Wars of the Roses*," and is "often cited as the most influential, if not the definitive, modern production of the

3. John Barton's "mirror image" production of 1973. Richard Pasco and Ian Richardson alternated the roles of King Richard and Bullingbrook. Here they enact the metaphor of the two characters as buckets in a well, one going down as the other is pulled up.

play."[58] The enduring significance of this production lies in its ability to make relevant the analysis of kingship so keenly worked by Shakespeare in the "now of Elizabethan England." The program for the 1973 production contains a short essay by Anne Barton entitled "The King's Two Bodies." Ernst H. Kantorowicz in *The King's Two Bodies* (1957) explores an idea of kingship found in Edmund Plowden's *Reports* (collected and written under Queen Elizabeth I) that "the King has in him two Bodies, viz., a Body natural, and a Body politic."[59] In Anne Barton's explication of the concept:

> One of these bodies is flawless, abstract and immortal. The other is fallible, individual and subject to death and time. These two natures are fused at the moment of coronation in a way that deliberately parallels the incarnation of Christ, whose representative on earth—as Richard continually reminds us—the king henceforth will be.[60]

For John Barton, as for Kantorowicz, the notion of kingship with its fusing of the king's two bodies is at the center of the play. To give this dramatic expression, Barton's production took up Shakespeare's own use of the parallel between monarch and actor with their common assumption of roles, but whereas previous directors had seen the acting imagery only as a key to Richard's histrionic personality, Barton applied it to his whole production and, most important, to the other king in the play—Bullingbrook: "The alternation of the two actors playing Richard and Bullingbrook constantly focussed attention on the theme of kingship."[61]

The set and stage blocking helped to formalize these relationships, working with the stylized and symmetrical pattern of the play:

> Symmetry, of course is a natural feature of the play (for example "On this side, my hand; and on that side, thine" [4.1.177]), and Barton developed this element and made it an important part of his production. The play began with a meta-theatrical device in which an actor representing Shakespeare (and carrying a large book) appeared to nominate one of the two Richards to play the King and to put on a mask, robe and

crown. Removing the mask the designated Richard assumed the role and the play began.[62]

In Act 1 Scene 3, two ladders rose up behind the combatants "with between them a platform on which Richard literally rose and fell."[63] B. A. Young of the *Financial Times* commented:

> On this eccentric set the scenes are strictly formalised. There is no furniture but a tall golden cenotaph standing for a throne which comes and goes. The attendant characters are mar-shalled into rigid military ranks.[64]

Theater historian Robert Shaughnessy describes how

> Movement, grouping and gesture were highly choreographed, formalised and symmetrical, with many speeches directed straight out to the audience, and others divided and distributed among the cast in choric fashion. Barons appeared on wooden horses or on stilts, the Queen and her attendants in half-masks . . . For the Flint Castle scene, Richard appeared on the bridge high above the stage wearing a huge circular golden cloak which transformed king and actor into "glistering Phaethon"—an image of the sun-king which "set" as the bridge descended to the floor.[65]

In the deposition scene, when Richard broke his mirror, Bulling-brook placed the empty frame over the king's head, creating a noose. At Pomfret, a ragged Richard unburdens his soul to the groom, who turns out to be Bullingbrook, eliciting sympathy for the variable for-tunes of the two "kings" but to some critics straining the text too far.[66] Michael Billington felt that Richardson's king "ranks with Red-grave and McKellen as one of the classic Richards,"[67] while J. C. Trewin observed that "Mr Pasco tastes every word as he moves from the contemptuous smiling sun-king, through the arias on the Welsh shore, to the agony of Westminster Hall and the ultimate time-spinning metaphysics at Pomfret."[68] However, Trewin's final praise was reserved for Richardson as Bullingbrook: "no actor in my memory has so governed the 'silent king' of Westminster Hall."

Terry Hands (1980)

Irving Wardle's review of *Richard II* for the London *Times* catches the way in which the highly unusual "cycle" directed by Terry Hands was to position the play:

> Having begun in the middle of the English histories with *Henry V* and worked outwards in both directions, Terry Hands now arrives simultaneously at the beginning and the end of the cycle with this production and tonight's *Richard III* . . . we have a version of *Richard II* which converts the play from a lyric prelude into a compressed epic.[69]

The "cycle" opened a season in 1975 celebrating the centenary of the Royal Shakespeare Theatre from its beginnings as the Shakespeare Memorial Theatre. The "asymmetrical, even arbitrary" cycle, directed by Hands, comprised the *Henriad* in 1975, the *Henry VI* plays in 1977, with *Richard II* and *Richard III* completing the histories in 1980. Alan Howard played the lead role in all eight plays. Hands disregarded historical chronology and "opened out of sequence with *Henry V* in order to let the Chorus provide a prologue to the whole enterprise with his appeal to 'imaginary puissance' and 'the brightest heaven of invention.'"[70] Hands also revived his 1968 *The Merry Wives of Windsor* to round off the cycle, making a connection between "a jaundiced depiction of the condition of England," emerging through the *Henriad*, and the "run-down England" which "was ripe for the reappearance of an enfeebled Falstaff."[71]

The pairing of *Richard II* and *Richard III* in 1980 suggests a compression of time, projecting a retrospective light on King Richard II's tenuous grasp of the political realities that will unseat him and unleash bitter power struggles for the throne in years to come. At the same time, the unlikely companion piece of *Richard III* offered "a chance of showing another actor-king."[72] Stuart Hampton-Reeves suggests that the productions were "a self-conscious challenge to the monumental histories of the 1960s. History was represented on a stage (designed by Farrah) which had been stripped to reveal the wood and brickwork of the theatre."[73]

4. Terry Hands' 1980 production: from affability to opportunism to "a haunted figure bent under the weight of a usurped kingdom."

B. A. Young described the effects of the minimalist staging in *Richard II*:

> As we begin, the King stands before a costly panel of gold inlay and dons his crown with a gesture that speaks wordlessly of his divine right. Later this panel inclines backward to give a big open stage to which men climb up unseen stairs upstage, sometimes to fine effect, as when the savage Welsh come, lit from behind, to learn that they are too late.[74]

Shaughnessy argues that Hands' approach repudiates the politics in the *Henriad* and *Henry VI* plays, "concentrating upon the private self rather than the public role."[75] In his production of *Richard II*, Hands shows the protagonists responding personally to the pressures of their situations. Thus, as Irving Wardle notes,

> The first thing to be said of Mr Howard's performance is that he does Richard out of the arias. "What shall the king do now?" is delivered in a terrified gabble. He really wants to know. It is the panic-stricken demand of an actor who has forgotten his lines.[76]

Wardle notes that the emotional journey for John Suchet's Bullingbrook moves from "an affable open-hearted invader" to "a coldly-masked opportunist" and, finally, "a haunted figure bent under the weight of a usurped kingdom."

Barry Kyle (1986)

Barry Kyle's production of *Richard II* opened with colorful medieval scenic splendor, announcing its distance from the harsh steel world of the history cycle, directed by Peter Hall and John Barton in 1963–64, and from the minimalist staging favored by Terry Hands (1975–80). As Margaret Shewring relates, "It was the stage picture for Barry Kyle's production that attracted most column inches of critical attention."[77] However, "This visual feast was not gratuitous. On the contrary, it was an essential image of the cultural richness of the Ricardian court."[78] Other critics were less impressed:

Barry Kyle has adopted a pop-up picture book approach to this play and William Dudley's set, steeped in the artificial world of "The Book of Hours," is an enclosed garden surrounded by castellated walls and turrets against a brilliant, azure background with the passage of time marked by an astrological arch which spans the stage. It is an exquisite set which becomes increasingly irrelevant as the tragedy moves out of the claustrophobic luxuriance of Richard's court to the reality of Bullingbrook's camp, not to mention Pontefract Castle. At times it is seriously counter-productive: "Come down—down court, down King, / For night-owls shriek where mounting larks should sing" [3.3.183–4]. And sure enough, Richard goes spiralling downwards on a miniature turret, the very same turret that Bullingbrook leaps onto later—going up naturally.[79]

Stanley Wells also found the set "less than wholly successful" where "Richard, facing the audience, addresses his abdication speeches to

5. Barry Kyle production, 1986. The "colourful medieval scenic splendour" of the set proved problematic for some, where "Richard, facing the audience, addresses his abdication speeches to Bolingbroke, who is seated above and behind him, through the back of his head."

Bullingbrook, who is seated above and behind him, through the back of his head," but argued that the production represented "an honest and intelligent attempt to objectify the style of this highly formalized play."[80]

The play started with Jeremy Irons' Richard

first discovered resplendent in peacock blue and gold, spread-eagled on the ground, the leopard encaged in his kingdom that will become his tomb. He looks up wearily, as if to say: I *know* I'm not playing the kingship game with the degree of serious-ness everybody else expects of me.[81]

Without the context of a history cycle, the production can suggest an elegiac response to the ending of a medieval kingship. However, the "startlingly messianic" portrayal by Jeremy Irons of the tragic downfall of a divine king, a man "more or less crucified by his assailants," is in fact "another aspect of the poseur."[82] Richard plays his role ineffectually and dangerously, misjudging the politi-cal climate. Critics were impressed with the ceremonial joust scene, "a public ritual whose essential meaning is obvious to every-one present and the actors brilliantly convey the sense of unspo-ken but thoroughly understood accusations," and Michael Kitchen's "mesmerising performance" as Bullingbrook, "a formi-dable figure: an unpleasant, unglamorous and devious man but one who simply radiates competence, shrewdness, and a cynical likeability."[83]

Ron Daniels (1990)

While Jeremy Irons suggested the self-destructive path taken by the last undisputed medieval English king, Alex Jennings showed the repercussions of a tyrannical regime on the people subjected to his rule. Ron Daniels' "stand-alone" production had a modern context: the world of realpolitik. The theater program included a double-page spread on tyrannical regimes throughout history with a printed quote across the centerfold in red: "Mussolini would have liked to have been a poet just as Hitler would have liked to have been a great painter—most dictators, it seems, are artists manqués."[84] Maria Jones describes the start of the performance:

> The tyranny of Richard's regime was suggested through his personal bodyguard, the Cheshire archers, who trained their crossbows on the audience . . . Sinister guards in greatcoats and fur helmets recalled East European guards and referenced the tyrannical regime in Romania under Nicolae and Elena Ceausescu who were executed in December 1989 . . . Richard (Alex Jennings) entered "magnificently attired," wearing "the kind of crown a Holy Roman Emperor might have worn." His divine authority was emphasized through the presence of the Bishop of Carlisle (John Bott) standing behind the throne in ceremonial robes and bishop's mitre. Sinking "voluptuously into the throne," Jennings portrayed a monarch "utterly entranced with the role, the power, the trappings of kingship."[85]

The presence of a "false" white proscenium arch cast Richard as the "leading actor" of an illusory world and the production conveyed the idea that dictators appropriate images to produce distorted versions of reality, feeding off illusionary visions of themselves.[86] A huge, extravagant baroque Guido Reni backdrop created an effect that mythologized Richard's tragic downfall through the story of Atalanta stooping to retrieve Hippomene's apples, creating "a pictorial analogue of Bullingbrook's ascendancy, an image of victory through flight from a diverted opponent. Atalanta stoops just as Richard, the glistering phaeton, descends."[87] Richard appeared like a spoiled child, jealously guarding his favorite "toys," the orb, scepter and crown, which he kept in his "toy-box" and that would later be carried into Westminster Hall. Michael Billington of the *Guardian* commented on "a highly exciting performance from Anton Lesser" who played Bullingbrook:

> Willing to wound and yet afraid to strike, like certain modern politicians, Mr Lesser's Bullingbrook exhibits a wonderful mix-

ture of power-hunger and residual guilt: the classic moment comes with Richard's ironic offer of "Here, cousin, seize the crown" when Mr Lesser instinctively backs off as if the diadem itself were charged with electricity.[88]

Jennings was praised as "a commanding presence throughout," but some thought "the fascist/Stalinist touch in the production is a touch over-done" with "every character, save Richard, dressed in black."[89]

Steven Pimlott (2000)

Steven Pimlott's production of *Richard II* in the intimate studio space of The Other Place was the first in the RSC's two-year project "This England: The Histories," a "cycle" of all eight plays in chronological order for which "there would be no attempt to impose a single directorial or design concept."[90] Puzzled by the decision to choose different directors, designers, and venues, one critic asked: "Why stage a cycle if you plan an anti-cyclical style?"[91] Another provided an answer: "This variety is in deference to the stylistic contrasts of the plays, but you can also see the fragmentation as a response to the devolving nature of Britain, and the evolving character of its monarchy."[92]

Pimlott's approach, it was suggested, "dramatically opened up *Richard II* to the present moment, and opened up the present moment to the play."[93] The permanent white-box set designed by Sue Willmington, with environment designed by David Fielding, released the actors to tell the story "in what was avowedly the same real time as that of the audience." The spectator might be asked to consider "the future of the monarchy," the "presentational style of New Labour or the current state of English national identity."[94]

In this Brechtian-style production, Richard, played by Samuel West, dragged around a wooden box that would serve as dais for the throne, mirror and coffin. The circularity of power play was emphasized when, at the close, Bullingbrook (David Troughton) took Richard's place on the end of the wooden crate and repeated lines from a "Prologue" (reassigned from 5.5.1–5):

6. Steven Pimlott's 2000 Brechtian-style production where Sam West "dragged around a wooden box that would serve as dais for the throne, mirror and coffin."

I have been studying how to compare
This prison where I live unto the world.
And for because the world is populous
And here is not a creature but myself,
I cannot do it. Yet I'll hammer't out.

At the start, strains of "Jerusalem," the sound of marching, followed by bells, offered a pastiche of emblematic associations of "England": patriotism, war, celebration, and ceremony. A purple light associated the set with the royal court as Richard, dressed in smart pullover and trousers, commenced his "Prologue" sitting on his box, then rose to put on his jacket hanging on the back of his "throne" (a gold-painted chair) and his crown, a thin band of gold. It had a powerful effect on the audience:

> Pimlott's *Richard II* at Stratford's Other Place is a powerful modern production in a merciless white box. The audience are at the closest quarters with the players in experiencing the "prison" which Samuel West's Richard compares to the world. West is utterly compelling through every stage of the character's progress from indecisive monarch, through the pretence of an almost Ophelia-like madness, St. George's flag wrapped about him, to being "eased with being nothing." When he enters bearing his coffin like a cross you are also caught up in a passion play about the killing of a king. David Troughton's Bullingbrook is no reluctant regicide but a hectoring tyrant on the make, a man who insists the audience should get to its feet to endorse his usurpation.[95]

Critics commented on "excellent performances from Christopher Saul (a bustling, creepy Northumberland) and David Killick (a shrewd, watchful York)"[96] and Catherine Walker's "touching" Queen Isabel,[97] and applauded Sue Willmington's design, which created "a lethal debating chamber"[98] for "a gripping distillation of the pomp and circumstance, disillusion, confusion, and cynicism that now beset the term 'Englishman.' "[99]

THE DIRECTOR'S CUT: INTERVIEWS WITH CLAUS PEYMANN AND MICHAEL BOYD

Claus Peymann was born in Bremen, Germany, in 1937. He studied in Hamburg, where he also joined a student theater company, and from 1966 to 1969 he was artistic director of Frankfurt's Theater am Turm (TAT). In 1971 he directed the world premiere of Peter Handke's *The Ride Across Lake Constance* at the Berlin Schaubühne am Halleschen Ufer, which he founded together with Peter Stein. He has been artistic director of the Staatstheater Stuttgart (1974–79), the Schauspielhaus Bochumer (1979–86), and Burgtheater, Vienna (1986–99). Since 1999 he has been artistic director of the Berliner Ensemble, where he staged his much acclaimed version of *Richard II* (discussed here), translated by Thomas Brasch. The production was awarded with the Berlin Critics' Award and was invited to the German Theatertreffen as well as many theaters worldwide, from Tokyo to Stratford. In 2010 the staging was taken to Vienna Burgtheater. He is known for producing both classical work and premieres of Austrian dramatists, including plays by Thomas Bernhard, Peter Handke, Elfride Jelinek, and Peter Turrini.

Michael Boyd was born in Belfast in 1955, educated in London and Edinburgh and completed his MA in English literature at Edinburgh University. He trained as a director at the Malaya Bronnaya Theatre in Moscow. He then went on to work at the Belgrade Theatre in Coventry, joining the Sheffield Crucible as associate director in 1982. In 1985 Boyd became founding artistic director of the Tron theater in Glasgow, becoming equally acclaimed for staging new writing and innovative productions of the classics. He was drama director of the New Beginnings Festival of Soviet Arts in Glasgow in 1999. He joined the RSC as an associate director in 1996 and has since directed numerous productions of Shakespeare's plays. He won the Laurence Olivier Award for Best Director for his version of the *Henry VI* plays in the RSC's "This England: The Histories" in 2001. He took over as artistic director of the RSC in 2003 and oversaw the extraordinarily successful Complete Works Festival in 2006–07. His own contribution to this, and the company's subsequent season, was a cycle of all eight history plays, from *Richard II* through to *Richard III*, with the same company of actors. This transferred to London's Roundhouse Theatre in 2008 and won multiple awards. He talks here about his production of *Richard II* as part of that cycle.

Richard is traditionally described as a "weak" king, but that doesn't seem a very rewarding place for a production to start, does it?

Peymann: It is precisely his weakness that makes Richard II the prototype of a modern-day politician. Isn't it a frightening symptom that many politicians are simply not suited to the importance of their office, its responsibilities and demands? Many of them simply can't fill those shoes. This is why the "weakling" Richard II was of particular interest to us and why the Berliner Ensemble decided to stage the play in 2000.

Boyd: Richard begins the play exercising considerable autocratic power with ruthless finesse. He has had his only perceived threat, Gloucester, assassinated, and when Mowbray, who carried out the political execution, is accused at court by Bullingbrook, Richard is able to silence Mowbray and exile him for life without being implicated himself. He also exiles the rising figure of Bullingbrook for ten years, commuted to six, and is able immediately to raise tax revenue to finance a war in Ireland. It is this very display of power that loses him allies and renders him weak.

From the first beat of our production there was an extreme tension around the tightly choreographed "submission" of the English Court to their absolute ruler.

The play is closely related to Christopher Marlowe's *Edward II*, in which the king has explicitly gay relationships. And the great critic Samuel Taylor Coleridge saw in Richard what he called "a kind of feminine friendism," whatever that means. Did you explore questions of the king's sexuality and effeminacy?

Peymann: Richard's sexuality is not in the foreground in Shakespeare's play—in contrast to Marlowe's *Edward II*, which is specifically focused on the emancipation of and discrimination against a homosexual. The struggle for the realization of his love for men is a central theme in Marlowe, whereas the supposed homosexuality of Shakespeare's King Richard II is rather an invention of literary criticism. Of course sexual ambivalence is an underlying theme in the Shakespearean human cosmos—evident also in his *Sonnets*. And it is obvious that King Richard feels happier in the male company of his courtiers than in the daily routine of his marriage. And—there is no heir to the throne. But gay?—No! Incidentally, there is also a tradition—similar to that in *Hamlet*—of casting a female actor in the title role. Fiona Shaw did a fantastic job of this a couple of years ago at the National Theatre in London. Although this is a tempting interpretation, it doesn't interest me as a director. The sad goodbye kisses between King Richard and his wife Isabel—he on his way to the Tower, she fleeing back to France—those show intimacy and love.

Boyd: Jonathan Slinger's Richard loved the camp splendor of court ceremony and "dressing up" and at times resembled Elizabeth I in her prime.

There was an implied hierarchy in his harem of supporters whereby Nick Asbury's Bushy was reconciled to being sexually sidelined, Forbes Masson's Bagot was not, and Anthony Schuster's Green was the young man of the moment. Isabella eventually won his deepest affection by loving him unconditionally through both her humiliation and his.

And his kingliness? He has a strong investment in the idea of the sacredness of monarchy and of the king having two bodies, one representing his personal self and the other his kingly embodiment of the state. Is it hard to put these very medieval ideas across to a modern audience?

Peymann: Richard has two souls: his personal ego and the divinely appointed body of the King of England. Here the individual—there the politician. That represents a very contemporary phenomenon, doesn't it? Today's politicians also distinguish between person and office. And their credibility suffers from this schizophrenia.

Boyd: The king's body is closely associated with the land, and our stage had two arms, two legs, a huge helmeted head, and a torso which was ripped open often in our Histories' cycle.

Richard began our production at the head of an elaborate body of court ritual which rendered vivid his "unearthly" status. Paradoxically, this was when he was at his most "worldly" in the play: modern, Machiavellian, and sensualist. Only when he shed the trappings of divine right did he discover his true divinity as a human and therefore as a king. Richard's spiritual authority dated in our production from the "cleansing" shower of dust or sand thrown upon him by the crowd. No makeup, no wig, no magnificent gown, just a man mortified under God's gaze and ours.

Jonathan Slinger began our production stepping gracefully over the body of the murdered Duke of Gloucester, played by Chuk Iwuji. Jonathan, playing Richard III, had murdered Chuk three and a half hours earlier as the sainted Henry VI; a character modeled consciously on Edward the Confessor, to whom people still pray at his shrine at the heart of Westminster Abbey. Jonathan ended *Richard II* with his blood spread over the stage in the same arc as Chuk's had been spread by him in *Henry VI Part III*.

The central scene, when the crown passes from Richard to Bullingbrook, is usually referred to as the "deposition" scene, but doesn't it in some respects seem more like an abdication?

Peymann: Bullingbrook forces Richard to abdicate. But Richard exploits this situation. He acts out a scene in front of the entire Parliament. He becomes an actor, using refinement and wit to turn his tragedy into a public victory over Bullingbrook. In the "mirror scene" he casts himself as the victim and publicly scorns Bullingbrook, leaving him speechless.

Boyd: Richard states publicly and clearly that he is being not just deposed, but "usurped," and responds to Bullingbrook's direct question "Are you contented to resign the crown?" with the ferocious ambiguity of "Ay, no; no, ay, for I must nothing be: / Therefore no 'no,' for I resign to thee." Given that "I," "Ay," "eye," and "aye" (for

7. Michael Boyd production: "Richard's spiritual authority dated in our production from the 'cleansing' shower of dust or sand thrown upon him."

ever) *all* sound identical, this reply could be read as "No." To the last, he calls himself "a true king."

And what about the development of Richard's language: the poetry is very formal at moments such as the one where he inverts the language of the coronation ceremony, but at other times—especially toward the end—it's much more personal and fragmented, isn't it?

Peymann: Richard II plays with all linguistic devices. He deftly juggles with courtly rituals and thereby questions their validity. He scorns all linguistic clichés. In the course of his political swansong his mental and linguistic ability to differentiate is increased. As so often in Shakespeare, he becomes more and more human. In the catastrophe he gains our sympathy. The translation—and the version used in our production—is by the significant German dramatist, poet, and translator Thomas Brasch (1945–2001). It sticks closely to the original and thereby stands in strong contrast to the Shakespeare image of the brothers Schlegel/Tieck and of Baudissin, which was heavily influenced by German Romanticism of the eighteenth century. Brasch's language is very poetic, full of comedy, direct and obscene. It is very "Shakespearean."

The language throughout is highly lyrical, heightened, poetic, isn't it? There's no prose at all: even the gardeners speak in elevated (and quite allegorical) verse! That's a far cry from the world of Eastcheap and Falstaff that will follow in the *Henry IV* plays, and indeed from the rough-edged commoner's voice of Jack Cade in *Henry VI*. Does this make *Richard II* somehow stand apart from the other history plays?

Peymann: Similar to the gravedigger scene in *Hamlet*, the gardener scene in *Richard II* fuses comedy, grandeur, and political polemics. The linguistic unity of Shakespeare's *Richard II* distinguishes it from the other history plays. It is in fact closer to Shakespeare's *Hamlet*. To put it bluntly: Richard II is a Hamlet come to power. That is an essential characteristic of this masterwork—which is unfortunately performed far too rarely. Similar to *Hamlet*, Shakespeare's *Richard II* is way ahead of its time. He endows the title characters with a psychological modernity that the contemporary modern psychodrama would only be able to show several centuries later.

Boyd: The language of *Richard II* is more refined and "exquisite" than the other history plays. This is partly a question of milieu: we barely ever leave the world of the court, and even the gardeners are gardeners to the Duke of York and Queen Isabella.

This is also a particular court and a play that is dominated by an intelligent and witty man who has cultivated a conscious courtly high style in those around him. The language of *Richard II* is designed to rise to metaphysics, to capture fine distinctions of thought on time, divinity, optics, music, and constitutional law.

It is even more potently a language of exquisite equivocation, with the refined vocabulary and subtle grammar that are necessary to tread the highwire over danger, to conceal one's true intentions, and avoid being condemned for perjury. It's a language equipped to walk on thin ice, or tiptoe through a minefield.

The first half of Act 4 Scene 1 is such a wonderful release for the audience as the language turns to direct abuse and mines explode all round the place.

Could we even say that it is a tragedy (the downfall of one man) more than a history play (the story of a nation)?

Peymann: In no other Shakespeare play are there more characters who cry or grow pale than in *Richard II*. The psychological richness of the characters—even going as far as self-analysis—gives this play such a modern character. *Richard II* is much more the tragedy of an individual than merely a station in the great carousel of power of the English kings.

Boyd: Richard II the character does earn tragic status, and we are privy to his insight and revelations as he falls.

Shakespeare's history plays are not just the story, but the tragedy (or downfall) of the nation, felt every bit as presently by the author and the audience, as the fate of Richard himself.

How much sympathy can we have for Bullingbrook?

Peymann: Through the injustice Bullingbrook experiences—banishment, emigration, and loss of his birthright—he evokes sympathy and understanding in an audience. Over the course of the play our perspective of Bullingbrook becomes more critical. Like so many fighters for justice and protesters against arbitrary rule, Bullingbrook leads a personal war, which becomes a civil war and eventually turns him into a criminal. It's the eternal struggle for power! Bullingbrook, too, must kill to stay at the top.

Boyd: If Shakespeare characterized the slaying of Richard II as the original Plantagenet "fratricide" in the *Henry VI/Richard III* quartet, he has become more circumspect by the time he writes his next cycle: Bullingbrook is no straightforward Cain, and Richard sure as hell is no Abel.

The "original sin" of the histories is revealed in *Richard II* as predating Richard's death. Now it has become Richard's sanctioned murder of his uncle, Gloucester. There are echoes of Elizabeth's equivocation over her sanctioning of Mary Stuart's execution.

Henry has our strong sympathy as a vigorous and unjustly exiled seeker-of-the-truth. He loses this sympathy when he, as Richard had done before him, makes an offstage request for the assassination of his chief threat. Shakespeare has a long, slow punishment in store for Bullingbrook in the two *Henry IV* plays. God will only seem to be appeased at Agincourt, and even then the Chorus has to warn us (remind us) that worse is yet to come.

And York, the turncoat?

Peymann: York is an opportunist, turning to whoever happens to be the most powerful person at any given moment. Beginning as a follower and supporter of Richard, he becomes one of Bullingbrook's men. In our production York even takes on the task of murdering the king. He carries out this job eagerly himself. Our production ends in a pitiless slaughtering of all of Richard's followers and Richard himself. York becomes an accomplice of the new King Henry IV, alias Bullingbrook. That is the logical career progression from opportunist to henchman of the new dictatorship. A butcher from a family of Nazi-killers in a white-tiled, bloody slaughterhouse.

Boyd: If any one character encompasses the "story of a nation," it is Edmund, Duke of York. He is shown tormented on the rack between a deep loyalty to the old dynastic certainties, and an equal repugnance toward the destructive tyranny of Richard. The closing movement of the play, where Edmund's attempts to maintain his old belief system in the new world of Bullingbrook lead him to betray his own son against his nature, is a brilliant portrait of the human cost of the Reformation on buckled English lives in Shakespeare's time.

What's going on in that very curious scene with Aumerle near the end?

Peymann: The central thought of this scene, in which Aumerle begs forgiveness, is "grace." The absurdity of this scene is more akin to the farces of Eugene Ionesco and Feydeau than to Shakespeare's history plays. Forgiveness and grace—the highest virtues of regal power which Bullingbrook, the new King Henry IV, must now learn. Grace and forgiveness: does this perhaps hint at the recurring speculation that Shakespeare was a Jesuit scholar and a secret Catholic? We don't know.

So, finally, how much does Richard change in the course of his journey?

Peymann: Through his fall the human side of Richard becomes visible—there was someone living in the crown who hid behind the mask of king. And as we come to see this person, he gains our sympathy. Henry IV's eulogy next to the bloody corpse of the king moves us: "March sadly after: grace my mourning here, / In weeping after this untimely bier."

Boyd: Richard never quite loses his arrogance. Shakespeare is rarely judgmental but does reserve a special room in purgatory for those who think themselves "wise" as Richard refers to himself as late as 5.5.63. He has perforce learned humility in other respects, and the self-knowledge that he has "wasted time." The humanity and the simplicity of his parting with Isabella: "hand from hand, my love, and heart from heart," are the most convincing symptoms of real change.

PLAYING RICHARD: AN INTERVIEW WITH FIONA SHAW

Fiona Shaw was born in Cork, Ireland, in 1958. She studied at RADA and has extensive experience with the National Theatre, as well as credits for a diverse range of films including *My Left Foot* (1989) and more recently a recurring role in the Harry Potter series. In the theater she has regularly collaborated with the director Deborah Warner, achieving great success in a variety of roles. Recently the pair revived their highly acclaimed production of T. S. Eliot's *The Waste Land*, first performed in New York in 1996. Fiona has won numerous awards for her acting and was awarded an Officier des Arts et Lettres in France in 2000 and an honorary CBE in the 2001 New Year's Honors. She talks her about her performance as Richard II at the National Theatre in London in 1995, in a production again directed by Warner, which was also filmed for the BBC.

Richard is traditionally described as a "weak" king, but that doesn't seem a very rewarding place for an actor to start, does it?

At the beginning of the play Richard seems more of a spoiled king than a weak king. He uses his power to banish Bullingbrook in the first act, which results in the world tumbling down on his head. His weakness lies in his abuse of power. He has none of the evenness that John of Gaunt describes in the beautiful "sceptred isle" speech. The play is about his journey to wisdom.

The play is closely related to Christopher Marlowe's *Edward II,* in which the king has explicitly gay relationships. And the great critic Samuel Taylor Coleridge saw in Richard what he called "a kind of feminine friendism," whatever that means. Did you explore questions of the king's sexuality and effeminacy?

Well, certainly the gender of the actress playing Richard meant that in our case we were obliquely sideswiping the thorny issue of Richard's sexuality. In historical terms Richard is said to have written the first cookbook, and he was also a king who prided himself on an England full of peace. As we know to our detriment, strong governments prefer war. My playing Richard did mean that I was free from using energy on the issue of effeminacy. And certainly I played the passionate affection for Bullingbrook, which was freed by the fact I was female so I could indulge the physicality of their affection; though it may have heightened the homoeroticism in the minds of the audience. What interested us was the way in which an intimate childhood friendship like Bullingbrook's and Richard's turned into a power battle later where neither party can win because both are fundamentally sympathetic to the other. I always felt Richard was both released in handing Bullingbrook the crown, the power reverting to the stronger member of the duo, as well as furious with himself in his famous "Ay, no; no, ay, for I must nothing be." There are very complex feelings at play in this section where love and revulsion meet.

And his kingliness? He has a strong investment in the idea of the sacredness of monarchy and of the king having two bodies, one representing his personal self and the other his kingly embodiment of the state. Is it hard to put these very medieval ideas across to a modern audience?

Again, being female meant that there was an iconoclastic element in tiptoeing into the area of "kingship" as opposed to "queenship." Richard speaks from the battlements with great fluency about the divine right of kings, which became his only protection against an insurgent group. His vulnerability and need to name God as the top of the pyramid in which he was second says a lot about how frail these notions are. The king is the servant of the will of the people as much as the people serve the king. There was a spectacular reply to this moment implicitly when the royal family reluctantly gathered for Princess Diana's funeral. The gift of kingship does lie with the people.

The central scene, when the crown passes from Richard to Bullingbrook, is usually referred to as the "deposition" scene, but, in the playing, did it seem more like an abdication?

The deposition scene is one of the greatest scenes ever written. Theatrically the audience has begun to turn its allegiance to Richard as he appears poor and a prisoner, broken from the previous "Down, down I come, like glist'ring Phaethon." He doesn't really abdicate because he asks Bullingbrook first to take up the crown and, finally, with his intellectually accurate contortions, he crowns the thieving cousin. But always on the edge of a dialectical ambiguity: "'God save King Henry,' unkinged Richard says."

And what about the development of Richard's language: the poetry is very formal at moments such as the one where he inverts the language of the coronation ceremony, but at other times—especially toward the end—it's much more personal and fragmented, isn't it?

The whole play is entirely in verse, which gives the impression that the world of the play is held in a more formal and perhaps more innocent time. There is no free prose, no breakages of line; it has a metronome, as if it is one long poem. Richard's language improves from the moment he returns from Ireland with the beautiful speech, "let us sit upon the ground / And tell sad stories of the death of kings." It is as if, when his wit meets sorrow, something beautiful is minted. By the time we meet him in the prison he has the gentle "aria": "I have been studying how to compare / This prison where I live unto the world." His fluency has the motor of a search rather than triumph, he uses his phenomenal mind to say something about the state of being; far too late for him, but not for us hearing it. We are privileged because we learn his lesson:

> . . . But whate'er I am,
> Nor I nor any man that but man is
> With nothing shall be pleased, till he be eased
> With being nothing. . . .

A very particular language question: what did you make of his shifts between the royal "we" and the personal "I"?

He uses the royal "we" during the first half of the play; his final speech before being killed is his discovery that he is not a god or a king, but a man, and that is enough. He sheds the "we" to become himself: this is very much the Christian model of having to lose everything to gain the eternal life.

So how much does Richard change in the course of his journey?

One of the reasons it is a spectacular part to play is that the play needs the actor playing Richard to be in flying colors from the top of the evening. It also needs the actor to know that you will lose the audience's sympathy very early on. The coup of the play is that Richard gains the sympathy of the audience by losing his seeming charms. Richard changes entirely from someone who does not

8. Fiona Shaw as Richard II, National Theatre, 1995. Richard leaves the audience asking the question "What do we do when we elevate people too high?"

notice what he eats to being someone who needs "bread like you."
From this access in the play onward he joins us, the ordinary people,
leaving us with the question: what do we do when we elevate people
too high? We map our aspirations onto them and punish them when
they fail us. Richard is a star that falls.

SHAKESPEARE'S CAREER IN THE THEATER

BEGINNINGS

William Shakespeare was an extraordinarily intelligent man who was born and died in an ordinary market town in the English Midlands. He lived an uneventful life in an eventful age. Born in April 1564, he was the eldest son of John Shakespeare, a glove-maker who was prominent on the town council until he fell into financial difficulties. Young William was educated at the local grammar in Stratford-upon-Avon, Warwickshire, where he gained a thorough grounding in the Latin language, the art of rhetoric, and classical poetry. He married Ann Hathaway and had three children (Susanna, then the twins Hamnet and Judith) before his twenty-first birthday: an exceptionally young age for the period. We do not know how he supported his family in the mid-1580s.

Like many clever country boys, he moved to the city in order to make his way in the world. Like many creative people, he found a career in the entertainment business. Public playhouses and professional full-time acting companies reliant on the market for their income were born in Shakespeare's childhood. When he arrived in London as a man, sometime in the late 1580s, a new phenomenon was in the making: the actor who is so successful that he becomes a "star." The word did not exist in its modern sense, but the pattern is recognizable: audiences went to the theater not so much to see a particular show as to witness the comedian Richard Tarlton or the dramatic actor Edward Alleyn.

Shakespeare was an actor before he was a writer. It appears not to have been long before he realized that he was never going to grow into a great comedian like Tarlton or a great tragedian like Alleyn. Instead, he found a role within his company as the man who patched up old plays, breathing new life, new dramatic twists, into tired repertory pieces. He paid close attention to the work of the university-educated dramatists who were writing history plays and tragedies for the public stage in a style more ambitious, sweeping, and poetically grand than anything that had been seen before. But he may also have noted that what his friend and rival Ben Jonson would call "Marlowe's mighty line" sometimes faltered in the mode of comedy. Going to university, as Christopher Marlowe did, was all well and good for honing the arts of rhetorical elaboration and classical allusion, but it could lead to a loss of the common touch. To stay close to a large segment of the potential audience for public theater, it was necessary to write for clowns as well as kings and to intersperse the flights of poetry with the humor of the tavern, the privy, and the brothel: Shakespeare was the first to establish himself early in his career as an equal master of tragedy, comedy, and history. He realized that theater could be the medium to make the national past available to a wider audience than the elite who could afford to read large history books: his signature early works include not only the classical tragedy *Titus Andronicus* but also the sequence of English historical plays on the Wars of the Roses.

He also invented a new role for himself, that of in-house company dramatist. Where his peers and predecessors had to sell their plays to the theater managers on a poorly paid piecework basis, Shakespeare took a percentage of the box-office income. The Lord Chamberlain's Men constituted themselves in 1594 as a joint stock company, with the profits being distributed among the core actors who had invested as sharers. Shakespeare acted himself—he appears in the cast lists of some of Ben Jonson's plays as well as the list of actors' names at the beginning of his own collected works—but his principal duty was to write two or three plays a year for the company. By holding shares, he was effectively earning himself a royalty on his work, something no author had ever done before in England. When the Lord Chamberlain's Men collected their fee for performance at court in the Christmas season of 1594, three of them went along to the Treasurer of the Chamber: not just Richard Burbage the tragedian and Will Kempe the clown, but also Shakespeare the scriptwriter. That was something new.

The next four years were the golden period in Shakespeare's career, though overshadowed by the death of his only son Hamnet, aged eleven, in 1596. In his early thirties and in full command of both his poetic and his theatrical medium, he perfected his art of comedy, while also developing his tragic and historical writing in new ways. In 1598, Francis Meres, a Cambridge University graduate with his finger on the pulse of the London literary world, praised Shakespeare for his excellence across the genres:

> As Plautus and Seneca are accounted the best for comedy and tragedy among the Latins, so Shakespeare among the English is the most excellent in both kinds for the stage; for comedy, witness his *Gentlemen of Verona*, his *Errors*, his *Love Labours Lost*, his *Love Labours Won*, his *Midsummer Night Dream* and his *Merchant of Venice*: for tragedy his *Richard the 2*, *Richard the 3*, *Henry the 4*, *King John*, *Titus Andronicus* and his *Romeo and Juliet*.

For Meres, as for the many writers who praised the "honey-flowing vein" of *Venus and Adonis* and *Lucrece*, narrative poems written when the theaters were closed due to plague in 1593–94, Shakespeare was marked above all by his linguistic skill, by the gift of turning elegant poetic phrases.

PLAYHOUSES

Elizabethan playhouses were "thrust" or "one-room" theaters. To understand Shakespeare's original theatrical life, we have to forget about the indoor theater of later times, with its proscenium arch and curtain that would be opened at the beginning and closed at the end of each act. In the proscenium arch theater, stage and auditorium are effectively two separate rooms: the audience looks from one world into another as if through the imaginary "fourth wall" framed by the proscenium. The picture-frame stage, together with the elaborate scenic effects and backdrops beyond it, created the illusion of a self-contained world—especially once nineteenth-century developments in the control of artificial lighting meant that the auditorium could be darkened and the spectators made to focus on the lighted stage. Shakespeare, by contrast, wrote for a bare platform stage with a standing audience gathered around it in a courtyard in full daylight. The audience were always conscious of themselves and their fellow spectators, and they shared the same "room" as the actors. A sense of immediate presence and the creation of rapport with the audience were all-important. The actor could not afford to imagine he was in a closed world, with silent witnesses dutifully observing him from the darkness.

Shakespeare's theatrical career began at the Rose Theatre in Southwark. The stage was wide and shallow, trapezoid in shape, like a lozenge. This design had a great deal of potential for the theatrical equivalent of cinematic split-screen effects, whereby one group of characters would enter at the door at one end of the tiring-house wall at the back of the stage and another group through the door at the other end, thus creating two rival tableaux. Many of the battle-heavy and faction-filled plays that premiered at the Rose have scenes of just this sort.

At the rear of the Rose stage, there were three capacious exits, each over ten feet wide. Unfortunately, the very limited excavation of a fragmentary portion of the original Globe site, in 1989, revealed nothing about the stage. The first Globe was built in 1599 with similar proportions to those of another theater, the Fortune, albeit that the former was polygonal and looked circular, whereas the latter was rectangular. The building contract for the Fortune survives and allows us to infer that the stage of the Globe was probably substantially wider than it was deep (perhaps forty-three feet wide and twenty-seven feet deep). It may well have been tapered at the front, like that of the Rose.

The capacity of the Globe was said to have been enormous, perhaps in excess of three thousand. It has been conjectured that about eight hundred people may have stood in the yard, with two thousand or more in the three layers of covered galleries. The other "public" playhouses were also of large capacity, whereas the indoor Blackfriars theater that Shakespeare's company began using in 1608—the former refectory of a monastery—had overall internal dimensions of a mere forty-six by sixty feet. It would have made for a much more intimate theatrical experience and had a much smaller capacity, probably of about six hundred people. Since they paid at least sixpence a head, the Blackfriars attracted a more select or "private" audience. The atmosphere would have been closer to that of an indoor performance before the court in the Whitehall Palace or at Richmond. That Shakespeare always wrote for indoor production at court as well as outdoor performance in the public theater should make us cautious about inferring, as some scholars have, that the opportunity provided by the intimacy of the Blackfriars led to a significant change toward a "chamber" style in his last plays—which, besides, were performed at both the Globe and the Blackfriars. After the occupation of the Blackfriars a five-act structure seems to have become more important to Shakespeare. That was because of artificial lighting: there were musical interludes between the acts, while the candles were trimmed and replaced. Again, though, something similar must have been necessary for indoor court performances throughout his career.

Front of house there were the "gatherers" who collected the money from audience members: a penny to stand in the open-air yard, another penny for a place in the covered galleries, sixpence for the prominent "lord's rooms" to the side of the stage. In the indoor "private" theaters, gallants from the audience who fancied making themselves part of the spectacle sat on stools on the edge of the stage itself. Scholars debate as to how widespread this practice was in the public theaters such as the Globe. Once the audience were in place and the money counted, the gatherers were available to be extras on stage. That is one reason why battles and crowd scenes often come later rather than early in Shakespeare's plays. There was no formal prohibition upon performance by women, and there certainly were women among the gatherers, so it is not beyond the bounds of possibility that female crowd members were played by females.

The play began at two o'clock in the afternoon and the theater had to be cleared by five. After the main show, there would be a jig—which consisted not only of dancing, but also of knockabout comedy (it is the origin of the farcical "afterpiece" in the eighteenth-century theater). So the time available for a Shakespeare play was about two and a half hours, somewhere between the "two hours' traffic" mentioned in the prologue to *Romeo and Juliet* and the "three hours' spectacle" referred to in the preface to the 1647 Folio of Beaumont and Fletcher's plays.

The prologue to a play by Thomas Middleton refers to a thousand lines as "one hour's words," so the likelihood is that about two and a half thousand, or a maximum of three thousand lines, made up the performed text. This is indeed the length of most of Shakespeare's comedies, whereas many of his tragedies and histories are much longer, raising the possibility that he wrote full scripts, possibly with eventual publication in mind, in the full knowledge that the stage version would be heavily cut. The short Quarto texts published in his lifetime—they used to be called "Bad" Quartos—provide fascinating evidence as to the kind of cutting that probably took place. So, for instance, the First Quarto of *Hamlet* neatly merges two occasions when Hamlet is overheard, the "Fishmonger" and the "nunnery" scenes.

The social composition of the audience was mixed. The poet Sir John Davies wrote of "A thousand townsmen, gentlemen and whores, / Porters and servingmen" who would "together throng" at the public playhouses. Though moralists associated female playgoing with adultery and the sex trade, many perfectly respectable citizens' wives were regular attendees. Some, no doubt, resembled the modern groupie: a story attested in two different sources has one citizen's wife making a post-show assignation with Richard Burbage and ending up in bed with Shakespeare—supposedly eliciting from the latter the quip that William the Conqueror was before Richard III. Defenders of theater liked to say that by witnessing the comeuppance of villains on the stage, audience members would repent of their own wrongdoings, but the reality is that most people went to the theater then, as they do now, for entertainment more than moral edification. Besides, it would be foolish to suppose that audiences behaved in a homogeneous way: a pamphlet of the 1630s tells of how two men went to see *Pericles* and one of them laughed while the other wept. Bishop John Hall complained that people went to church for the same reasons that they went to the theater: "for company, for custom, for recreation . . . to feed his eyes or his ears . . . or perhaps for sleep."

Men-about-town and clever young lawyers went to be seen as much as to see. In the modern popular imagination, shaped not least by *Shakespeare in Love* and the opening sequence of Laurence Olivier's *Henry V* film, the penny-paying groundlings stand in the yard hurling abuse or encouragement and hazelnuts or orange peel

at the actors, while the sophisticates in the covered galleries appreci-
ate Shakespeare's soaring poetry. The reality was probably the other
way around. A "groundling" was a kind of fish, so the nickname
suggests the penny audience standing below the level of the stage
and gazing in silent open-mouthed wonder at the spectacle unfold-
ing above them. The more difficult audience members, who kept up
a running commentary of clever remarks on the performance and
who occasionally got into quarrels with players, were the gallants.
Like Hollywood movies in modern times, Elizabethan and Jacobean
plays exercised a powerful influence on the fashion and behavior of
the young. John Marston mocks the lawyers who would open their
lips, perhaps to court a girl, and out would "flow / Naught but pure
Juliet and Romeo."

THE ENSEMBLE AT WORK

In the absence of typewriters and photocopying machines, reading
aloud would have been the means by which the company got to
know a new play. The tradition of the playwright reading his complete script to the assembled company endured for generations. A
copy would then have been taken to the Master of the Revels for
licensing. The theater book-holder or prompter would then have
copied the parts for distribution to the actors. A partbook consisted
of the character's lines, with each speech preceded by the last three
or four words of the speech before, the so-called "cue." These would
have been taken away and studied or "conned." During this period of
learning the parts, an actor might have had some one-to-one
instruction, perhaps from the dramatist, perhaps from a senior actor
who had played the same part before, and, in the case of an apprentice, from his master. A high percentage of Desdemona's lines occur
in dialogue with Othello, of Lady Macbeth's with Macbeth, Cleopatra's with Antony, and Volumnia's with Coriolanus. The roles would
almost certainly have been taken by the apprentice of the lead actor,
usually Burbage, who delivers the majority of the cues. Given that
apprentices lodged with their masters, there would have been ample
opportunity for personal instruction, which may be what made it
possible for young men to play such demanding parts.

9. Hypothetical reconstruction of the interior of an Elizabethan playhouse during a performance.

After the parts were learned, there may have been no more than a single rehearsal before the first performance. With six different plays to be put on every week, there was no time for more. Actors, then, would go into a show with a very limited sense of the whole. The notion of a collective rehearsal process that is itself a process of discovery for the actors is wholly modern and would have been incomprehensible to Shakespeare and his original ensemble. Given the number of parts an actor had to hold in his memory, the forgetting of lines was probably more frequent than in the modern theater. The book-holder was on hand to prompt.

Backstage personnel included the property man, the tire-man who oversaw the costumes, call boys, attendants, and the musicians, who might play at various times from the main stage, the rooms above, and within the tiring-house. Scriptwriters sometimes made a nuisance of themselves backstage. There was often tension between the acting companies and the freelance playwrights from whom they purchased scripts: it was a smart move on the part of

Shakespeare and the Lord Chamberlain's Men to bring the writing process in-house.

Scenery was limited, though sometimes set pieces were brought on (a bank of flowers, a bed, the mouth of hell). The trapdoor from below, the gallery stage above, and the curtained discovery-space at the back allowed for an array of special effects: the rising of ghosts and apparitions, the descent of gods, dialogue between a character at a window and another at ground level, the revelation of a statue or a pair of lovers playing at chess. Ingenious use could be made of props, as with the ass's head in *A Midsummer Night's Dream*. In a theater that does not clutter the stage with the material paraphernalia of everyday life, those objects that are deployed may take on powerful symbolic weight, as when Shylock bears his weighing scales in one hand and knife in the other, thus becoming a parody of the figure of Justice who traditionally bears a sword and a balance. Among the more significant items in the property cupboard of Shakespeare's company, there would have been a throne (the "chair of state"), joint stools, books, bottles, coins, purses, letters (which are brought on stage, read or referred to on about eighty occasions in the complete works), maps, gloves, a set of stocks (in which Kent is put in *King Lear*), rings, rapiers, daggers, broadswords, staves, pistols, masks and vizards, heads and skulls, torches and tapers and lanterns which served to signal night scenes on the daylit stage, a buck's head, an ass's head, animal costumes. Live animals also put in appearances, most notably the dog Crab in *The Two Gentlemen of Verona* and possibly a young polar bear in *The Winter's Tale*.

The costumes were the most important visual dimension of the play. Playwrights were paid between £2 and £6 per script, whereas Alleyn was not averse to paying £20 for "a black velvet cloak with sleeves embroidered all with silver and gold." No matter the period of the play, actors always wore contemporary costume. The excitement for the audience came not from any impression of historical accuracy, but from the richness of the attire and perhaps the transgressive thrill of the knowledge that here were commoners like themselves strutting in the costumes of courtiers in effective defiance of the strict sumptuary laws whereby in real life people had to wear the clothes that befitted their social station.

To an even greater degree than props, costumes could carry symbolic importance. Racial characteristics could be suggested: a breastplate and helmet for a Roman soldier, a turban for a Turk, long robes for exotic characters such as Moors, a gabardine for a Jew. The figure of Time, as in *The Winter's Tale*, would be equipped with hourglass, scythe, and wings; Rumour, who speaks the prologue of *2 Henry IV*, wore a costume adorned with a thousand tongues. The wardrobe in the tiring-house of the Globe would have contained much of the same stock as that of rival manager Philip Henslowe at the Rose: green gowns for outlaws and foresters, black for melancholy men such as Jaques and people in mourning such as the Countess in *All's Well That Ends Well* (at the beginning of *Hamlet*, the prince is still in mourning black when everyone else is in festive garb for the wedding of the new king), a gown and hood for a friar (or a feigned friar like the duke in *Measure for Measure*), blue coats and tawny to distinguish the followers of rival factions, a leather apron and ruler for a carpenter (as in the opening scene of *Julius Caesar*—and in *A Midsummer Night's Dream*, where this is the only sign that Peter Quince is a carpenter), a cockle hat with staff and a pair of sandals for a pilgrim or palmer (the disguise assumed by Helen in *All's Well*), bodices and kirtles with farthingales beneath for the boys who are to be dressed as girls. A gender switch such as that of Rosalind or Jessica seems to have taken between fifty and eighty lines of dialogue—Viola does not resume her "maiden weeds," but remains in her boy's costume to the end of *Twelfth Night* because a change would have slowed down the action at just the moment it was speeding to a climax. Henslowe's inventory also included "a robe for to go invisible": Oberon, Puck, and Ariel must have had something similar.

As the costumes appealed to the eyes, so there was music for the ears. Comedies included many songs. Desdemona's willow song, perhaps a late addition to the text, is a rare and thus exceptionally poignant example from tragedy. Trumpets and tuckets sounded for ceremonial entrances, drums denoted an army on the march. Background music could create atmosphere, as at the beginning of *Twelfth Night*, during the lovers' dialogue near the end of *The Merchant of Venice*, when the statue seemingly comes to life in *The Winter's Tale*, and for the revival of *Pericles* and of *Lear* (in the Quarto text, but not the Folio). The haunting sound of the hautboy suggested a realm beyond the human, as when the god Hercules is imagined deserting Mark Antony. Dances symbolized the harmony of the end of a comedy—though in Shakespeare's world of mingled joy and sorrow, someone is usually left out of the circle.

The most important resource was, of course, the actors themselves. They needed many skills: in the words of one contemporary commentator, "dancing, activity, music, song, elocution, ability of body, memory, skill of weapon, pregnancy of wit." Their bodies were as significant as their voices. Hamlet tells the player to "suit the action to the word, the word to the action": moments of strong emotion, known as "passions," relied on a repertoire of dramatic gestures as well as a modulation of the voice. When Titus Andronicus has had his hand chopped off, he asks, "How can I grace my talk, / Wanting a hand to give it action?" A pen portrait of "The Character of an Excellent Actor" by the dramatist John Webster is almost certainly based on his impression of Shakespeare's leading man, Richard Burbage: "By a full and significant action of body, he charms our attention: sit in a full theatre, and you will think you see so many lines drawn from the circumference of so many ears, whiles the actor is the centre. . . ."

Though Burbage was admired above all others, praise was also heaped upon the apprentice players whose alto voices fitted them for the parts of women. A spectator at Oxford in 1610 records how the audience were reduced to tears by the pathos of Desdemona's death. The puritans who fumed about the biblical prohibition upon cross-dressing and the encouragement to sodomy constituted by the sight of an adult male kissing a teenage boy on stage were a small minority. Little is known, however, about the characteristics of the leading apprentices in Shakespeare's company. It may perhaps be inferred that one was a lot taller than the other, since Shakespeare often wrote for a pair of female friends, one tall and fair, the other short and dark (Helena and Hermia, Rosalind and Celia, Beatrice and Hero).

We know little about Shakespeare's own acting roles—an early allusion indicates that he often took royal parts, and a venerable tradition gives him old Adam in *As You Like It* and the ghost of old King Hamlet. Save for Burbage's lead roles and the generic part of the clown, all such castings are mere speculation. We do not even know for sure whether the original Falstaff was Will Kempe or another actor who specialized in comic roles, Thomas Pope.

Kempe left the company in early 1599. Tradition has it that he fell out with Shakespeare over the matter of excessive improvisation. He was replaced by Robert Armin, who was less of a clown and more of a cerebral wit: this explains the difference between such parts as Lancelet Gobbo and Dogberry, which were written for Kempe, and the more verbally sophisticated Feste and Lear's Fool, which were written for Armin.

One thing that is clear from surviving "plots" or storyboards of plays from the period is that a degree of doubling was necessary. *2 Henry VI* has over sixty speaking parts, but more than half of the characters only appear in a single scene and most scenes have only six to eight speakers. At a stretch, the play could be performed by thirteen actors. When Thomas Platter saw *Julius Caesar* at the Globe in 1599, he noted that there were about fifteen. Why doesn't Paris go to the Capulet ball in *Romeo and Juliet?* Perhaps because he was doubled with Mercutio, who does. In *The Winter's Tale*, Mamillius might have come back as Perdita and Antigonus been doubled by Camillo, making the partnership with Paulina at the end a very neat touch. Titania and Oberon are often played by the same pair as Hippolyta and Theseus, suggesting a symbolic matching of the rulers of the worlds of night and day, but it is questionable whether there would have been time for the necessary costume changes. As so often, one is left in a realm of tantalizing speculation.

THE KING'S MAN

On Queen Elizabeth's death in 1603, the new king, James I, who had held the Scottish throne as James VI since he had been an infant, immediately took the Lord Chamberlain's Men under his direct patronage. Henceforth they would be the King's Men, and for the rest of Shakespeare's career they were favored with far more court performances than any of their rivals. There even seem to have been rumors early in the reign that Shakespeare and Burbage were being considered for knighthoods, an unprecedented honor for mere actors—and one that in the event was not accorded to a member of the profession for nearly three hundred years, when the title was bestowed upon Henry Irving, the leading Shakespearean actor of Queen Victoria's reign.

Shakespeare's productivity rate slowed in the Jacobean years, not because of age or some personal trauma, but because there were frequent outbreaks of plague, causing the theaters to be closed for long periods. The King's Men were forced to spend many months on the road. Between November 1603 and 1608, they were to be found at various towns in the south and Midlands, though Shakespeare probably did not tour with them by this time. He had bought a large house back home in Stratford and was accumulating other property. He may indeed have stopped acting soon after the new king took the throne. With the London theaters closed so much of the time and a large repertoire on the stocks, Shakespeare seems to have focused his energies on writing a few long and complex tragedies that could have been played on demand at court: *Othello, King Lear, Antony and Cleopatra, Coriolanus,* and *Cymbeline* are among his longest and poetically grandest plays. *Macbeth* only survives in a shorter text, which shows signs of adaptation after Shakespeare's death. The bitterly satirical *Timon of Athens,* apparently a collaboration with Thomas Middleton that may have failed on the stage, also belongs to this period. In comedy, too, he wrote longer and morally darker works than in the Elizabethan period, pushing at the very bounds of the form in *Measure for Measure* and *All's Well That Ends Well.*

From 1608 onward, when the King's Men began occupying the indoor Blackfriars playhouse (as a winter house, meaning that they only used the outdoor Globe in summer?), Shakespeare turned to a more romantic style. His company had a great success with a revived and altered version of an old pastoral play called *Mucedorus.* It even featured a bear. The younger dramatist John Fletcher, meanwhile, sometimes working in collaboration with Francis Beaumont, was pioneering a new style of tragicomedy, a mix of romance and royalism laced with intrigue and pastoral excursions. Shakespeare experimented with this idiom in *Cymbeline* and it was presumably with his blessing that Fletcher eventually took over as the King's Men's company dramatist. The two writers apparently collaborated on three plays in the years 1612–14: a lost romance called *Cardenio* (based on the love-madness of a character in Cervantes' *Don Quixote*), *Henry VIII* (originally staged with the title "All Is True"), and *The Two Noble Kinsmen*, a dramatization of Chaucer's "Knight's Tale." These were written after Shakespeare's two final solo-authored plays, *The Winter's Tale*, a self-consciously old-fashioned work dramatizing the pastoral romance of his old enemy Robert Greene, and *The Tempest*, which at one and the same time drew together multiple theatrical traditions, diverse reading, and contemporary interest in the fate of a ship that had been wrecked on the way to the New World.

The collaborations with Fletcher suggest that Shakespeare's career ended with a slow fade rather than the sudden retirement supposed by the nineteenth-century Romantic critics who read Prospero's epilogue to *The Tempest* as Shakespeare's personal farewell to his art. In the last few years of his life Shakespeare certainly spent more of his time in Stratford-upon-Avon, where he became further involved in property dealing and litigation. But his London life also continued. In 1613 he made his first major London property purchase: a freehold house in the Blackfriars district, close to his company's indoor theater. *The Two Noble Kinsmen* may have been written as late as 1614, and Shakespeare was in London on business a little over a year before he died of an unknown cause at home in Stratford-upon-Avon in 1616, probably on his fifty-second birthday.

About half the sum of his works were published in his lifetime, in texts of variable quality. A few years after his death, his fellow actors began putting together an authorized edition of his complete *Comedies, Histories and Tragedies*. It appeared in 1623, in large "Folio" format. This collection of thirty-six plays gave Shakespeare his immortality. In the words of his fellow dramatist Ben Jonson, who contributed two poems of praise at the start of the Folio, the body of his work made him "a monument without a tomb":

And art alive still while thy book doth live
And we have wits to read and praise to give . . .
He was not of an age, but for all time!

SHAKESPEARE'S WORKS:
A CHRONOLOGY

1589–91	? *Arden of Faversham* (possible part authorship)
1589–92	*The Taming of the Shrew*
1589–92	? *Edward the Third* (possible part authorship)
1591	*The Second Part of Henry the Sixth*, originally called *The First Part of the Contention Betwixt the Two Famous Houses of York and Lancaster* (element of coauthorship possible)
1591	*The Third Part of Henry the Sixth*, originally called *The True Tragedy of Richard Duke of York* (element of co-authorship probable)
1591–92	*The Two Gentlemen of Verona*
1591–92; perhaps revised 1594	*The Lamentable Tragedy of Titus Andronicus* (probably cowritten with, or revising an earlier version by, George Peele)
1592	*The First Part of Henry the Sixth*, probably with Thomas Nashe and others
1592/94	*King Richard the Third*
1593	*Venus and Adonis* (poem)
1593–94	*The Rape of Lucrece* (poem)
1593–1608	*Sonnets* (154 poems, published 1609 with *A Lover's Complaint*, a poem of disputed authorship)
1592–94/ 1600–03	*Sir Thomas More* (a single scene for a play originally by Anthony Munday, with other revisions by Henry Chettle, Thomas Dekker, and Thomas Heywood)
1594	*The Comedy of Errors*
1595	*Love's Labour's Lost*

1595–97	*Love's Labour's Won* (a lost play, unless the original title for another comedy)
1595–96	*A Midsummer Night's Dream*
1595–96	*The Tragedy of Romeo and Juliet*
1595–96	*King Richard the Second*
1595–97	*The Life and Death of King John* (possibly earlier)
1596–97	*The Merchant of Venice*
1596–97	*The First Part of Henry the Fourth*
1597–98	*The Second Part of Henry the Fourth*
1598	*Much Ado About Nothing*
1598–99	*The Passionate Pilgrim* (20 poems, some not by Shakespeare)
1599	*The Life of Henry the Fifth*
1599	"To the Queen" (epilogue for a court performance)
1599	*As You Like It*
1599	*The Tragedy of Julius Caesar*
1600–01	*The Tragedy of Hamlet, Prince of Denmark* (perhaps revising an earlier version)
1600–01	*The Merry Wives of Windsor* (perhaps revising version of 1597–99)
1601	"Let the Bird of Loudest Lay" (poem, known since 1807 as "The Phoenix and Turtle" [turtledove])
1601	*Twelfth Night, or What You Will*
1601–02	*The Tragedy of Troilus and Cressida*
1604	*The Tragedy of Othello, the Moor of Venice*
1604	*Measure for Measure*
1605	*All's Well That Ends Well*
1605	*The Life of Timon of Athens*, with Thomas Middleton
1605–06	*The Tragedy of King Lear*
1605–08	? contribution to *The Four Plays in One* (lost, except for *A Yorkshire Tragedy*, mostly by Thomas Middleton)

1606	*The Tragedy of Macbeth* (surviving text has additional scenes by Thomas Middleton)
1606–07	*The Tragedy of Antony and Cleopatra*
1608	*The Tragedy of Coriolanus*
1608	*Pericles, Prince of Tyre*, with George Wilkins
1610	*The Tragedy of Cymbeline*
1611	*The Winter's Tale*
1611	*The Tempest*
1612–13	*Cardenio*, with John Fletcher (survives only in later adaptation called *Double Falsehood* by Lewis Theobald)
1613	*Henry VIII (All Is True)*, with John Fletcher
1613–14	*The Two Noble Kinsmen*, with John Fletcher

KINGS AND QUEENS OF ENGLAND: FROM THE HISTORY PLAYS TO SHAKESPEARE'S LIFETIME

	Lifespan	Reign
Angevins:		
Henry II	1133–1189	1154–1189
Richard I	1157–1199	1189–1199
John	1166–1216	1199–1216
Henry III	1207–1272	1216–1272
Edward I	1239–1307	1272–1307
Edward II	1284–1327	1307–1327 deposed
Edward III	1312–1377	1327–1377
Richard II	1367–1400	1377–1399 deposed
Lancastrians:		
Henry IV	1367–1413	1399–1413
Henry V	1387–1422	1413–1422
Henry VI	1421–1471	1422–1461 and 1470–1471
Yorkists:		
Edward IV	1442–1483	1461–1470 and 1471–1483
Edward V	1470–1483	1483 not crowned: deposed and assassinated
Richard III	1452–1485	1483–1485
Tudors:		
Henry VII	1457–1509	1485–1509
Henry VIII	1491–1547	1509–1547
Edward VI	1537–1553	1547–1553

	Lifespan	*Reign*
Jane	1537–1554	1553 not crowned: deposed and executed
Mary I	1516–1558	1553–1558
Philip of Spain	1527–1598	1554–1558 co-regent with Mary
Elizabeth I	1533–1603	1558–1603

Stuart:

	Lifespan	*Reign*
James I	1566–1625	1603–1625 James VI of Scotland (1567–1625)

THE HISTORY BEHIND THE HISTORIES: A CHRONOLOGY

Square brackets indicate events that happen just outside a play's timescale but are mentioned in the play.

Date	Event	Location	Play
22 May 1200	Truce between King John and Philip Augustus	Le Goulet, Normandy	*King John*
Apr 1203	Death of Arthur	Rouen	*King John*
1209	Pope Innocent III excommunicates King John		*King John*
18/19 Oct 1216	Death of King John	Swineshead, Lincolnshire	*King John*
Apr–Sep 1398	Quarrel, duel, and exile of Bullingbrook and Mowbray	Coventry	*Richard II*
3 Feb 1399	Death of John of Gaunt	Leicester	*Richard II*
Jul 1399	Bullingbrook lands in England	Ravenspur, Yorkshire	*Richard II*
Aug 1399	Richard II captured by Bullingbrook	Wales	*Richard II*
30 Sep 1399	Richard II abdicates	London	*Richard II*
13 Oct 1399	Coronation of Henry IV	London	*Richard II*
Jan–Feb 1400	Death of Richard II	Pontefract Castle	*Richard II*
22 Jun 1402	Owen Glendower captures Edmund Mortimer	Bryn Glas, Wales	*1 Henry IV*
14 Sep 1402	Henry Percy defeats Scottish army	Homildon Hill, Yorkshire	*1 Henry IV*

Date	Event	Location	Play
21 Jul 1403	Battle of Shrewsbury; death of Henry Percy (Hotspur)	Battlefield, near Shrewsbury, Shropshire	*1 & 2 Henry IV*
Feb 1405	Tripartite Indenture between Owen Glendower, Edmund Mortimer, and Northumberland (Henry Percy)	Bangor	*1 Henry IV*
May–Jun 1405	Rebellion of Archbishop of York (Richard Scroop), Earl of Norfolk (Thomas Mowbray), and Lord Bardolph	Yorkshire	*2 Henry IV*
8 Jun 1405	Trial and execution of Archbishop of York and Earl of Norfolk	York	*2 Henry IV*
20 Mar 1413	Death of Henry IV	Westminster Abbey	*2 Henry IV*
9 Apr 1413	Coronation of Henry V	Westminster Abbey	*2 Henry IV*
c.1415–16?	Death of Owen Glendower	Wales?	*2 Henry IV*
Early Aug 1415	Execution of Earl of Cambridge, Lord Scroop, and Sir Thomas Grey	Southampton	*Henry V*
14 Aug–22 Sep 1415	Siege of Harfleur	Harfleur, Normandy	*Henry V*
25 Oct 1415	Battle of Agincourt	Agincourt, Pas de Calais	*Henry V*
31 Aug 1422	Death of Henry V	Bois de Vincennes, near Paris	*1 Henry VI*
18 Jan 1425	Death of Edmund Mortimer	Ireland	*1 Henry VI*
Oct 1428–May 1429	Siege of Orléans	Orléans	*1 Henry VI*
17 Oct 1428	Death of Lord Salisbury	Orléans	*1 Henry VI*

Date	Event	Location	Play
18 Jun 1429	Capture of Lord Talbot at battle of Patay	Patay, near Orléans	*1 Henry VI*
18 Jul 1429	Coronation of Charles VII	Rheims Cathedral	*1 Henry VI*
6 Nov 1429	Coronation of Henry VI as King of England	Westminster Abbey	[*1 Henry VI*]
23 May 1430	Capture of Joan of Arc	Compiègne, near Soissons	*1 Henry VI*
30 May 1431	Execution of Joan of Arc	Saint-Ouen, near Paris	*1 Henry VI*
16 Dec 1431	Coronation of Henry VI as King of France	Notre Dame Cathedral, Paris	*1 Henry VI*
14 Sep 1435	Death of Duke of Bedford	Rouen	*1 Henry VI*
Summer–Autumn 1441	Arrest and trial of Eleanor Cobham and accomplices	London	*2 Henry VI*
20 May 1442	Lord Talbot created Earl of Shrewsbury	Paris	*1 Henry VI*
23 Apr 1445	Marriage of Henry VI and Margaret of Anjou	Titchfield, Hampshire	*2 Henry VI*
23 Feb 1447	Death of Humphrey, Duke of Gloucester	Bury St. Edmunds	*2 Henry VI*
11 Apr 1447	Death of Cardinal Beaufort	Winchester	*2 Henry VI*
2 May 1450	Death of Earl of Suffolk	English Channel	*2 Henry VI*
Jun–Jul 1450	Rebellion of Jack Cade	Kent and London	*2 Henry VI*
Spring 1452	Richard, Duke of York, marches on London	London	*2 Henry VI*
17 Jul 1453	Death of Lord Talbot at battle of Cantillon	Cantillon, Gascony	*1 Henry VI*
22 May 1455	First battle of St. Albans	St. Albans, Hertfordshire	*2 Henry VI*

Date	Event	Location	Play
10 Jul 1460	Battle of Northampton	Northampton	[*3 Henry VI*]
Oct 1460	Richard, Duke of York, holds Parliament	London	*3 Henry VI*
30 Dec 1460	Battle of Wakefield	Wakefield, Yorkshire	*3 Henry VI*
2 Feb 1461	Battle of Mortimer's Cross	Near Wigmore, Herefordshire	*3 Henry VI*
29 Mar 1461	Battle of Towton	Near Tadcaster, Yorkshire	*3 Henry VI*
28 Jun 1461	Coronation of Edward IV	Westminster Abbey	*3 Henry VI*
1 May 1464	Marriage of Edward IV and Elizabeth Woodville	Northamptonshire	*3 Henry VI*
Jul 1465	Henry VI captured	Lancashire	*3 Henry VI*
26 Jul 1469	Battle of Edgecote Moor	Near Banbury, Oxfordshire	*3 Henry VI*
Oct 1470–Apr/May 1471	Readeption (restoration) of Henry VI	London	*3 Henry VI*
14 Apr 1471	Battle of Barnet; death of Warwick	Barnet, near London	*3 Henry VI*
4 May 1471	Battle of Tewkesbury; death of Edward, Prince of Wales	Tewkesbury, Gloucestershire	*3 Henry VI*
21 May 1471	Death of Henry VI	Tower of London	*3 Henry VI*
12 Jul 1472	Marriage of Richard, Duke of Gloucester, to Anne	Westminster Abbey	*Richard III*
18 Feb 1478	Death of Duke of Clarence	Tower of London	*Richard III*
9 Apr 1483	Death of Edward IV	Westminster	*Richard III*
Jun 1483	Death of Lord Hastings	Tower of London	*Richard III*

Date	Event	Location	Play
6 Jul 1483	Coronation of Richard III	Westminster Abbey	*Richard III*
2 Nov 1483	Death of Duke of Buckingham	Salisbury	*Richard III*
16 Mar 1485	Death of Queen Anne	Westminster	*Richard III*
22 Aug 1485	Battle of Bosworth Field	Leicestershire	*Richard III*
30 Oct 1485	Coronation of Henry VII	Westminster Abbey	[*Richard III*]
18 Jan 1486	Marriage of Henry VII and Elizabeth of York	Westminster Abbey	[*Richard III*]
Jun 1520	Meeting of Henry VIII and Francis I	"Field of the Cloth of Gold," near Calais, France	[*Henry VIII*]
17 May 1521	Death of Duke of Buckingham	Tower Hill, London	*Henry VIII*
29 Nov 1530	Death of Wolsey	Leicester	*Henry VIII*
25 Jan 1533	Marriage of Henry VIII and Anne Bullen (Boleyn)	Whitehall	*Henry VIII*
1 Jun 1533	Coronation of Anne Bullen (Boleyn)	Westminster Abbey	*Henry VIII*
7 Sep 1533	Birth of Princess Elizabeth	Greenwich Palace	*Henry VIII*
10 Sep 1533	Christening of Princess Elizabeth	Greenwich Palace	*Henry VIII*

FURTHER READING
AND VIEWING

CRITICAL APPROACHES

Brooke, Nicholas, ed., *Shakespeare: Richard II: A Casebook* (1973). Invaluable collection of early criticism.

Coyle, Martin, ed., *William Shakespeare: Richard II*, Icon Critical Guides (1998). Informative introduction with useful collection of historical criticism of play.

Fanell, Kirby, ed., *Critical Essays on Shakespeare's Richard II* (1999). Useful collection of influential late twentieth-century essays.

Hattaway, Michael, ed., *The Cambridge Companion to Shakespeare's History Plays* (2002). Excellent general introduction to the histories with illuminating essays on individual plays.

Hodgdon, Barbara, *The End Crowns All: Closure and Contradiction in Shakespeare's History* (1991). Thoughtful general introduction plus chapters on individual history plays, focusing on theatrical conclusions: chapter 5 on *Richard II*, pp. 127–50.

Holderness, Graham, *Shakespeare's History Plays: Richard II to Henry V*, New Casebooks (1992). Theoretically informed collection of important late twentieth-century critical essays.

Holderness, Graham, *Shakespeare: The Histories* (2000). Useful account of historical context and a chapter on each of the individual plays, *Richard II* at pp. 175–216.

Kantorowicz, Ernst H., *The King's Two Bodies: A Study in Mediaeval Political Theology* (1957). Influential development of the thesis of the natural versus the political body of the king.

Lopez, Jeremy, *Richard II*, The Shakespeare Handbooks (2009). Useful guide with chapters on early performance, sources, context, criticism, key productions, and textual commentary.

Sieman, James R., *Word Against Word: Shakespearean Utterance* (2002). Fascinating detailed linguistic account.

THE PLAY IN PERFORMANCE

Brooke, Michael, "*Richard II* on Screen," www.screenonline.org.uk/tv/id/1027840/. Overview of television versions, with clips.

Hattaway, Michael, Boika Sokolova, and Derek Roper, eds., *Shakespeare in the New Europe* (1994). Fascinating account of the continuing international significance of Shakespeare's plays; includes Nicholas Potter, "'Like to a Tenement or Pelting Farm': *Richard II* and the Idea of the Nation," pp. 130–47; Michael Hattaway, "Shakespeare's Histories: The Politics of Recent British Productions," pp. 351–69.

Jones, Maria, *Shakespeare's Culture in Modern Performance* (2003). Thoughtful introduction with detailed account of recent performances; the chapter on *Richard II* focuses on the use of the crown as a prop.

Page, Malcolm, *Richard II: Text and Performance* (1987). Good basic introduction to the text in Part 1 with a detailed discussion of important performances from 1973 to 1984.

Rauen, Margarida Gandara, *Richard II Playtext, Promptbooks and History 1597–1857* (1998). Detailed account of early texts and editions of play.

Shewring, Margaret, *Shakespeare in Performance: King Richard II* (1996). Useful introduction—Part 1 discusses the text, Part 2 individual productions and performances, Part 3 the play in other cultural contexts.

Smallwood, Robert, ed., *Players of Shakespeare 6* (2004). Actors discuss their performances: Sam West on Richard II, pp. 85–99, David Troughton on Bullingbrook/Henry IV, pp. 100–16.

AVAILABLE ON DVD

Richard II, directed by Deborah Warner (1997). Recording of successful stage production with Fiona Shaw as Richard; contentious cross-casting produced a haunting performance, discussed above.

Richard II, directed by David Giles (1978, DVD 2005). Part of the

BBC Shakespeare series. Derek Jacobi gives a bravura performance as Richard in a star-studded cast with John Gielgud as Gaunt.

Richard the Second, directed by John Farrell (DVD 2001). Updated, contemporary version: reasonable performances but sound levels poor. Not for purists.

Richard II, directed by William Woodman (1982, DVD 2001). Well-meaning but misguided.

The Wars of the Roses, directed by Michael Bogdanov (1989, DVD 2005). Recording of English Shakespeare Company's eclectic stage production with Michael Pennington, a compelling Richard.

REFERENCES

1. Tim Carroll, "'Practising Behaviour to His Own Shadow,' " in Christie Carson and Farah Karim-Cooper, eds., *Shakespeare's Globe: A Theatrical Experiment* (2008), pp. 40–1.
2. Nahum Tate, *The History of King Richard the Second Acted at the Theatre Royal Under the Name of the Sicilian Usurper* (1681), sig. A2.
3. Charles Beecher Hogan, *Shakespeare in the Theatre 1709–1800* (1952).
4. Lewis Theobald, *The Tragedy of King Richard the II; As It Is Acted at the Theatre in Lincoln's-Inn-Fields* (1720), sig. A2.
5. Theobald, *The Tragedy of King Richard the II*, p. 59.
6. Thomas Davies, *Dramatic Miscellanies* (1783–84), Vol. 1, pp. 151–3.
7. Davies, *Dramatic Miscellanies*, p. 124.
8. Margarida Gandara Rauen, *"Richard II": Playtexts, Promptbooks and History: 1597–1857* (1998), pp. 141–9.
9. William Hazlitt, *A View of the English Stage* (1818), p. 100.
10. Leah Scragg, "Introduction," *King Richard II: Richard Wroughton 1815* (1970).
11. Theodor Fontane, *Shakespeare in the London Theatre 1855–58* (1999), pp. 52–3.
12. *Punch* 32 (January–June 1857), p. 124.
13. *Birmingham Daily Gazette*, 24 April 1896.
14. Malcolm Page, *Richard II* (1987), p. 48.
15. *The Times*, 19 November 1929.
16. *The Times*, 30 December 1952.
17. *Birmingham Mail*, 22 April 1933.
18. *Stratford-upon-Avon Herald*, 25 April 1941.
19. *Evening Dispatch*, Birmingham, 24 May 1944.
20. *Birmingham Mail*, 14 June 1947.
21. Quoted in Margaret Shewring, *Shakespeare in Performance: King Richard II* (1996), p. 97.
22. *News Chronicle*, 26 March 1951.
23. Shewring, *King Richard II*, p. 88.
24. Shewring, *King Richard II*, p. 335.
25. Shewring, *King Richard II*, p. 231.
26. Eve-Marie Oesterlen, *Cahiers Élisabéthains*, Special Issue (2007), pp. 69–70.

27. Page, *Richard II*, p. 54.

28. *The Times*, 30 March 1972.

29. Henry Fenwick, *Richard II: The BBC TV Shakespeare* (1978), p. 24.

30. Michael Bogdanov and Michael Pennington, *The English Shakespeare Company: The Story of "The Wars of the Roses" 1986–1989* (1990), p. 107.

31. Bogdanov and Pennington, *The Story of "The Wars of the Roses,"* p. 139.

32. John Pettigrew and Jamie Portman, *Stratford: The First Thirty Years* (1985), Vol. I, p. 175.

33. Terry Doran, *Buffalo News*, quoted in Pettigrew and Portman, *Stratford*, Vol. II, p. 159.

34. James Fenton, *You Were Marvellous* (1983), p. 257.

35. *Independent*, 14 June 1995.

36. Shewring, *King Richard II*, p. 182.

37. *Observer*, 9 October 2005.

38. *Independent*, 9 October 2005.

39. *Sunday Times*, 9 October 2005.

40. *Telegraph*, 6 October 2005.

41. *Royal Shakespeare Company Season Guide 2007–2008*, p. 7.

42. The queen is reported to have said this to William Lambarde, the keeper of the records of the Tower.

43. *RSC Season Guide 2007–2008*, p. 2.

44. Stuart Hampton-Reeves, "Theatrical Afterlives," in Michael Hattaway, ed., *The Cambridge Companion to Shakespeare's History Plays* (2002), p. 229.

45. Theater program, 1951.

46. Hattaway, *The Cambridge Companion to Shakespeare's History Plays*, p. 354.

47. Jan Kott, *Shakespeare Our Contemporary*, trans. Boleslaw Taborski (1964), p. 10.

48. Colin Chambers, *Inside the Royal Shakespeare Company* (2004), p. 36.

49. Shewring, *King Richard II*, p. 98.

50. *Coventry Evening Telegraph*, 16 April 1964.

51. *Birmingham Post*, 16 April 1964.

52. Shrewring, *King Richard II*, pp. 100–1.

53. Harold Hobson, *Sunday Times*, 16 April 1964.

54. *The Times*, London, 16 April 1964.

55. Alan Dent, *Financial Times*, 16 April 1964.

56. *Warwick Advertiser*, 17 April 1964.

57. Irving Wardle, *The Times*, London, 11 April 1973.

58. Robert Shaughnessy, *Representing Shakespeare: England, History and the RSC* (1994), p. 91.

59. Ernst H. Kantorowicz, *The King's Two Bodies: A Study in Mediaeval Political Theology* (1957), p. 7.

60. James Stredder, "John Barton's Production of *Richard II* at Stratford-on-Avon, 1973," *Shakespeare Jahrbuch* (1976), p. 24.

61. Stredder, "John Barton's Production of *Richard II*," p. 25.

62. Stredder, "John Barton's Production of *Richard II*," p. 29.

63. Andrew Gurr, ed., *King Richard II* (1984), p. 48.

64. B. A. Young, *Financial Times*, 11 April 1973.

65. Shaughnessy, *Representing Shakespeare*, p. 94.

66. Stanley Wells found the scene "illustrates a danger of Mr. Barton's production methods; that, at their extremes, they were directing their audience what to think" (quoted in Shewring, *King Richard II*, pp. 124–5).

67. Michael Billington, *Guardian*, 12 April 1973.

68. J. C. Trewin, *Birmingham Post*, 11 April 1973.

69. Irving Wardle, *The Times*, London, 4 April 1980.

70. Chambers, *Inside the Royal Shakespeare Company*, p. 70.

71. Shaughnessy, *Representing Shakespeare*, pp. 64–5.

72. Irving Wardle, *The Times*, London, 5 November 1980.

73. Hampton-Reeves, "'Theatrical Afterlives," p. 239.

74. B. A. Young, *Financial Times*, 4 April 1980.

75. Shaughnessy, *Representing Shakespeare*, p. 61.

76. Wardle, *The Times*, 4 April 1980.

77. Shewring, *King Richard II*, p. 59.

78. Nicholas Shrimpton, "Shakespeare Performances in London, Manchester and Stratford-upon-Avon 1985–6," *Shakespeare Survey* 40 (1988), p. 180.

79. Jane Edwardes, *Time Out*, 17 September 1986.

80. Stanley Wells, *Times Literary Supplement*, 26 September 1986.

81. Giles Gordon, *Plays & Players*, November 1986.

82. Eric Shorter, *Daily Telegraph*, 12 September 1986.

83. John Peter, *Sunday Times*, 14 September 1986.

84. RSC program, *Richard II* (1990). The quote is from Marie Louise Bruce, *The Usurper King: Henry Bolingbroke 1366–99* (1986).

85. Maria Jones, *Shakespeare's Culture in Modern Performance* (2003), p. 152, quoting Harry Eyres, *The Times*, London, 13 September 1991.

86. Jones, *Shakespeare's Culture in Modern Performance*, p. 153.

87. Michael Coveney, *Observer*, 11 November 1990.

88. Michael Billington, *Guardian*, 9 November 1990.

89. Malcolm Rutherford, *Financial Times*, 12 September 1991.
90. Russell Jackson, "Shakespeare at Stratford-upon-Avon: Summer and Fall, 2000," *Shakespeare Quarterly* 52 (2001), p. 114.
91. Alastair Macaulay, *Financial Times*, 31 March 2000.
92. Susannah Clapp, *Observer*, 2 April 2000.
93. Michael Dobson, "Shakespeare Performances in England, 2000," *Shakespeare Survey*, 45 (2001), p. 276.
94. Dobson, "Shakespeare Performances in England, 2000," p. 276.
95. Patrick Carnegy, *Spectator*, 8 April 2000.
96. John Peter, *Sunday Times*, 9 April 2000.
97. John Gross, *Sunday Telegraph*, 2 April 2000.
98. Clapp, *Observer*, 2 April 2000.
99. Carole Woddis, *Stratford Herald*, 4 April 2000.

ACKNOWLEDGMENTS AND PICTURE CREDITS

Preparation of "*Richard II* in Performance" was assisted by a generous grant from the CAPITAL Centre (Creativity and Performance in Teaching and Learning) of the University of Warwick for research in the RSC archive at the Shakespeare Birthplace Trust.

Thanks as always to our indefatigable and eagle-eyed copy editor Tracey Day and to Ray Addicott for overseeing the production process with rigor and calmness.

Picture research by Michelle Morton. Grateful acknowledgment is made to the Shakespeare Birthplace Trust for assistance with picture research (special thanks to Helen Hargest) and reproduction fees.

Images of RSC productions are supplied by the Shakespeare Centre Library and Archive, Stratford-upon-Avon. This Library, maintained by the Shakespeare Birthplace Trust, holds the most important collection of Shakespeare material in the UK, including the Royal Shakespeare Company's official archive. It is open to the public free of charge.

For more information see www.shakespeare.org.uk.

1. London Princess Theatre, directed by Charles Kean (1857). Reproduced by permission of the Shakespeare Birthplace Trust
2. Directed by Anthony Quayle (1951). Angus McBean © Royal Shakespeare Company
3. Directed by John Barton (1973). Joe Cocks Studio Collection © Shakespeare Birthplace Trust
4. Directed by Terry Hands (1980). Joe Cocks Studio Collection © Shakespeare Birthplace Trust
5. Directed by Barry Kyle (1986). Reg Wilson © Royal Shakespeare Company